AGING AND PUBLIC POLICY

Social Control or Social Justice?

By

JOHN B. WILLIAMSON

Department of Sociology
Boston College

JUDITH A. SHINDUL

School of Nursing
Boston College

LINDA EVANS

Department of Sociology
Central Connecticut State University

CHARLES C THOMAS • PUBLISHER
Springfield • Illinois • U.S.A.

Published and Distributed Throughout the World by

CHARLES C THOMAS • PUBLISHER

2600 South First Street

Springfield, Illinois 62717

© *1985 by* CHARLES C THOMAS • PUBLISHER

ISBN 0-398-05104-6

Library of Congress Catalog Card Number: 84-26735

With THOMAS BOOKS *careful attention is given to all details of manufacturing and design. It is the Publisher's desire to present books that are satisfactory as to their physical qualities and artistic possibilities and appropriate for their particular use.* THOMAS BOOKS *will be true to those laws of quality that assure a good name and good will.*

Printed in the United States of America
Q-R-3

Library of Congress Cataloging in Publication Data

Williamson, John B.
  Aging and public policy.

  Bibliography: p.
  Includes indexes.
    1. Aged — Government policy — United States.
  2. Pensions — Government policy — United States.
  3. Medical care — Government policy — United States.
  I. Shindul, Judith A. II. Evans, Linda. III. Title.
  HQ1064.U5W5923 1985   362.6'0973   84-26735
  ISBN 0-398-05104-6

AUTHORS

JOHN B. WILLIAMSON
    Professor
    Department of Sociology
    Boston College
    B.S., Massachusetts Institute of Technology
    Ph.D., Harvard University

JUDITH A. SHINDUL
    President, Massachusetts Nurses Association
    Instructor, Boston College School of Nursing
    B.S., Boston College
    M.S.N., Yale University
    Ph.D. (Candidate), Boston College

LINDA EVANS
    Professor
    Department of Sociology
    Central Connecticut State University
    B.A., Mount Holyoke College
    M.A., Boston College
    Ph.D., Boston College

For Bette and Kate

J.B.W.

For my parents, Maye and Arnold

J.A.S.

For my little troopers. Bartholomew and Charlie

L.E.

PREFACE

IN RECENT years we have witnessed a dramatic change in public policy toward the elderly, a shift from a focus on questions of social justice to questions of cost containment. While this shift is unprecedented in recent times, it is not the first time the nation has experienced a realignment toward greater restrictiveness in public policy toward the elderly. An equally dramatic shift took place during the early nineteenth century. One goal of this book is to explain how and why these and other major shifts in public policy toward the aged have taken place. Particular attention is given to the question as to why, of late, concerns about distribution, equity, and social justice are increasingly being superceded by concerns about cost containment and efficiency.

Our explanations draw extensively on three theoretical perspectives — political economics, functionalism, and labeling theory — which are outlined in Chapter 2. These perspectives are used in an explication of the concept of social control and in an analysis of the social control aspects of various public policies affecting the aged. They are also used in an assessment of government's reluctance to give more attention to issues of equity and justice in the shaping and implementation of these policies.

We begin our historical analysis by considering the evolution of aging policy in England. Chapter 4 shows how these English ideas about aging policy were adapted to the needs of the American colonies. It goes on to offer an explanation of why the ideology of individualism had an even greater impact in America than in England and how this led to even more restrictive old-age relief policies.

Chapter 5 discusses the origins of private pensions. Private pensions facilitate control over workers, capital accumulation, and profit maximization — all requisites of a capitalist economy. Because the value of the pension is related to income, job tenure, and labor market location, the private pension system fails to provide adequate income maintenance for most Americans. In light of these inadequacies, reforms are suggested which would enable the elderly to gain greater control over their pension rights. In Chapter 6 we shift to a consideration of public pensions, specifically Social Security, and the extent to which the program acts as a bureaucratic form of social control. The dysfunctions inherent in the system and its role in maintaining social order are discussed. Ways in which the changing needs of corporate America are likely to affect the Social Security program in the years ahead are also explored.

The next three chapters deal with various aspects of health care policy. Chapter 7 reviews the history of health care policies toward the aged, the role of the government in these policies, the influence of the medical establishment, and the manner in which various corporate interests have been successful in restructuring health care delivery to the detriment of the elderly. Ways in which the government could deal with such conflicting forces as growing demand, limited resources, and escalating health care costs, without placing undue hardship on the aged are also discussed. The chapter on long-term care expands on some of these same themes. The problem of increasing demand and of increasing costs is reaching ominous proportions and it has the potential for pitting one generation of Americans against another unless there is a major restructuring of the long-term care system. Policymakers must either increase regulation or take steps to promote much greater competition among vendors; we explore the potential efficacy of each of these alternatives.

The social and economic impact of advances in medical technology on the elderly is considered in Chapter 9. Medical technology can either empower or seriously reduce the autonomy of the elderly. The profit motive leads to the proliferation and unnecessary use of technologies while at the same time, due to cost considerations, the elderly, particularly the elderly poor, end up being undeserved relative to the extent of their actual health care needs.

The following chapter deals with the impact of technology in another sphere. Messages contained in the mass media which rationalize the subordinization, economic exploitation, and devalued status of the elderly are examined. This labeling process can be linked to both the market-based economy and the libertarian tradition of a relatively unregulated press. Given the ageism apparent in the mass media today, we ask if there are any recent developments in telecommunications that might counter these distorted media portrayals.

The chapter on ageism brings together a number of themes considered throughout the book. We argue that ageism is an outgrowth of nineteenth century liberalism which was used to explain and justify capitalist expansion. Both liberalism and ageism arose in response to economic transitions.

In the final chapter we assess the prospects for future public policy gains. With the deterioration of the American economy during the late 1970s and early 1980s came a number of questions about the elderly's "deserving" status. Increasing skepticism about the intensity of the elderly's needs and concern over the growing costs of existing programs present major challenges for the elderly's public policy advocates in the years ahead. In the future it may be wise for the elderly and their advocates to promote two quite different types of policy reforms at the same time. One would emphasize programs for the aged that are particularistic in the sense that they are aimed at segments of the aged that are very needy. The other would emphasize programs and policies that are universalistic in the sense of providing benefits to individuals of all ages and in all income groups. Ultimately, trade-offs will have to be made between the needs of the elderly on the one hand and the needs of other age groups, corporate American, and of elected political officials on the other, choices which we would like to see increasingly governed by considerations of equity and social justice rather than political and economic expediency.

J.B.W.
J.A.S.
L.E.

ACKNOWLEDGMENTS

JOHN WILLIAMSON is author of Chapters 1, 3, and 4; he is also coauthor of Chapter 12 and a contributor to all other chapters. Judith Shindul is author of Chapters 7 and 8; she is also the primary author of Chapter 12 and a contributor to several others. Linda Evans is author of Chapters 2, 6, and 11. Lawrence Powell is author of Chapter 10. Avery Gordon is author of Chapter 5. Kathryn Lasch is author of Chapter 9.

A number of people have commented on drafts of all or part of the manuscript or in other ways contributed to our thinking about these issues. For their interest, insights, and efforts we would like to thank: Stuart Altman, Severyn Bruyn, Charles Derber, John Donovan, Rose Frey, Jay Greenberg, Leonard Hausman, Elizabeth Johnson, Beth Hess, David Karp, Joanna Lion, Stephen Pfohl, and Ithiel Pool. A number of people have been of very great assistance in typing, editing, and other aspects of manuscript preparation. In this context we are particularly appreciative of the contributions of Alice Close, Shirley Urban, Sara White and Pui Yee Wong. Arlene Butler made major editorial contributions to Chapter 1 and significant editorial contributions to a number of others. Joseph Costa contributed to the preparation of this manuscript in a number of ways including playing a major role in the preparation of the bibliography. We wish also to thank Payne Thomas, Michael Thomas, and William Bried of our publisher's editorial staff for their assistance and support throughout this project.

CONTENTS

AGING AND
PUBLIC POLICY

CHAPTER 1

INTRODUCTION

A S PEOPLE grow old they often experience a loss of autonomy, power, influence, and authority which contribute to a reduction in quality of life (Linden, 1956). Many of these losses can be linked to and are consequences of social control at both an interpersonal and a societal level. Much of the social control that the elderly encounter in everyday living can be accounted for in terms of broader structural and cultural sources.

All social interaction involves a certain amount of mutual influence. It is appropriate to refer to this influence as social control when the element of constraint is present. Thus, this book deals with the various social mechanisms by which the elderly are constrained and their options limited. In this analysis we will consider the social relationships of influence, power, persuasion, force, manipulation, and authority, as well as the issues of autonomy and empowerment.

We analyze the development of public policy toward the elderly with a focus on the often unintended negative side effects for some (or many) of the aged. Who is responsible for the original formulation of the policy? What are the sources or agents of control? What is the process by which the mechanisms of control exert their influence? Which groups in society benefit from the policy? Which segments of the elderly are most vulnerable to the negative aspect of this policy? Are there significant variations among subgroups? What role does the state play in control of the elderly? Whose interests are being served by the state's involvement? What can people who are concerned with empowering the elderly do to facilitate and assure

3

this alternative in the development of public policy? Using empirical evidence drawn from a wide range of sources and a variety of theoretical perspectives, this book attempts to answer these and other closely related questions. We also discuss proposals for minimizing the social control aspects of programs and policies for the aged.

Most of the early work on social control was done by those working in what today we refer to as the functionalist tradition. Mechanisms of social control were viewed as essential for the maintenance of social order. More recently, functionalists have focused on mechanisms for the social control of deviance. This work assumes that there is some sort of normative consensus in society about what constitutes appropriate behavior (Spencer, 1961). From this perspective it is argued that if informal mechanisms of social control (such as socialization) are successful, then there will be less need for the formal mechanisms (such as police force and the legal system) (Durkheim, 1938).

Social control has also been of interest to those working in the symbolic interactionist tradition. Here the concern has been with the ways in which deviance is created by society's labeling of certain behavior as deviant. This process can lead to isolation and stigmatization of the offender (Lemert, 1967). In this context one can view growing old as a form of deviance; the elderly are punished by isolation and stigmatization for this "deviant" act.

In recent years political economy theorists have also taken up the issue of social control. From this perspective social control is viewed as the regulation of groups with less power by other groups with more power (Braverman, 1974). Economic stratification serves as the principle determinant of where the power lies and what form it takes (Marx, 1906b). The state rather than being viewed as a neutral broker of interests is seen as using its legitimated authority to rationalize and supplement the exploitation of some groups by others (Gough, 1979).

While we make extensive use of political economy theory, our analysis is not restricted to this perspective. There are many aspects of social control of the elderly that do not lend themselves to analysis from this perspective. Our major goal is to analyze social control aspects of public policy toward the elderly. To the extent that other theoretical perspectives suggest interesting questions or offer important insights, those perspectives are used.

In addition to describing the forms that social control takes in the everyday lives of elderly persons, we discuss the sources of this control and why it exists. Our goal is to account for the social control the elderly experience in broader cultural, historical, and social structural terms. In many instances we find a relationship between the sources of social control and the imperatives of the American polity and economy. For example, we argue that discrimination against older job applicants can be linked to the imperatives of a capitalist economy (Lubove, 1968; Fischer, 1978; Haber and Cohen, 1960). Many employers believe that it is more efficient and profitable to hire and train younger workers. Health care policies, now focused on containing costs, are not directed at the perpetrators of escalating costs but rather the recipients of medical care (Ehrenreich and Ehrenreich, 1971). Cost-containment policies, which increase co-payments and deductibles, essentially blame the victims and avoid entirely the issue of restricting profitability.

Many of the sources of social control we consider also contribute to an increase in autonomy among the elderly. For example, we analyze the social control aspects of the Social Security program. In this analysis we would not want to suggest that the program does little or nothing to increase the autonomy of the elderly. To the contrary, the program has been a major source of the increase in autonomy that the elderly have experienced during the past fifty years. However despite its making a significant net contribution to autonomy, it does have some very important social control aspects. Our goal is to bring to light these often neglected aspects of the program. When a program, policy, or innovation has made a significant contribution to the autonomy, power, or influence of the elderly, we say so; but this does not prevent us from going on to uncover its important social control aspects.

The inherent limitations of old age are based on losses. Physical health is lost through the aging process of the body. Social contacts are lost through the death of friends and family. Familiar roles of breadwinner and parent are lost through mandatory retirement and changes in the family structure. Financial security is lost through dependence on a relatively fixed income and no assurance of fixed prices. Independence and power are lost through needing to rely on family, friends, and government in a society that values self-reliance. As a result of these losses, the elderly end up with less economic, social and political clout than they would otherwise have.

Public policy has done a great deal to lessen the losses of the elderly. Certainly, the health and quality of life of the elderly are better because of Medicare, Medicaid, and Social Security pensions, but such policies also have negative side effects that often go unnoticed. Policies that are supposed to improve the quality of life sometimes end up harming those they are designed to help. The benefits of such programs are well known to professional gerontologists and the general public, but the negative side effects are difficult to see and are often overshadowed by the benefits. In our opinion, these require much more attention than they have been given to date.

Who is responsible for the development of public policy for the elderly? Public policy, as discussed here, not only includes laws and regulations made by federal, state and local government, it also includes certain policies made by private industry because these decisions can have as significant an impact on the aged as those made by the government. It is sometimes difficult to distinguish where governmental policies end and private industry policies begin. Through an analysis of the retirement system, and the institutionalization of ageism, we begin to see how difficult it is to draw a line between governmental and private industry's interests in the economic, social, and political arenas.

Some analysts argue that mandatory retirement rules help deal with the problem of unemployment among younger workers (Graebner, 1980; Sclar, 1980). However, such policies create economic problems for older workers. One governmental response has been the development of the Social Security system. Private industry's response has been to develop private pension plans. Both contribute to a perpetuation of class differences in economic status into old age due to the relationship between retirement income and wages during the working years (O'Connor, 1973; Gough, 1979). Such policies are part of the reason that retirement is a life stage of dependency for many, particularly those at the lower end of the income distribution.

Who benefits from mandatory retirement policies? Some would

say elected officials benefit because mandatory retirement gives the illusion that the unemployment rate is lower than it actually is. Others point out that private industry benefits by being able to hire inexperienced people and paying them less than older workers (Graebner, 1980).

In 1978, the minimum age of mandatory retirement was raised from 65 to 70 for many workers. More recently, serious consideration has been given to legislation that would eliminate all mandatory retirement age regulations for most categories of workers (U.S. Senate Special Committee on Aging, 1982). While this would increase the options and quality of life for some who are aged, such a policy shift would have its negative consequences for others. This will be particularly evident when workers who are anxious to retire at age 65 find that the age of eligibility for various pension and health care benefits has been raised. Those who have had the most routine jobs, the lowest paying jobs, and the jobs that most adversely affect one's health will end up paying the price for a policy shift that increases options and opportunities for those in the most desirable jobs.

Health insurance is another public policy arena in which there are a variety of unintended adverse effects to explore. By the 1960s it was clear that the existing health care system was not adequately meeting the needs of the middle and lower income elderly (Stevens and Stevens, 1974). The government response was to develop a health insurance system financed in part by Social Security funds and premiums (Medicare) and in part by general revenues (Medicaid) (Sundquist, 1968). Private industry's response was to use a corporate, free-market model to infuse competition into the system and presumably improve efficiency. Both responses worked together to inflate the cost of health care far beyond anyone's expectations.

When the elderly's health problems get to the point at which they are no longer able to care for themselves, for many the only option available is a nursing home placement paid for by Medicaid. A nursing home placement typically results in a rapid liquidation of the patient's life savings (Leonard, 1982). Some who recover to the point that they are physically able to live independently find that it is no longer financially feasible given the exhaustion of their personal assets.

Who benefits from this policy? Government benefits by being able to say that it provides health insurance for the elderly. Physicians and health care industries have an opportunity to make tremendous profits. The aged benefit, too, but not as much as had originally been anticipated. Out-of-pocket health care expenses are actually greater today than they were before enactment of the Medicare and Medicaid legislation in 1965.

The public image of the elderly as unhappy, diminishing in physical vigor, lessened sensory pleasures and being only a short distance from death contributed to a constriction of the autonomy and options available to the elderly. The government's response to these stereotypes was for many years to promote mandatory retirement, as the elderly were not viewed as productive as younger workers. The aged were transformed into a special category subsidized by the tax dollars of younger workers. The response of the mass media suggests that the elderly are incompetent but benevolent and preoccupied with bodily functions such as constipation and loose dentures (Francher, 1973). Both responses portray the elderly as unable to think clearly or care for themselves and as in need of protection from the rigors of the world. Unfortunately, many of the elderly have internalized these images and have been co-opted into assuming these roles. These public images and the self- images have reduced the autonomy and influence of the aged in American society.

The examples of mandatory retirement, health insurance, and the public image of the elderly illustrate the need to expand our view of who actually benefits from public policy toward the elderly. In order to more fully understand how we got to where we are, it is essential that we take a close look at the origins of public policy toward the elderly.

What are the origins of the public policies that limit the autonomy, authority, and influence of the elderly? The United States has a relatively short history, so we can easily trace our public policy toward the elderly back to colonial times. But it turns out that policies in colonial America were strongly influenced by those of England.

By considering developments in England from the medieval era through the nineteenth century and by considering developments in America from the colonial era through the nineteenth century, the link between the development of a capitalist economy and trends in public policy toward the aged becomes evident. This analysis provides a number of insights for understanding the development of contemporary aging policies and the link between these policies and the structure of our economy. This historical analysis also casts light on contemporary attitudes toward the dependent elderly and the relationship between such attitudes and public policy.

On feudal manors in Medieval England, neither the serfs nor the lords were responding to outside markets. The relationship between serf and lord was based on exchange, albeit one that clearly favored the lord. Serfs were needed to work the land and were difficult to replace. Thus, it was in the interest of the lord to be concerned with their health and well-being. Serfs who were "impotent" (a category which included the infirm elderly) were taken care of by the church and the lord of the manor (Tierney, 1959; de Schweinitz, 1943).

By the seventeenth century a market economy was clearly evolving. As a consequence workers became increasingly vulnerable to changes in international markets and the cyclical trends of capitalistic economies. The relationship between the capitalist and the worker was based on the exchange of money. It was necessary to control the able-bodied poor because they were prone to violence and destruction directed against the interests of property owners during economic downturns. They were controlled by laws prohibiting begging and laws introducing relief for all except outsiders and those able but unwilling to work (de Schweinitz, 1943). A new religious ideology emphasized the importance of hard work for eventual salvation (Webb and Webb, 1910). Children were required to provide for elderly parents, and the infirm were provided for either at home or in an almshouse supported by the community (Leonard, 1900).

Throughout the twentieth century the United States has had a fully developed capitalist economy. The able-bodied unemployed are still prone to cause social disorder during severe and prolonged depressions such as that the nation experienced during the 1930s. Today, they are regulated by a wide variety of social welfare programs including Social Security, by sophisticated rules and procedures in the workplace, and by an elaborate criminal justice system.

A close look at the evolution of public policy toward the elderly reveals a number of interesting findings of which one of the most important is the link between shifts in the economy and corresponding shifts in policy. As the market economy has evolved, the needs of those with economic power have changed. One of the transformations that has taken place in response to these changes has been the reduction in the power, influence, authority, and status of the elderly. This is particularly evident in the case of America from the colonial era up through the middle of the twentieth century.

There are many reasons that public policy toward the aged ends up being a source of social control. One is that public policies in the form of programs, laws, and regulations are used as mechanisms to maintain order in society. They are also used by groups with more power to regulate those with less power. The case of public policy dealing with the problem of unemployment can be used to illustrate this point. Cyclical unemployment is endemic to market economies, and the problem of mass unemployment has concerned public policymakers since the sixteenth century. One approach for dealing with the problem that emerged during the Great Depression of the 1930s is to make it possible for some of the aged to withdraw from the labor force by providing public pensions. Once such a pension system is established, it also served to legitimize industrial policies and regulations designed to remove older workers from the work force. This makes it possible to replace expensive workers with lower paid workers and it also provides work incentives for younger workers in the form of opportunities for mobility within the organization. Resistance to this social control aspect of Social Security pensions is undercut to the extent that policymakers have been able to define these pensions as a reward for good work done rather than as welfare for those who are no longer of use to industry.

It is our hope that many readers of this book will be concerned with the goal of empowering the elderly. We believe that an understanding of the social control aspects of various public policies that affect the elderly is essential to any effort to bring about changes in these policies, changes aimed at minimizing the most oppressive control aspects of these policies. While it is utopian to expect to remove all sources of social control for all persons affected by these policies, this is no justification to abandon efforts to minimize the most oppressive aspects of those policies. Some would argue that it is inappropriate to call attention to the social control aspects of a public policy that on balance greatly benefit the aged. We disagree. Our goal is to point the way for those who seek to make basically good programs and policies better. In the present analysis we take a critical look at a number of programs and policies which to this point have generally been the object of praise by those concerned with the welfare of the aged. The strengths and benefits of these programs are well known, and there is already a great deal of literature available documenting these strengths. Our goal is to take a more critical look at these programs and policies, not to provide evidence for those seeking to reduce the public committment to such efforts, but rather to provide guidance to those who seek to improve them.

CHAPTER 2

SOCIAL CONTROL OF THE ELDERLY

I T IS the purpose of this chapter to examine the origins and uses of social control as interpreted by three theoretical perspectives. This chapter will lay the groundwork for concepts used throughout the book. We shall begin by defining social control and briefly distinguishing it from other concepts such as power, influence, and authority. We shall then outline the analytical framework of political economists, functionalists, and labeling theorists on social control and explain why the emphasis throughout this book will reflect a political economy perspective.

Social control is a concept which describes how groups and individuals are impacted and constrained by other groups and individuals within a society. Social interactions involve demands and expectations from the actors toward one another, and not infrequently resistance results (Wrong, 1979:3). Norms and values, for example, represent efforts to control the behavior and ideas of group members, and rewards and punishments may be implied or invoked to encourage compliance or deter resistance. The means by which group members are controlled or compelled to conform to the will of the group can range from brute force and denial of a livelihood to persuasion, ridicule, and gossip (Berger, 1963).

Essentially, social control encompasses such concepts as power, influence, and authority. A major distinction between power and influence is that power involves the ability to bring about intended and foreseen effects on others, while someone may either intentionally or unintentionally influence the views and actions of others (Wrong, 1979:3-4). In either case, an individual's perceived options, real options, and personal autonomy may be reduced through this interaction. If an old person is advised by a bureaucratic official, for example, that his benefits will be reduced if he earns above a certain amount, then power has been exercised and autonomy lessened. In this instance, the intended and foreseen outcome will be "voluntary" absence from meaningful employment. The same result might occur, unintentionally, through repeated exposures to television ads depicting sick old persons and sitcoms in which all elderly characters are retired. Sometimes people attempt to influence others by persuasion where they rely upon the content of their arguments, and sometimes manipulation is used and the object of control is not aware of the attempt (Wrong, 1979:21-34). In all of these transactions, behaviors and beliefs may be impacted.

While social control is thought of as a collective term describing group processes that is analytically distinct from self-control (Roucek, 1956), at the core the success of either depends upon socialization of members toward their own containment. Social control begins as a structural relationship of power in the form of rules, customs, and ideologies surrounding such institutions as the economy, the polity, and the family. Its ultimate success is dependent upon the belief among subordinates within these institutions that their regulation and subordination are legitimate (Weber, 1947). When group members internalize the prevailing rules and invest those who invoke them with authority or the right to do so, then more direct and obvious forms of social control, such as force, are not needed (Wrong, 1979:24-28, 35-64). Nursing home residents, for example, who accept the prevailing regimen and the right of their caretakers to enforce it, can exercise only certain discretions within an otherwise predictable day. Those who interfere with the daily routine may be physically or chemically constrained and prohibited from displaying any autonomy whatsoever. At its root, social control reflects a tension between the group and the individual, between coercion and self-containment. Not incidentally, social control also reflects unequal power, authority, and ability to influence or define appropriate behavior.

A presumed tension between the group and the individual has been a subject of study for centuries and has often been debated in terms of social order versus individual freedom. Plato's REPUBLIC addressed the subject (Plato, 1930; 1935), and by the seventeenth century European political theorists, such as Hobbes (1958), were elaborating on the theme to be followed by eighteenth century political economists (Ricardo, 1951; Smith, 1937). It is important to note that while the formal concept of social control did not appear until the early twentieth century, nineteenth century concern about the issue underpinned the emergence of sociology as a discipline as well as the three theoretical perspectives employed throughout this book.

Comte, the "father of sociology," Marx, the initiator of radical political economy, Durkheim, the forerunner of functionalism, and Weber, a pioneer of interactionist theory, were all preoccupied with the relationship between economy and civil society, between capitalism and community, and between growth and social cohesion. In general, these Europeans took a critical stance towards emerging capitalism, in particular, the domination of society by economic relationships.[1] Also of concern was an expansion of the state to protect national and international capitalist markets — an expansion which could concentrate "legitimate" coercive power within one universalistic institution, the state (Weber, 1979).

American sociologists, inspired to some degree by England's Herbert Spencer, presented a slightly different focus in trying to identify strategies by which an emergent mass society comprised of diversified immigrants could be ordered.[2] Sociologists, on both sides of the ocean, noted the transition to wage labor which had occurred with the rise of capitalism and the accompanying growth of factory work and urban communities. Many also observed increased reliance upon formal rules for the maintenance of social order both within the workplace and the community (Durkheim, 1951; Marx, 1961; Weber, 1947).

As economies moved from an agricultural basis where families represented the primary work unit, societies were characterized by the existence of a group of people, laborers, who had to sell their labor power — their capacity to work — in order to survive materially (Marx, 1906a:186-189, 785-786).[3] While Marx, Durkheim, and Weber were preoccupied with how capitalism and increased reliance on formal rules were impacting the quality of individuals' lives and community integration, the prevailing question among early American sociologists was how those who were different — deviant — could be made to fit into a rule-oriented and wage-dependent society. This emphasis upon individual deviance, atavism, or pathology provided the concept of social control with decisively conservative undertones in America, where the term was first formally defined.[4]

Differences in the way European and American sociologists used such terms as pathology, deviance, and atavism are indicative of their varying interpretations of Darwinism and ideological applications. When Durkheim made his famous distinction between normal and pathological social facts (Durkheim, 1938:47-75), he used the word *normal* to describe that which was statistically normative — that behavior, for example, marrying, which occurs most often among a population, as opposed to the statistically infrequent behavior or pathology of remaining single. Both deviance and pathology went beyond this meaning of non-normativeness as used by early American sociologists. They carried perjorative connotations, sometimes implied atavism, and invariably called for the rehabilitation of individuals, not changes in the social structure. Labeling theory focuses on the study of deviance, and as we shall see, it too confines analysis to individual and group interactions, not to social structures.[5]

Use of the word atavist or throwback stemmed from Darwin's evolutionary theory of the species and suggested that a so-identified individual was not fully human and in need of reformation.[6] Certainly, Durkheim reflected the impact of Darwin in describing that form which is most prevalent within a society as normal. Functionalist theorists in America, who took their lead from Spencer, eventually tightened the social application of Darwinism and described society as an organism whose elements were the most evolutionary, progressive, and functional (Spencer, 1961). Thus, a positive value was imputed to social arrangements as they stood.

Marx's theory was also evolutionary in depicting history as a series of progressions of how humans combined with nature to provide for their material survival; but in refuting the idea of early political economists and later functionalists that existing economic and social arrangements were inevitable or functional, his analysis is better described as revolutionary than evolutionary (Gough, 1979:5-6). The concepts of deviance and social pathology are entirely absent from Marx's analyses.

For all of their differences, nineteenth century observers agreed that emergent industrial capitalism and increased reliance on formal rules (rationalization) were changing the face of social control. Most acknowledged the state's growing role as a regulator of social control. Throughout the discussion, we shall be concerned with how these two major loci of control — the world of work and the state — have exercised power over the elderly separately and collectively and how they continue to do so today. Building upon the concerns of these early observers, three major perspectives on social control have emerged. We shall first present separately the basic ideas of the political economy, functionalist, and labeling schools of thought and then suggest their points of convergence and relative merits.

POLITICAL ECONOMY AND SOCIAL CONTROL

A major distinction between the Marxist political economy theory of social control and others is its fusion of economics and sociology. While early sociologists registered concern about changes in civil society being wrought by the growth of capitalism, they essentially staked out the social relations and social structures of capitalist society as their targets for investigation. Economists, simultaneously, abstracted their analyses of capitalist production from the social relations generated by capitalism.[7] Marx, building upon and yet significantly altering earlier theories of political economy, evolved an entirely new social theory, often referred to as "historical materialism." This theory was also informed by Marx's familiarity with German philosophy and French socialism (Marx, 1968:1-64). Before discussing the forms of social control which are of most interest to neo-Marxists today, it is necessary to first explain some major departure points of historical materialism.

Originally, the term *political economy* referred to the works of such classical British economists as Adam Smith and David Ricardo (Ricardo, 1951; Smith, 1937). In analyzing the growing economic system of capitalism, they emphasized that the production of goods and services was for sale rather than for direct use by the producers (as under feudalism) and that all commodities involved in capitalist production could ultimately be analyzed according to their underlying objective cost with respect to human labor. This was the labor theory of value. Marx altered this concept of labor value in working out his historical materialism.

Marx's theory is materialist because he views the mode of production of a society as the basis of all other social institutions. A mode of production refers to the means by which humans interact with nature in producing goods to satisfy their material needs. It involves not only the way the labor process is organized (relations in production) but also the social relations between the classes created by a specific mode (relations of production) (Marx, 1906b). Of pivitol importance to Marx's analysis of capitalism is the concept of labor's surplus value.

Capitalism is not only a system in which human labor is a commodity, as early political economists noted, but also one whose surplus depended upon capitalists' ability to extract surplus value from the labor power which workers must sell to capitalists in order to live. Capitalism begins as a two-track class system where one group's means for survival is based on the privilege of owning the means of survival, and the other group gets by through selling its capacity to work — or labor power. According to Marx, the basis of the system rests on owners' ability to extract surplus value from workers by getting workers to produce more value than they recoup in wages and to claim this surplus (profits) as theirs by virtue of owning the means of production.

The major difference between Marx and traditional economists is his refusal to accept capitalism as a neutral system of exchange by which abstract commodities, such as labor, materials, and products, settle at market-defined value levels. While workers have the appearance of freedom to sell or not sell their labor power and the equality of exchanging wages for goods in the marketplace, most are not free to withhold their labor and cannot prevent their own exploitation within the sphere of production.[8] Workers generate surplus value — profits — over which they have no claim. The major difference between Marx and most sociologists is his contention that the mode of production, or the way in which one class extracts surplus value from another class, in the last analysis, determines the nature and form of the entire social structure. This constitutes the famous Marxian distinction between the infrastructure — the means of production — and the superstructure — the state, the family, religion, education, and ideology, and his argument that the latter reflect the interests of the dominant economic class.

It is important to note that Marx's materialism is not simplistic and addresses system contradictions, dialectics, and reflexiveness.[9] For example, within the workplace employers may be motivated to constantly increase profits and thereby try to extract more and more surplus value from workers, but they must obscure this dynamic or risk worker upheavals. Similarly, the state, according to Marxian analysis, is not a neutral arbitrator of class interests but rather a facilitator of the capital accumulation process and the recreation of the existing class system. Any given government operating within the state structure purports to represent all of the people but must play off competing class interests at times and mask certain capital accumulation functions.[10] Some state activities, such as overseeing public education, help subsidize the costs of employee training for capitalists while bolstering the state's appearance of class neutrality.

These kinds of contradictions will be explored in the following discussions of social control in the workplace and within the state. For now, it is important to stress that while both the marketplace and the government are typically depicted as neutral arbitrators of good, services, and policies, Marxian analysts argue that both are underpinned by inherently unequal social class relations, dialectical tensions, and interdependent mechanisms for socially controlling groups and being controlled.

The workplace is thus an important setting for social control. According to radical political economy theorists, control is exercised over workers in the workplace through two primary and interrelated mechanisms: one is management control over the work process, and the other is the existence of a reserve army of workers, that is, the unemployed (Braverman, 1974; Edwards, 1979). An apparent contradiction of capitalism is that in theory its harnessing of nature could enhance economic security and free humans for greater personal development. In practice, workers experience sizable insecu-

rity and have increasingly lost control over a more and more fragmented labor process (Marx, 1906a). Both results stem from the
need of capitalists to extract surplus value from their workers.

While employers purchase the labor power of workers through
employing them, they do not contract for a certain amount of labor.
The amount of labor an employer receives is directly related to the
generation of surplus labor value for the employer. Employers have
focused their efforts to control the workplace through controlling the
work process itself. For example, piece work used by some employers represented an attempt to purchase finished labor instead of
directly controlling the labor process. The employer could limit costs
this way but could in no way control the amount of labor, output,
and thus surplus value or profits.[11] Radical political economists argue that many of the changes in the production process over the past
100 years represent in fact a history of increased control of labor, and
while these observers have different terms depicting these changes,
they are in essential agreement on most transitions. Not incidentally,
older workers were the primary targets of some transitions and the
principal victims.

One area of agreement among radical political economists is that
the transition from competitive to monopoly capitalism between
1890 and 1920 spurred not only new forms of labor process control,
it also increased unemployment, intensified class conflict, and led to
broader state controls to deal with these by-products (Buraway,
1978; Edwards, 1979). In the early stages of this transition when
competition was fierce, employers frequently attempted to extract
surplus value from workers through direct exploitation — that is,
they increased the hours and intensity of work. Taylorism, developed by Frederick Winslow Taylor, for example, was an effort to systematically apply science to production by dividing work skills into
abilities, determining the maximum speed with which each ability
could humanly be executed, and attempting to force employees to
produce at these maximum speeds (Braverman, 1974:85-123;
Leutz, 1978:60). Although this system generated intense labor resistance from its primary targets — craft and semi-skilled workers —
and was eventually discarded, many seasoned workers were victimized in the meantime.

This kind of crude and obvious labor exploitation only furthered union growth and thus had to be abandoned by management for more subtle techniques. The idea of dividing a craft or skill into individual parts, however, took root among employers as a vehicle for controlling the labor process and was relied upon as a means of cheapening labor, creating interchangeable employees, and using unemployed persons as a threat to the employed. Braverman, one of the first neo-Marxists to analyze social control within the labor process, has described this job subdividing as the separation of conception from execution in labor, and he argues that most white- and blue-collar jobs today have been subjected to this process (Braverman, 1974:50-51). Buraway counters that employers must constantly mask the exploitation of workers' surplus value and must therefore adhere to limits in trying to reduce jobs into boring, interchangeable and externally paced tasks[12]. A distinction between Taylorism and externally paced or technical control is that Taylorism was enforced through human or hierarchical control, while technical control is administered through machinery.

Edwards, in his typology of work control, identifies four major and chronologically overlapping modes: entrepreneurial control, hierarchical control, technical control, and bureaucratic control (Edwards, 1979). Entrepreneurial control occurs in small enterprises where all employees are relatively powerless before the owners or supervisors. This kind of direct personal control was prevalent in the early to mid-nineteenth century and was relied upon as a means for encouraging "voluntary" retirement from older workers. As employers targeted skilled and craft workers for more control, they often relied on a hierarchical model. Skilled workers, many of whom were older, were viewed as too autonomous, too niggardly in transmitting their skills, and too unwilling to embrace technological innovation or drive themselves toward ever-rising output (Edwards, 1979:31). According to Edwards, hierarchical control was modeled on the army, and thus the supervisory ranks were expanded and each person was accountable to the individual above. It was within this context that Taylorism was implemented.

Whereas hierarchical control relies upon human supervision for speedups, technical control mandates speedups through machine pacing of the work process. Technical control was used as early as the first decades of the nineteenth century within Rhode Island textile plants, but its origin is usually associated with Fordism (Edwards, 1979:113). Although Taylorism had represented an attempt to subdivide work, cheapen labor, and deskill older craft workers, it was not nearly as successful in doing so as Fordism. Fordism was a major step toward structural control of the workplace. Mechanization allowed for a uniform work force comprised of unskilled and semiskilled operatives who were virtually interchangeable, They had no unique skills to barter with in wage negotiations, and Henry Ford and followers succeeded in their effort to create an enormous reserve of laborers to be played off against the employed.[13] Skilled older workers were dealt a particularly harsh blow by this turn of events.

Edwards's fourth type of work control, bureaucratic control, is built into job categories, work rules, promotion procedures, wage scales, and definitions of job responsibilities. While technical control rests on the design of machines, bureaucratic control is ascribed to "company rules," and individuals' powers are presented as impersonally and impartially based. Class interests become masked by bureaucratic rules, and the process of extracting surplus value from laborers is obscured by a vast system of internal stratification and preoccupation with job status distinctions. Edwards argues that all of these modes of control co-exist today, depending upon the enterprise.

Most radical political economists contend that as the exploitation of labor has become more obscured within the workplace through technical and bureaucratic controls, class conflicts are more frequently expressed within the political arena (Wolfe, 1977; O'Connor, 1973; Offe, 1975; Poulantzas, 1973). Another reason given for this shift is a presumed "social contract" made by labor unions and owners within the monopoly sector of the economy in the 1930s — an understanding whereby management guaranteed rising real wages for workers in the monopolized sector in exchange for labor's acknowledgement of management's prerogatives in the work process, the firm, and the economy.[14] Of particular interest is the role the state has played in this deflection of class tension from the workplace to the state itself, the topic to which we now turn.

Earlier, we noted a contradiction within the capitalist state of needing to assist capitalists in their accumulation process while simultaneously masking this goal so that the state's legitimacy as a neutral representative of all can be maintained. During the transition from competitive to monopoly capitalism which involved a drive among corporate employers for increased control over markets and employees, certain dynamics were set in motion that altered the state. Instead of merely assisting the accumulation process through such mechanisms as tax policies and subsidization of labor training in the form of public education, the state assumed responsibility for stabilizing the economy and managing those not absorbed by the economic system. These activities paralleled the "social contract" referred to earlier between monopoly sector labor and management and set the stage for bureaucratic controls within the workplace and the government.

As employers attempted to increase surplus labor value by introducing such methods as Taylorism, union activity only intensified, and their deskilling of labor generated ever-growing numbers of unemployed workers. A vanguard of corporate leaders openly looked to the state for assistance in salvaging their dominance, while workers and displaced workers also sought government protections (Kolko, 1971; Wolfe, 1977).

By the 1930s, the state was closely involved in trying to stabilize or rationalize the economy by overseeing the implementation of collective bargaining processes and providing for the unemployed old and disabled (Edwards, 1979; O'Connor, 1973). By legitimizing unions, mediation and reform of class conflict were improved.

Political economists point out various forms of social control which were generated by this shift in responsibility. In exchange for a loss of workplace control, labor received the beginnings of a welfare state through the Social Security Act of 1935. The price they paid for rationalization (bureaucratization) of the workplace and a seniority system was removal of the upper end of that system, that is, the elderly. As we shall see, this disenfranchised group was eventually subjected to bureaucratic control by a burgeoning state. A major argument made by radical political economists is that the "welfare state" itself is a major means by which the capitalist system is stabilized and social class inequities are maintained.

Gough defines the welfare state as "the use of state power to modify the reproduction of labor power and to maintain the non-working population in capitalist societies" (Gough, 1979:44-45). The expression "reproduction of labor power" here refers to efforts to provide for the social welfare of workers to the extent necessary so as to assure an adequate supply of workers over the years. O'Connor (1973) points out that although the welfare state contributes to capital accumulation through reproduction of labor, it is not the state's only method. The state, for example, makes social investments in the form of highways and research which subsidize profits, and the state provides social consumption items, such as housing and education, which reduce the costs to employers of reproducing labor power (O'Connor, 1973). The welfare state attempts to reproduce labor power by providing work-related subsidies, that is, employment training and worker's compensation. These help restore laborers for the workplace while simultaneously underscoring the state's legitimacy as a provider for all.

The other major function of social welfare policy is to maintain nonworking groups so as to dissipate any potential threat to social stability. Spitzer (1975) argues that the existence of (indeed the need for) unemployment within capitalist economies leads to two categories of nonconformists: "social junk" and "social dynamite." The first group is made up of those who withdraw, lose out, or are forced out of production — the handicapped, the ill, and the aged. The second or social dynamite group are those who call the economic system into question due to their experiences or their beliefs about system inequities and dysfunctions. Juvenile delinquents, criminal offenders, and political radicals fall into this group. The control of social junk is relegated to medical personnel, bureaucrats, and social welfare workers; control of social dynamite falls within the aegis of law enforcement agencies.

In addition to maintaining the capitalist system through the subsidization of labor reproduction and surplus labor, the state also assists capitalists in choosing policies which will benefit the system as a whole and yet exclude anti-capitalist alternatives.[15] For example, while the American Medical Association vehemently opposed Medicare legislation, they lost out to other groups who believed high medical costs could incite the elderly towards challenging the entire health care system. By establishing the program on the entrepreneurial fee-for-service basis, Congress excluded "anti-capitalist" alternatives, such as creation of a national health insurance program.

In America, the most potent political battles have revolved around issues of private versus public solutions to problems (Derthick, 1979; Piven and Cloward, 1977) and, more recently, about the permissible boundaries of state involvement. As radical political economists suggest, the expanded role of the state since the 1930s has served to stabilize the economic system; yet, in the absence of a genuinely progressive tax system or alternative state revenues, the fiscal cost has been great. Despite recent efforts to get the state's boundaries back to pre-1930 levels, both capitalists and workers have come to expect assistance from the government in their struggles.[16]

Throughout the book, we shall employ concepts introduced by the political economy perspective. For example, we shall examine the relationship between bureaucratic controls and the elderly and mechanisms whereby the state constrains them. We shall also want to know whether or not the elderly constitute "social junk," and if so, why, how, and for how long.

FUNCTIONALISM AND SOCIAL CONTROL

A second interpretation of social control comes from the functionalist approach to nonconformity. This school has its genesis in early applications of Darwinism to society. As noted, Marx borrowed from Darwin in emphasizing the concept of progress and suggesting that all of human history could be viewed in terms of progressively fruitful economic systems, yet he introduced a revolutionary note in saying that the most "fit" system for workers was yet to come.

A different application of Darwin's theory was provided by those social control analysts in America who stressed individual pathology as the cause of nonconformity. Essentially, those who deviated from the norm were seen as throwbacks to a less socialized form, and emphasis was placed on trying to adjust these individuals to the evolving modern era. An additional interpretation of Darwin stressed the normative aspect of his theory. Just as the human species was supposed to be in its most internally logical and strongest form as a result of natural selection, so could society's customs, behavioral rules, and values be seen as the most appropriate for continued survival. Their mere existence implied a rational or functional basis for their evolution (Abrahamson, 1978; Davis, 1975).

While both the individual pathology and the pre-normative or status quo perspectives on the origins of deviance inform the functionalist school, a third emphasis has emerged as the major interpretation. Based upon the ideas of Emile Durkheim and Talcott Parsons, functionalists argue that not only are individual deviance and social control two sides of the same coin, rule breaking is itself essential (functional) to the very structure of society (Durkheim, 1938; Parsons, 1951). Thus, deviant behavior is elevated to system-sustaining behavior, and the existence of deviants is considered necessary for maintaining an equilibrium or balance in society.

Durkheim proposed that a social mind or collective moral authority provides the basis for individual restraint within a society (Durkheim, 1951). The collective moral authority is expressed through efforts to socialize members of society to the prevailing values, attitudes, and behavioral patterns. This socialization results in the integration of individuals to society (Parsons, 1949:327-338). The state, according to Durkheim, embodies the social ego or consciousness of the collectivity. It reinforces this socialization process with both covert and overt means of social control (Durkheim, 1958). Legislation, administration, and law enforcement efforts comprise some of the overt control mechanisms.

Durkheim noted that despite society's formidable powers to control members' behaviors, ultimately, rule conformity is dependent upon the existence of norm breakers. Since collective moral authority or consciousness rests upon the successful diffusion of values, society needs to point out unacceptable behaviors in order to delineate what ideas and behaviors are valued. Durkheim is referring here to definition through negation (Durkheim, 1938). Through the designation of deviant behavior and activity, society makes known its acceptable behavioral standards. The deviant then comes to represent that for which society does not stand. Conceptually, this process is akin to the male sex role being defined and learned largely in terms of what it is not to be, for example, any behavior thought of as feminine or sissy-like. Similarly, youth is highly valued within

American culture not only because it is positively associated in the media with beauty, competency, and consumption, but also because old people are depicted as nonproductive, noncompetent, and pre-occupied with ailments, wrinkles, and gray hairs.

In addition to clarifying behavioral boundaries, the existence of deviants contributes to group cohesion. In-group members, identifying and focusing upon out-groups and norm-breakers, can simultaneously feel self-righteous and minimize their own differences (Mead, 1918). This is the well-known scapegoating dynamic. One of the most important ideas advanced by functionalists is that social systems are organized to produce or assure necessary levels of nonconformity, causing some groups or behaviors to be set up as examples of what not to be or do. We shall expand this idea in our discussion of Social Security legislation and show that one of its functions was to reinforce productivity among younger age groups by establishing the elderly as a negative referent.

Parsons has identified two major mechanisms — insulation and isolation — for containing deviant populations and stresses role performance, particularly the work role, as the goal or deviant creation devices (Parsons, 1951:301-310). One strategy is to insulate groups which threaten the existing economic organization by trying to depict their cause and the participants as "radical." The group goals are portrayed as marginal or contrary to the American way of life. To the extent that these groups are political, some rudimentary organization presumably exists, so insulation rather than the second strategy — isolation — is used. At the same time, attempts are made to co-opt group leaders by giving some token victories and by incorporating a few into the legitimized political network. Group leaders will presumably then control their more demanding members.

A case can and will be made throughout this book that Social Security and ensuing legislation and policies have helped to insulate America's old as an economic and political force and have contributed to their isolation individually. Those who come under the care of welfare, medical, or nursing home personnel are particularly isolated. As Parsons has suggested, by placing individuals under the care of experts and stressing their need for adjustment, successful coping becomes an effective way to render them politically impotent (Parsons, 1951:319). Such persons look to themselves as the cause of their problems, not to the social structure, and they also serve as examples of what becomes of nonproductive members of society.

If deviants respond to this insulation and/or isolation by forming subcultures, Parsons believes they are merely participating in a ritual pattern of control (Parsons, 1951:304). The elderly subculture, to the extent that one exists, reflects a permissible way to act out strain, just as youth cultures do, and its existence would reinforce the prevailig economic, power, and social arrangements.

A major difficulty with the functionalist perspective on social control is its premise that social values, ideologies, and behavioral rules are consensually derived. Consensus about what behavior is appropriate or inappropriate may be possible within small groups or rural communities, but within large industrialized societies a different process underpins social control. It will be recalled that Durkheim suggested that the state is the conscience of the collective moral authority and thus implied a process whereby the people's will is reflected in government policy. This bottom-to-top model parallels the pluralist model of power proposed by many political scientists in characterizing American society.

A more realistic model suggests that with so many formal mechanisms of social control in place today, such as various government bureaucracies, the media, and caretaking agencies, organized groups compete for access and direction of these social control institutions (Farrell and Swigert, 1982). Thus, standards of behavior represent the result of power struggles among unequal groups rather than a society-wide consensus.

One manifestation of this process, to be explored in this book, is the redefinition of deviance from a legal to a medical phenomenon, a redefinition that has been prompted, sold, and sizably controlled by mental health practitioners (Scull, 1977). With this transition, political issues are increasingly defined as personal issues[17] and potential "social dynamite" is rendered "social junk." We shall want to know whether gerontologists' packaging of the elderly as a "social problem" is part of this trend (Estes, 1979; Levin and Levin, 1980:41-48) and whether such a definition both reflects and tightens social control of the old.

LABELING THEORY AND SOCIAL CONTROL

While functional theorists view deviance and social control as reciprocal, interdependent, and inevitable elements of a social system, labeling theorists argue that deviance is the result of social control.[18] The relationship is one way rather than two way. Unlike functionalism which stresses the functions of social control for society, labeling theory focuses on its effects in the lives of those who are designated to a deviant status. Both schools believe definitions of deviance reflect moral meanings, but they differ on whose meanings they are — the larger society's or dominant group's.

Labeling theory developed out of symbolic interactionism, an approach which assumes that social reality is comprised of shared symbols — that is, mutually understood verbal and nonverbal signs. People learn these symbols through interaction with others and, through internalizing these symbols, come to recognize what is meaningful (Cooley, 1902; Mead, 1918). Behavioral categories are determined by social definitions whose meaning is passed along through symbolic communication. Since social control, according to labeling theorists, is the effective use of definitions or labels in discrediting some groups as opposed to others, two key questions are whose definitions are accepted and toward what ends?

Howard Becker argues that those with political and economic power are able to force their definitions upon others (Becker, 1963:16-17). Thus, for example, whites, males, and middle-aged persons are able to label blacks, women, and the elderly as less socially valuable than themselves. The meaning of being black, female, or old takes on negative, perjorative, and morally inferior connotations and this meaning is recognized by all. A major rationale for this discrediting process is difference or deviation from a norm, in this instance the declared norm being white, male, and middle-aged. Labeling on the basis of difference is termed *primary deviance,* and while being defined as such may be undesirable, it can ususally be dealt with through a normalizaton process by which the deviance is viewed as a normal everyday variation.[19]

The real difficulty arises, according to Lemert (1967), when a disvalued status due to some primary deviation becomes the basis for stigmatization, sanctions, segregation, and social control. Thus, a set of role expectations gets assigned to occupancy of the disvalued status, and the original deviance becomes a master status reinforced by public stereotypes. For example, age is a basis for deviation within any society, depending upon the age distribution. Old age can and continues to be viewed, within many cultures, as a normal variation. Perhaps old people's work loads are lightened, but their social roles remain basically constant (Treas, 1979; Davies, 1975).

When old age comes to be used as the basis for specific role expectations and is used by old persons as a referent for self-attitudes, then secondary deviation has occurred. A successfully labeled deviant has difficulty engaging in valued group activities, is usually stereotyped in terms of a broad range of imperfections (Simmons, 1965), and a self-fulfilling prophecy snowballs. By being labeled, the deviant is denied access to legitimate or valued social roles, comes to approximate the stereotype, and may eventually only feel comfortable with similarly labeled individuals (Goffman, 1963). Becker refers to this interaction process between the labeled individual and the group as a career path in which each successive step of exclusion and deviant identity is predetermined by previous events (Becker, 1963:101-119).

An important argument here is that the labeling process is arbitrary and today's deviants might be tomorrow's normals. What begins as a difference — that is, a limp, gender, race, or age — comes to be used as a justification for excluding deviant group members from powerful social positions.[20] The labeling process reflects a relative powerlessness among the labeled which becomes increased and systemitized powerlessness. As Goffman notes, the irony and impossibility of this situation is that labeled persons, particularly disvalued ones such as the handicapped and the old, continue to be told that they are normal and are encouraged to act like normals at the same time that the social structure is organized to preclude their acceptance or normalcy (Goffman, 1963:116-124). A phantom normalcy underlies a phantom acceptance. Once difference has become the basis for discrediting, stereotyping, stigmatization, and exclusion, maneuverability around the label is very difficult.

Labeling theorists make two additional observations. First, the labeling process is rationalized through laws, policies, and ideologies and usually involves public or private agencies as vehicles for defining and classifying people (Clinard, 1974; Lemert, 1967; Miller, 1979). Delinquents, criminals, the mentally ill, welfare recipients, and the old, for example, are classified as such by officials, who then impose punishments or curtail access to rewards. Some groups are incarcerated, others are subject to close surveillance, and still others must work or not work for benefit eligibility, depending upon official policy and the purposes each group serves within the social order. Welfare recipients are supposed to work, and old people lose Social Security benefits if they earn more than a minimal amount. Members of all of these groups are subject to publicly promoted stereotypes, carry a stigma, and tend to be segregated from mainstream life by official policy.

A second point made by labeling theorists is that the stigmatization process will affect the way group members feel about themselves. Our self-concepts are products of how we believe others perceive us. Some discredited persons will try to pass as "normals," others will keep their deviance a secret, and still others will want to interact with similarly labeled peers (Goffman, 1963). There are old people, for example, who compulsively try to carry all prior activities into old age, misrepresent their age, or seek out the company of older people almost exclusively.[21] In each of these cases, age is the major status referent.

One of the most chilling aspects of social control is the complicity of the controlled in their own containment. To the extent that old people internalize public stereotypes and respond to them as a basis for action or reaction, they are being controlled. Family members also contribute to this process when they encourage conformity to age norms among older members with the retort, "Act your age." As labeling theorists suggest, behavior is frequently guided by meanings which have been learned in interaction with significant others, and because this kind of social control is more subtle than official policies, it is very difficult to address.

Thus far in our discussion, we have emphasized the distinctive features of these social control perspectives so that their respective contributions to later discussions will be evident. There are, in fact, many areas of agreement among theorists from these schools and still other theories which link components of each.[22] Social control theorists generally concur, for example, on the importance of resource control, whether it is money, expertise, or prestige which is employed, as a basis for everyday transactions.[23] All emphasize exclusion from the work force as the major impetus for a "deviant" label and/or its effect. Work is the central vehicle for organizing the social order (Piven and Cloward, 1971:7), and those who are perceived as unfit (the handicapped and the elderly) or as willfully unattached to the labor force (criminals and welfare recipients) become objects for separation and stigmatization (Clinard, 1974; Parsons, 1951; Spitzer, 1975). This insulation in turn assures difficulty in returning to the labor force and other legitimizing social roles.

A second area of agreement between functionalist and labeling theorists is that a deviant, disvalued, discredited, or nonconformist label is an arbitrary matter (Durkheim, 1938:70-71; Simmons, 1969:120-126). Radical political economists would expand on Becker's idea that the dispensing of labels reflects economic and political power and argue that the structural dominance of business owners and managers gives them the edge in successfully labeling others. Differences among individuals always exist, and whether age, gender, race, religion, thievery, or corruption lead to a labeling and exclusion process depends upon the needs of the capitalist system (radical political economists), what behaviors are to be encouraged (functionalists), or who is in a position to dispense labels (labeling theory).

We have used the terms *deviant, disvalued,* and *nonconformist* interchangeably throughout this discussion because the dynamics of social control are similar no matter what the label. Today, the word *deviant* often suggests someone who violates a law, but the process of discrediting and trying to contain group members follows parallel patterns when a characteristic such as age, gender, deformity, social class origin, or mental health provides the rationale.

A third area of convergence among social control theorists is their belief that social control involves blaming the target, not the system. As Ross noted many years ago, in a society such as the United States where discrimination is frowned upon in the ideal, it is rationalized by the belief that the target deserves it (Ross, 1928). This focus serves many purposes simultaneously. The policies which solidify the discrimination go unchallenged, those who are discriminated against are told to adjust to their situation since their "difference" has

brought on their problems, and specialized caretakers and bureaucrats can be employed to assure their distance from the rest of the
community (Lemert, 1967:48-52). In this way, those who are responsible for the discriminatory policy do not have to observe the
consequences of their acts (Hughes, 1964).

Probably the most important point made by theorists of social
control is that the nature or face of control has changed over the past
100 years; not only are targets told they are responsible for their
plight, they are also led to believe that their loss of autonomy and relegation to others' care is for their own good (Schrag, 1978; Parsons,
1951; Lemert, 1967; Goffman, 1961). Essentially, social control
mechanisms have been altered in two major, yet overlapping ways.
First, enlightened bureaucratic management, through the use of policy and law, has replaced informal controls of the primary group and
overtly coercive powers of the state as the most pervasive sources of
control (Poulantzas, 1973; Berger, 1963).

Individuals are not thrown into dungeons for nonpayment of
debts or into workhouses for nonparticipation in the productive
force. Instead, they are relegated to an agency set up for the purposes of counseling, advising, and rehabilitating them for community integration. Or if their "proper place" is outside the productive
force, they will be encouraged to look for meaning in life elsewhere
and not notice that they are officially marginal. Within the workplace itself, employees control themselves through compliance with
bureaucratic rules that proscribe worker determination of production outputs and processes (Edwards, 1979). This bureaucratic
model of control is difficult to target for change.

Second, the major agents of control are no longer sweatshop employers or law enforcement agents. Rather, the benign bureaucratic
model overlaps with a medical model of control, and psychiatrists
and other medical personnel play a major part in defining people's
possibilities in life (Szasz, 1963). Davis noted many years ago that
mental hygiene is not so much a science for preventing mental disorder as a science for the prevention of moral delinquency (Davis,
1938:60-61).

By suggesting that something so arbitrary as mental illness is a
"disease" which can be rationally treated, medical personnel
managed to legitimize their turf and guarantee an endless supply of

patients (Szasz, 1963). Every new edition of the American Psychiatric Handbook for diagnoses includes additional categories of mental illness which ideally would be "treated" by psychiatrists. Two recent entries, for example, include coffee-drinking and smoking disorders.

Not only was this transition in social control mechanisms a major coup for medical professions, but, more importantly, political and social problems have come to be labeled medical problems.[24] Mental health means conformity to the demands of society (Davis, 1938:60-61), and the therapeutic function is to isolate potential nonconformists and forestall or reverse their tendencies to deviate (Parsons, 1951:308-319). By labeling and discrediting, psychiatrists legitimize and illegitimize the social aspirations of and roles available to individuals (Szasz, 1970:206). For example, they can decide who can go to trial, drive a car, execute a will, or successfully challenge nursing home policies; to the extent that they or their diagnostic instruments are used by employers, they also directly impact a person's ability to make a living.

Mental health practitioners look within individuals for all explanations of behavior, so the focus is removed from what people say, to why they say it. As Szasz suggests, the medical model leads people to conclude that a person is "mentally ill" or senile, not that the person's arguments are "wrong" or "threatening" (Szasz, 1963:204-206). Political convictions, beliefs, and actions are often reduced to symptoms of illness (nonconformity) rather than respected as self-expressions. Nursing homes present an unusually graphic example of bureaucratic, medical, profit-oriented, and labeling control mechanisms in operation as we shall see in later chapters.

Now that we have outlined each theoretical perspective and noted their differences and similarities for analyzing social control, we shall briefly mention some of their relative strengths and weaknesses. In addition to sharing observations, such as the prevalence of bureaucratic control in modern America, these theories complement one another at certain points. For this reason, all will be employed throughout the book. Labeling theorist, Becker (1963), for example, suggests that the ability to label results from structural power, and yet the labeling pespective does not shed light on who has structural power or why. This school of thought is also ahistorical in that it analyzes the interaction dynamics of control as they exist at one point in time. Political economy theory will be our preferred analytical tool throughout because it is both historical and capable of locating structural power among owners, managers, and their representatives within a capitalist society. Labeling theory will be very useful in exploring how ideological control is exercised and legitimated through internalization of symbols and shared meanings on an everyday basis and how deviant or disvalued persons might empower themselves by refusing to accept a negative definition.

Functional theory is helpful in showing how certain social facts, such as age norms, can promote society equilibrium; yet, it is less useful in explaining why norms take their present form or whose interests might be best served by their existence. Again, the political economy perspective could assist in answering such questions. For example, functionalists might explain mandatory retirement at age 65 in terms of society's need to replace its producers before their deaths so that the ongoing work of society would not be disrupted.[25] Political economists would want to know how this policy fits in with managements' attempts to extract surplus value from workers and whose class positions were bolstered or reduced as a result.

While functional theory is oriented toward equilibrium and is basically conservative, a radical analysis can be done using its concepts. Gans, for example, outlines the "positive functions" of poverty for upper-, middle-, and working-class Americans, and in so doing, he alludes to structural power in the hands of economic elites (Gans, 1981:61-63). Using a functionalist approach, we shall analyze various twentieth century policies for the elderly, but our emphasis will be on how these policies perpetuate the class system, transform class issues into political issues, and help to splinter working-class Americans. Our bias throughout will be toward critically analyzing old age policy rather than merely describing it.

CONCLUSION

Using such concepts as modes of control, social functions, and secondary deviations or gains, we shall explore the ways in which older Americans have been successfully controlled as an economic, political, and social force. We shall rely heavily upon the political economy perspective throughout so that we may go beyond description of what programs, policies, ideologies, and norms exist toward an understanding of .why. We shall be particularly interested in fusing economics and sociology in our analyses, as Marx did,[26] so that we can better understand the relationship between the system needs of capitalism and all other social facts and between class dynamics and the politics of aging. To begin this process, we need to examine the historical foundation of public policy for the aged.

NOTES

1. For selected works on these topics, see Comte (1896), Durkheim (1951), Marx (1961), and Weber (1947).
2. For example, see Gerver (1963) for how Lester Ward adapted Spencer (1961) to some extent.
3. Giddens (1971:164) argues that Weber agrees with Marx on ownership versus nonownership of production constituting the major class determinant within capitalist societies.
4. See Bernard and Bernard (1965) for an analysis of the rise of sociology in America, and Davis (1975:14-35) for a critique of the "social pathologists" in America. Ross (1928) made the first major study of social control as a formal concept.
5. Our own use of the term *deviance*, unless otherwise specified, refers to the broad interpretation of non-normative behavior.
6. An example of an exception to Europeans' usual emphasis on the social structure was Lombroso (1918), who identified "stigmata" or physical characteristics associated with criminality and which represented atavism.
7. Gough (1979:1-7) provides a good overview of this splintering of the political economy perspective into the disciplines of economics and sociology.
8. Gough (1979:23) elaborates on this apparent anomaly.
9. See Buraway (1978) and Edwards (1979) for discussions of how workers can and do impact the work process; O'Connor (1981), Offe (1975), and Wright (1979b) all provide excellent analyses of the ways in which workers impact state policy and how efforts by the state to assist capital accumulation invariably lead to problems which generate additional pressure on the state by the working class.
10. See O'Connor (1973) for one of the most thorough developments of

this capital accumulation versus legitimacy trade-off problem of the state.

11. Braverman (1974) gives one of the first and most thorough Marxian analyses of workplace transitions between the later 1800s and the 1960s.

12. Buraway (1978:271-276) elaborates on this in his discussion of games within the workplace.

13. The use of Fordism to make workers interchangeable and therefore intimidated by their easy replacement is a major point made by both Braverman (1974) and Edwards (1979).

14. This thesis is argued in Herman (1982).

15. For a discussion of state strategies of control from a neo-Marxist perspective with a Hegelian influence, see Wolfe (1977).

16. See O'Connor (1981) for a discussion of structural obstacles to Reagan's attempts to place state involvement in class issues back on a pre-1930 basis.

17. See Schrag (1978) for an interesting discussion of this transition of issues from the political to the personal realm.

18. See Becker (1963), Clinard (1974), and Lemert (1967) for examples of this argument.

19. See Lemert (1967:40-64) for the discussion of primary and secondary deviance upon which this presentation is based.

20. See Clinard (1974), Simmons (1969), and Lemert (1967) for analyses of the labeling process as arbitrary.

21. See Clark and Anderson (1967) for case histories of how individual old persons deal with this perceived stigma.

22. Although these microtheories of interpersonal power will be explored in later discussions of how old people negotiate with others in everyday life, we shall briefly provide an example. Exchange theory suggests that in all relationships individuals try to balance the rewards and costs involved. See Blau (1964) and Homans (1960). Rewards include such factors as respect, deference, assistance (emotional or monetary), knowledge, or a sense of reciprocity. Costs might take the form of unreasonable demands, a lack of reciprocity, and unmet expectations. Dowd (1980:38) has pointed out that the resources people have available will impact their exchange currency and thus their negotiating ability in everyday relationships. He cites several types of resources which people call upon to bolster their interpersonal power. These include personal resources, such as strength, beauty, intelligence, charm and knowledge; material possessions in the form of money or property; authority conferred by one's positions; family

and friend relationships, and generalized reinforcers, such as approval, respect, and support. A case can and will be made that social policies have conspired in such a way as to reduce the elderly's share of some valued resources. Removal from the producer role, for example, obviously reduces material possessions and any authority gained from that role. Social contacts can also be sizably impacted. Generalized reinforcers in the form of deference, respect, or approval are frequently relied upon by older Americans to assure continued relationships with more socially powerful friends and family members.

23. See Archibald (1976), Borgatta amd Meyer (1959), Parsons (1951), Goffman (1963); each of these sources directly or indirectly introduces the issue of resources control into the analysis.

24. It should be noted that the economic repercussions of this redefintion of deviance exceeded mere revenues for health care workers. It has resulted in an enormous health care industry whose rate of inflation runs well ahead of other industrial sectors. See Ehrenreich and Ehrenreich (1971). If the costs involved in the third-party payment system were better controlled by the government, greater reductions in inflation and tax expenditures would occur than with most Social Security revisions advanced so far. See Myles (1981b).

25. The disengagement theory of aging in Cumming and Henry (1961) is a functionalist theory which could support this argument.

26. Gough (1979:7) discusses linkages between economics and sociology and Marx's fusion of the two.

CHAPTER 3

THE ORIGINS OF ENGLISH AGING POLICY

PRIOR to the twentieth century the primary public policies dealing with the elderly were relief policies. In order to understand the origins of public policy toward the elderly in the United States, it is necessary to consider the development of English Poor Law, which played a profound role in shaping this policy.

We begin our analysis with the twelfth century because there is no systematic statement of poor relief policy prior to the *Decretum* written in 1140. This is also the first time that a distinction is made for policy purposes between the elderly and other categories of the poor. To understand the significance of the policy changes embodied in the Elizabethan Poor Law of 1601, which was to have a major impact on relief legislation in both England and the American colonies, it is essential to compare it with the medieval relief policies which had preceded it. The analysis in this chapter ends with a discussion of the Poor Law Reform of 1834, as that was the last piece of nineteenth century English relief legislation to have a significant impact on the development of policy in the United States.

In the present analysis the term *poor* refers to persons who are dependent on alms for subsistence.[1] In preindustrial England the porportion of the population in this situation ranged from 5 percent during good times to as high as 50 percent during some of the famines.[2] Due to crop failures, wars, epidemics, and the economic cycles, rapid fluctuations in the proportion destitute were common. The term *old* refers to people unable to support themselves through work due to the infirmities of old age. It includes most of those over

38

age 60 and virtually all of those over age 65. The proportion age 60 and over was typically between 8 and 12 percent in preindustrial England.[3] In most of the literature the reference is not to the "aged" but rather to the "aged and impotent." Simply being 60 or 65 years old did not in itself put one into this category.[4]

MEDIEVAL RELIEF POLICY

As early as the sixth century, the Christian Church was actively involved in poor relief through a system of largely rural monasteries (Webb and Webb, 1927:6). In fact, because Church policy dictated public policy, relief for the indigent remained relatively stable from the twelfth through the middle of the fourteenth century.[5] In 1140, an Italian monk, Gratian, codified Church law into a document termed the *Decretum* (Tierney, 1959:7-67). The *Decretum*, by thoroughly stating policies toward poor relief, served as a foundation for all relief policy throughout the medieval period.

Because everyone was a member of the Church and potentially eligible for relief, the Crown and the feudal lords viewed relief as solely a function of the Church. The Church administered relief by two different ecclesiastical hierarchies: the monasteries and the parish churches. The medieval monasteries were powerful and wealthy institutions; in 1430 they owned 15 percent of the land in England.[6] Large feudal estates run by the monasteries generated revenues which were used for a variety of purposes, including poor relief (Cipolla, 1976:57). The system of parish churches was financed by the tithe. Unfortunately, there was no systematic effort to coordinate the relief efforts of the monasteries with those of the parish churches.[7]

The alms provided by the Church or monastery typically did not provide sufficient income for subsistence. This source had to be supplemented by some combination of help from family and begging. There was substantial variation among serfs in land holding (Bennett, 1937:63). The better off were undoubtedly more likely to provide for their elderly parents, yet many were so poor themselves that they were unable to support dependent parents.[8]

The practice of begging was viewed very differently in medieval England that it is today. The practice had a long Church heritage.

The teachings of St. Paul, St. Augustine, St. Bernard, St. Francis, and St. Thomas Acquinas were frequently cited when discussing relief policy and they all spoke about the virtues of poverty, particularly voluntary poverty (Tierney, 1959:11; de Schweinitz, 1943:17). Begging was consistent with the Church tradition of the mendicant friar and the religious pilgrim to the Holy Land.

Another reason for the Church's accepting view toward poverty was its static view of the social order. Some were born rich and some were born poor; poverty was seen as part of God's design, not as a reflection of personal failure or moral turpitude. The existence of poverty provided an opportunity for others to demonstrate Christian charity.

Medieval relief policy toward the aged poor was not sharply differentiated from policy toward other dependent individuals such as the blind and the disabled. Under ordinary circumstances, not much was made of the distinction between the infirm elderly poor and the able-bodied poor.[9] Church law and relief practice tended to favor alms to all who were in need, even if able-bodied.

In most areas the parish priest was in charge of relief. He tended to know those who were seeking alms and their individual situations (Coll, 1969:3). For this reason it was not necessary to depend upon formal categorizations when deciding how much assistance a person was to be given. Able-bodied beggars were typically urged to find work or were given a job, yet they were not categorically denied relief.[10] In the *Decretum* the distinctions that were made among various categories of the poor were to be used only when resources for relief were limited. In such situations, infirm elderly were to be given a higher priority than were the able-bodied (Coll, 1969:2; Tierney, 1959:58).

A great deal of attention is given in the *Decretum* to the question of when charity will or will not contribute to the salvation of the donor.[11] In view of the medieval concern with doing "good works" and on the benefits of such efforts for the donor, it is not surprising that relatively little attention is given to assessing the consequences for recipients (Webb and Webb, 1927:4-5). This conclusion is particuarly true with respect to monastic relief toward the end of the Middle Ages. It is also true of individual almsgiving. For example, it was common for the affluent to sponsor feasts for the poor as acts of charity in connection with weddings and particularly funerals (Tierney, 1959:66-67). Feudal lords also had a clear economic interest in keeping their serfs in good health so they would be able to work the land.[12] Thus, they could be expected to participate in relief efforts in times of need, often by providing food or money to the parish church for distribution (de Schweinitz, 1943:17). However, the feudal economy had not evolved to the point where it had any significant impact on the incidence of poverty or on relief policy.

During he late Middle Ages the feudal social order began to disintegrate.[13] The rise of towns and the development of an international market for English woolen cloth contributed to the change, as did the shift from sharecropping and feudal services to a system of cash payments (Bennett, 1937:227). This emergence of a money economy provided a means for serfs to buy their freedom and created job opportunities for those able to escape bondage. London, York, and other such towns were places with a new set of norms, values, and opportunities for advancement, which were very attractive to the newly freed serfs (Cipolla, 1976:139-145).

The social disorder that resulted from the transition to a money economy led to the enactment of statutes that changed policies toward relief. The first major shift in public relief policy came with enactment of a series of laws referred to as the Statutes of Laborers between 1349 and 1388 (Nicholls, 1898:36-38; Leonard, 1900:3-4). These laws were primarily designed to deal with the social disorder caused by a sharp increased in the movement of labor and marauding bands of beggars. The 1388 statute prohibited begging by the able-bodied, yet permitted begging by the infirm elderly and other categories of the impotent poor (e.g. the blind and the disabled) so long as it was done in the place of current residence or place of birth (de Scweinitz, 1943:8).

In 1348 the bubonic plague reached England causing a sharp reduction in population which turned out to have some positive consequences for the peasants who survived.[14] The shortage of labor dramatically drove up wages which in turn accelerated the long-term social changes associated with the decline of feudalism that were already in process. It became increasingly easy and attractive to escape bondage for work as an artisan in town or as a free laborer on another estate (Coulton, 1925:137). Strong economic incentives encouraged laborers to move from one region to another in search of higher-paying jobs. Between jobs, many turned to begging. Some joined vagrant bands which led to an increase in thievery and banditry (Coll, 1969:4).

The Statutes of Laborers were repressive measures designed to control the geographic mobility, wage demands, vagrancy, and begging of the peasants. The motive for this first instance of state involvement in the regulation of begging was in no sense a humanitarian concern for the plight of destitute beggars. These statutes were aimed primarily at sturdy beggers, the younger able-bodied unemployed. The legislation would not have been enacted if most beggars had been disabled, blind, or elderly. The goal was to force the able-bodied to work at "reasonable" wages. The provisions for the elderly and other impotent beggars were included more as an afterthought. These statutes were not successful in eliminating begging by the able-bodied, yet they probably did help elderly beggars by reducing the competition. The statutes had another serendipitous consequence: children were discouraged from leaving the local area and, as a result, were more likely to be available to provide help to elderly parents.

During the fifteenth century, economic conditions were generally favorable for peasants in England and throughout Europe. Braudel and Coulton argue that conditions were as good at this time as they would be until late in the nineteenth century (Braudel, 1967:129-130; Coulton, 1925:9). If we look at the amount of wheat a day's wages bought or at per capita meat consumption, we found evidence of a decline in the standard of living for peasants from this time through the middle of the nineteenth century.[15]

ELIZABETHAN POOR LAW OF 1601

The sixteenth century, in contrast, brought a marked deterioration in economic conditions for the laboring class (Oxley, 1974:15). A number of factors contributed to this change but of particular importance was increased dependence on a market economy.[16] The evolving market economy was making the nation increasingly vulnerable to the vicissitudes of international markets and the cyclical trends of capitalist economies. This led to a sharp increase in the number of vagrants and beggars, which contributed to an upswing in social disorder, crime, and food riots (Hampson, 1934; Webb and Webb, 1927:42).

Something had to be done to maintain social order. The first attempts were similar to the fourteenth century Statutes of Laborers: the emphasis was on the suppression of begging, particularly by the able-bodied.[17] Now conditions were different. The basic problem was too many laborers, not too few. Repression alone was not working even though the sanctions were severe.

Between 1531 and 1576 several Poor Law statutes were enacted that were synthesized in the comprehensive statute of 1597. With minor changes this became the Elizabethan Poor Law of 1601 — the foundation for English relief policy during the next two hundred years (Leonard, 1900:134).

The Poor Law of 1601 called for a poor tax to generate the revenues needed to provide relief. The poor were divided into three categories: (1) children, (2) the able-bodied, and (3) the impotent (infirm). Different policies were suggested for each. The able-bodied were not denied relief so long as they were willing to accept work provided by poor relief officials. The statute prohibited begging and it provided relief for all categories of the poor except those who were able, yet unwilling, to work. Children were required to provide for their elderly parents (Webb and Webb, 1927:62-65). The infirm elderly were grouped with the disabled, the blind, and the ill as well as others unable to provide for themselves (de Schweinitz, 1943:27). Such persons were provided for at home or in an almshouse (Leonard, 1900:213-214).

While the Poor Law of 1601 was more generous and less harsh than the Statutes of Laborers, the social control objective was still important. The legislation was enacted in response to food riots, looting, and other crimes against property. Begging was prohibited. If found begging, the able-bodied were sent in jail. Throughout this period, relief policy was closely linked to concerns about law and order.

Had all of the poor been infirm elderly, blind, or disabled, it is likely that their destitution would have gone all but unnoticed. This legislation was designed primarily as a way to control the able-bodied; they were the ones most likely and most able to turn to the violence and destruction that threatened the interests of property owners. The elderly were included in this legislation, but they were not the focus. For policy purposes a distinction was made between the infirm elderly poor and the able-bodied elderly poor, but no distinction was made between the elderly and other categories of the impotent poor.

The next major piece of legislation of interest to us was the Law of Settlement and Removal enacted in 1662 (Henriques, 1979:13-14). It was a response to labor mobility and the desire of taxpayers in one area to avoid paying relief for recent migrants from other areas (Webb and Webb, 1927:314-349). Public officials were given the right to make recent migrants leave the parish if it seemed likely that they would become public dependents (de Schweinitz, 1943:39-47). Such persons were required to return to their parish of legal settlement.[18] The Law of Settlement and Removal had particularly adverse consequences for older laborers. The older, less productive workers had to search longer and further for employers when the market was tight. They were also viewed as potential dependents and thus were more vulnerable than were younger workers to the provisions of the statute. The most important aspect of this act is that it signals a shift toward a more restrictive policy toward the poor. It is indicative of a generally more punitive policy that characterized the period from the mid-seventeenth century to the late eighteenth century.

One factor contributing to this shift in attitude and policy was the Protestant Reformation. The Puritans and other sects inspired by Calvinstic ideology became popular among merchants, craftsmen, and small landholders (de Beauvoir, 1972:178). The Calvinist stress on thrift, industry, and sobriety fit well with the entrepreneural orientation of the growing and increasingly influential middle class (Coll, 1969:7). The Calvinist conception of predestination was also important, as it led to the search for signs that one had been selected for salvation; economic success was taken as one such sign (Weber, 1958:98-128). These values led to the practice of blaming the victim. It was assumed destitute elderly were responsible for their improvidence by not having made a sufficient effort to accumulate assets to subsist on during their later years.

EIGHTEENTH CENTURY RELIEF POLICY

Policymakers became obsessed with the prospect of malingering on the part of the able-bodied poor. In 1722 a statute was passed which required that all recipients move into the workhouse as precondition for relief. All who sought relief, the elderly as well as the able-bodied, were to be subjected to the indignity, stigma, loss of autonomy, regimentation, and social control associated with such institutions. One goal was to make relief so unattractive that only those who were truly needy would apply; another was to provide that relief which was necessary at the minimum possible expense. The hope was that this approach would reduce the cost of relief and the related tax burden. In many areas the relief applicant was given the option of continued outdoor (at home) relief but at a much lower benefit level (de Schweinitz, 1943:58-66). Overall, these policy changes had a dire effect on the infirm elderly and other categories of the impotent poor.

High infant mortality rates were used by social reformers to discredit these shifts in policy and the notion of the workhouses (de Schweinitz, 1943:65-68). Persuaded by their arguments, in 1782 the Parliament enacted the Gilbert Act, which no longer required the poor to enter the workhouse as a precondition for relief (de Schweinitz, 1943:65-68). Although the effects of the Statute of 1722 were greatly reduced, it was not because of any heightened concern for the squalid conditions of the elderly but rather the young.

In 1795 Parliament approved a system of wage supplements referred to as the Speenhamland system. This new approach allowed local relief officials to supplement wages when they fell below a specific minimum level based on the price of wheat and the size of the laborer's family (Polanyi, 1944:77-85). The most radical aspect of this new policy is that it did not discourage the able-bodied from seeking relief; to the contrary, it made relief more or less automatic with none of the stigma of the workhouse. This liberalization of relief policy was in response to outbreaks of violence and social disorder, particularly in rural areas. The late eighteenth century was a period of mass unemployment and sharp fluctuations in the price of food.

Urban industrial growth stimulated a new round of enclosure.

The earlier and more well-known round took place during the late medieval period in response to the demand for wool. At that time, many peasants were forced out of the countryside and into towns, as small subsistence farms were combined into large enclosed tracts for sheep herding. This new eighteenth century round of enclosure eliminated much of the commons and waste lands. For centuries these lands were considered public, and many of the poor had come to depend on resources obtained from these lands to supplement meager wages and to tide them over during periods of unemployment. In the eighteenth century, large landowners bought the right to enclose these lands for private use. In addition, a shift to cereal cash crops from mixed subsistence farming meant that there was less year-round employment.

Rural overpopulation also contributed to an increase in povety (Henriques, 1979:18). Much of the surplus population was drained off by the expansion of industry in the towns and cities, but during the periodic depressions many of the unemployed would attempt to return to the rural areas from which they had previously migrated making an already serious overpopulation problem catastrophic.

At first the impact of the Speenhamland system on the elderly poor was positive. It made up the difference between what the worker was able to earn and what was needed for subsistence. Thus older, less productive workers could remain in the labor force longer. Eventually, the system severely depressed wages and ceased to adequately make up the difference between wages paid and subsistence. Opinions differ as to why this happened. Some argue that employers began to reduce wages in response to the availability of this new system of relief. Others argue that workers themselves became less productive in response to the security provided (Polanyi, 1944:86-102).

POOR LAW REFORM OF 1834

The liberalization of relief policy during the late eighteenth century was reversed with the enactment of the Poor Law Reform of 1834 (Rose, 1971:95-100). The most important policy change was that able-bodied relief applicants were now required to enter the workhouse as a condition for the receipt of relief.[19] This new policy was not as harsh as that in response to the 1722 statute, yet it was a definite step back in that direction.

Another important policy outlined in the Royal Commission Report of 1834, which served as the basis for the Reform Act of 1834, was that the condition of those on relief was to be less desirable ("less eligible") than that of the lowest paid laborers not on relief (Webb and Webb, 1910:3). The goal was to avoid making the workhouse an attractive option for able-bodied laborers working at low wages.

More directly affected than the infirm elderly were older able-bodied agricultural workers. Long before a worker was in any obvious way disabled by the infirmities of old age, he became less productive and thus less attractive to employers than younger workers. These landless older agricultural workers were often forced into beggary or the workhouse. As they were not suffering from the infirmities of extreme old age, for purposes of relief they were classified as able-bodied. Not only these workers but also their dependents were forced to make a choice between the workhouse and starvation.[20]

This new legislation did not call for any change in poor law provisions dealing with the infirm elderly (Webb and Webb, 1910:51), but it did have the effect of increasing the proportion of the elderly who ended up in the workhouse. One reason was that the legislation was part of a more general shift in the direction of harsher attitudes and policies toward the poor (Coll, 1969:9; Polanyi, 1944:82; de Schweinitz, 1943:114-120). All categories of the poor including the infirm elderly were more likely to be blamed and held in contempt for being paupers. Local poor relief authorities had a great deal of discretion in the implementation of poor relief policy. This shift in attitude toward the poor made even the elderly poor vulnerable to these more restrictive policies. In many areas the workhouse became the first choice rather than last resort not only for the able-bodied but also for the elderly and other infirm categories.[21]

A major stimulus to the enactment of the 1834 reform was the rapid increase in poor taxes since the turn of the century (Webb and Webb, 1927:418; de Schweinitz, 1943:114). During this same period there was a marked increase in the number of persons on relief, particularly in areas which had implemented the Speenhamland system (Hammond and Hammond, 1911:153). The conclusion reached by many policymakers (and taxpayers) was that the liberal Speenhamland system was causing pauperization.[22] Tax monies could be saved and the able-bodied could be saved from a life of dependency if only a more restrictive relief policy were implemented.

If the elderly were required to move into the workhouse, this would provide a strong incentive to find some alternative means of subsistence. Some would do without, some would turn to their children, and some would find yet other ways to avoid institutionalization. It would also provide an incentive to children both to support their elderly parents and to set aside funds for their own old age (Webb and Webb, 1929:351).

INTERPRETATION AND ANALYSIS

Between the twelfth and the nineteenth centuries, English public policy toward the elderly poor was residual in nature. The focus of all major relief legislation after the fourteenth century was on the able-bodied poor. There were a number of reasons for this focus, but certainly one of the most important is that the able-bodied were the greatest threat to the social order. The demands of the infirm elderly, the blind, and the disabled could be ignored, but the demands of the able-bodied could not. They could cause too much damage when they turned to rioting, looting, and other forms of mass violence.

Another reason that the able-bodied were always the focus is that they were central to the work process. In times of labor shortage such as the fourteenth century, the able-bodied were in a position to drive up wage levels with adverse consequences for the profits of landowners and employers more generally. In times of labor surplus, it was the able-bodied of the relief population that fluctuated most erratically in response to the cycles of the market economy.

As a result of the legislative focus on the able-bodied, the infirm elderly were shunted to the background with other categories of the impotent poor. In some instances, as is the cases of the 1795 statute legalizing wage supplements, there were benefits for the elderly even though such benefits were not intended. More frequently, as in the case of the Reform Act of 1834, there were adverse consequences for the elderly that again were not intended by those formulating the legislation.

Looking at the long-term trend in poor relief policy for England from the twelfth through the nineteenth century, the pattern is clearly cyclical. The most useful theoretical account of this pattern is that proposed by Piven and Cloward (Piven and Cloward, 1971:3-42). According to their account, when mass unemployment leads to outbreaks of civil disorder, ruling elites expand relief programs as a mechanism of social control designed to restore political stability. In the English case there is much evidence to support this interpretation of poor relief efforts. It fits well with the liberalization of relief policies during the early seventeenth century (the Elizabethan Poor Law) and the late eighteenth century (the Speenhamland system).

There are, however, also a number of major policy shifts that are not explained by their model. It does not offer an adequate account for the punitive response to civil disorder during the fourteenth century (the Statutes of Laborers) and the early sixteenth century (the early poor law statutes). It also does not adequately deal with the Poor Law Reform of 1834 which was a distinctly restrictive response to the civil disorder and turmoil of the era. In England, a policy of repression was preferred to a policy of liberalization, at least for the period from the fourteenth through the nineteenth centuries. The policy of liberalization was an alternative resorted to when repression alone would not restore social order.[23]

In addition to the cyclical trend between more liberal and more restrictive relief policies, there was also a long-term trend from less restrictive old-age relief policies to more restrictive policies. To analyze this long-term trend, it is useful to compare policy toward the aged poor at three points in time: (1) the medieval period prior to the fourteenth century, (2) the early seventeenth century, and (3) the mid-nineteenth century.

Could it be that harsher policies were needed as the proportion who were old increased? Age structure estimates for England prior to 1841 are only available for selected villages, but there is sufficient evidence to conclude that there was little if any increase in the proportion of elderly between the sixteenth and the middle of the nineteenth centuries (Laslett, 1976:97-103). Similarly, we have no reason to believe that there was any increase in the proportion of elderly from the twelfth through the sixteenth centuries. Thus, it is unlikely that changes in demographics were responsible for the long-term trend toward harsher policies. Nor is it likely that the market economy, which had just started to emerge, made a significant impact on relief.

The Church had by far the greatest influence upon relief policies. The Church viewed poverty as part of God's design and as an opportunity to demonstrate Christian charity (Marshall, 1926:16). It was not a sign of personal failure, a crime, or a sign of immorality. Begging and voluntary poverty had a distinguished church heritage.[24] The feudal manor was largely self-sufficient; neither the serfs nor the lords were attempting to respond to outside market demands. The relationship between serf and lord was based on an exchange, albeit one that much favored the lord. Serfs were needed to work the land and were often difficult to replace, so the lord had an economic interest in their health and well-being.

By the early seventeenth century the more developed market economy began to have a greater effect on poor relief policy. As an increasing proportion of the population were drawn into the market economy, more people became vulnerable to periodic cycles of unemployment. The resulting mass unemployment was more than church relief could handle (Leonard, 1900:18-19). In the Elizabethan Poor Law of 1601 the able-bodied were put in a distinct relief category and they were not given relief unless they were willing to work. A public relief system based on a compulsory poor tax offered an alternative approach more consistent with the economic realities of the early seventeenth century. During this era of mercantilism markets became a concern of the government, but there was little awareness of the influence that markets would soon exert over all spheres of social life. The idea of a self-regulating economy was not yet affecting public policy.[25]

The Poor Law Reform of 1834 was formulated at a time when England had a well-developed market economy. The Reform Act of 1834 reflected the priorities of the self-regulating economy. While it did not call for a total end to government involvement in poor relief as some laissez-faire advocates were suggesting (de Schweinitz, 1943:116), it did represent the minimum public poor relief possible at the time given the need to maintain social order. Relief was now intentionally made stigmatizing and degrading to discourage all but the "truly needy" from becoming paupers (public dependents). Relief had come to be viewed as a necessary evil that represented an undesirable reduction in the economic return due the industrious. Many of the infirm elderly and many older workers had no choice but to accept these indignities as the price for a meager subsistence.

These nineteenth century changes in relief policy also reflected the imperatives of capitalism. The industrial revolution of the eighteenth century and the emergence of the factory system led to the total dominance of the capitalist mode of production. Virtually the entire economy was now based on work relations between capitalists and wage earners (Dobb, 1963:19, 255-319). Efforts to minimize relief and minimize the consumption of unproductive groups such as the elderly poor were entirely consistent with an economy dominated by competitive capitalism.

CONCLUSION

In this chapter we analyze the development of English aging policy between 1140 and 1834. To fully understand the early development of public policy toward the aged in the United States, it is essential to understand these early developments in England. We examine the explanatory power of Piven and Cloward's cyclical theory of social relief. While there is evidence of a cyclical trend between restrictiveness and liberal policies during this period, we find that these shifts cannot consistently be explained by the social turmoil hypothesis. There is also evidence of a long-term trend toward a more restrictive aging policy which is unaccounted for by the cyclical theory. This trend can be better explained by a more basic set of ideas, the emergence of a market economy and capitalist economic structures.

As shall be demonstrated in the next chapter, poor relief policy in the American colonies was greatly influenced by English Poor Law policy. The colonists drew heavily on the Elizabethan Poor Law of 1601, the 1662 Law of Settlement and Removal, and the English Poor Law Reform of 1834. Although there were some minor differences attributable to environmental or culture conditions, for the most part, the policies towards relief were remarkably similar between these two nations.

NOTES

1. In much of the literature considered here the term "poor" referred to the destitute, not to persons with very low incomes. By contemporary standards most people in preindustrial England had very low incomes, yet only a fraction were so poor that they had to rely on a combination of begging and public relief for subsistence.
2. Cipolla (1976:18-19) estimates that in England 25 percent of the population were poor at the end of the seventeenth century and that the number periodically increased to as high as 50 percent during depressions. However, in France during the sixteenth and seventeenth centuries, he estimates a range from 6 to 8 percent poor during good times to from 15 to 20 percent during famine years. The discrepancy between England and France with respect to the upper limit suggests a substantial margin of error.
3. See Laslett (1976:100). By contemporary standards the elderly made up a small proportion of the population in preindustrial Europe, yet at some times and in some areas the elderly made up a surprisingly large fraction of the population due to the demographic consequences of wars, epidemics, and famines. In the Italian town of Arezzo, 15.9 percent of the popultion was over 60 and 10.1 percent over age 65 in 1427. In the English town of Ringmore, 19.1 percent of the population was over age 60 and 11.2 percent over age 65 in 1698. In contrast, we find that 5.9 percent were over age 60 and 1.4 percent over age 65 in the English town of Ealing in 1599 (Laslett, 1976:98-100).
4. See Webb and Webb (1910:51). In 1871 in some areas of England being age 60 was considered a partial infirmity for relief purposes. Yet, in other areas persons over age 70 were still being refused relief on the grounds that they were able-bodied (Webb and Webb, 1929:1048).
5. See Cipolla (1976:44) for evidence supporting the argument that there was no distinction between the public and the private sector prior to the twentieth century. Tierney (1959:3) argues that in medieval society there were two public authorities, the secular and the ecclesiastical. The claim that church policy was public policy is most accurate when applied to rural areas, which included most of the English population during the medieval era and 80 percent of the population as late as 1600 (Jordan, 1961:17). In the emerging towns

we do find organized relief activities being carried out by a number of groups in addition to the church; for example, private philanthropic foundations, municipal authorities, craft guilds, and merchant guilds (Webb and Webb, 1927:19-22).

6. See Cipolla (1976:55-57). The parish churches owned another 10 percent of English land. The church owned about four times as much land as did the crown.

7. There is some disagreement as to whether it was the parish churches or the monasteries that played a greater role in medieval poor relief. Some authorities (e.g. de Schweinitz, 1943:17) argue that the monasteries were more important; others (e.g. Coll, 1969:3) argue that the parish churches played a more central role. As far as relief to the elderly was concerned, both made significant contributions.

8. The best evidence on family relations among peasants in preindustrial England describes a later era, but there is reason to believe that many of the conclusions also apply to the medieval era. See Laslett (1976:87-116) and de Beauvoir (1972:126-130).

9. The term "able-bodied" was used extensively in discussions of relief policy. It does not distinguish between voluntary and involuntary unemployment. One reason is that there was very little involuntary unemployment in the modern sense of the term. There was no use of the term "unemployed."

10. However, there are statements in the *Decretum* which can be interpreted as urging that alms be withheld from able-bodied beggars (Tierney, 1959:58-59).

11. For example, do charitable works contribute to one's salvation if the funds were illicitly obtained or if the recipient was only pretending to be needy.

12. See Webb and Webb (1927:43-44). For a comprehensive social history of feudal society, see Bloch (1961).

13. By 1350 only 50 percent of the English population were serfs (Coulton, 1925:2), and by 1600 there were no serfs (Bennett, 1937:227). Between the mid-fourteenth and the mid-fifteenth centuries there was a complete breakdown of the feudal order in England (Coulton, 1925:137; Tierney, 1959:113). Dobb (1963:37-40) agrees with most authorities that the revival of commerce and the growth of markets had a generally adverse effect on feudal society. He goes on to argue that this was not always the case. In this context he points to the revival of servile obligations in fifteenth century Poland in response to the expanding market for grain exports. In his review of Dobb's book, Sweezy (1976:42-44) outlines a number of factors con-

tributing to the decline of feudalism. One point he makes is that it became more efficient to buy certain goods from a nearby town than to make them on the feudal estate. This desire to buy created a pressure to sell, thus drawing the feudal estate into a market economy.

14. See de Schweinitz (1943:5). By 1349 the population was reduced by one-third (Trattner, 1974:7), and by 1400 it was down to just over half the pre-plague level (Coll, 1969:4). Between 1351 and 1485 there were epidemics of the bubonic and other plagues during thirty different years (Cipolla, 1976:154).

15. Focusing on how well the destitute were looked after, Tierney (1959:109) comes to a somewhat different conclusion. He points to the thirteenth century as being superior to any other prior to the twentieth.

16. The growth of the international market for English woolen cloth and the enclosure of land for sheep herding were two important factors which contributed to the development of a market economy. Other important factors were: (1) the discharge of feudal retainers and soldiers; (2) the rapid increase in commerce with its disruptive influence on one industry after another; (3) inflation due to an increase in the supply of precious metals; (4) periodic food shortages; and (5) King Henry the VIII's expropriation of the monasteries and the reduction in church resources available for relief (de Schweinitz, 1943:19; Webb and Webb, 1927:42-43, 61-62).

17. The marked upswing in begging and vagrancy in the sixteenth century was not unique to England. It was considered a serious problem throughout Europe at this time (Ashley, 1893:350). The first of these statutes, the Poor Law of 1531, called for public whipping of all able-bodied beggars. Those who were "impotent to serve" (the elderly, the blind, and the disabled) could apply for permission to beg. The sharp distinction in policy toward those considered able-bodied and others is noteworthy. The Poor Law of 1536 entirely prohibited begging; even the infirm elderly were prohibited from begging. For those caught begging it established an elaborate schedule of sanctions starting with whipping and then moving on to branding and if necessary execution. More significant than the punishments called for was the requirement that each parish collect contributions to pay for the relief of the impotent poor. In 1563 these "contributions" became mandatory (de Schweinitz, 1943:20-25).

18. The parish had become the smallest administrative unit for local government. It was no longer restricted to the catchment area for a particular church.

19. The Reform Act of 1834 itself did not specify this change. Rather, it gave the Central Authority a great deal of discretion and power. It was correctly assumed that the Central Authority would execute the reforms outlined in the 1834 Report of the Royal Commission. It is this report that recommends the workhouse for the able-bodied (Webb and Webb, 1910:1-20).

20. Despite the intentions of the 1834 legislation, local relief boards did not always require that the able-bodied enter the workhouse. Some found it less expensive to provide small wage supplements as outdoor relief (Rose, 1966:608-613). Because of this variation between local areas with repsect to implementation of the 1834 statute, most relief continued to be given on an outdoor basis. In 1848, for example, only 16 percent of relief recipients were living in the workhouse (Nicholls, 1898:391; Leonard, 1900:13-14). Discrimination against older workers was also a serious problem in Ireland (O'Neill, 1984).

21. It became particularly common between 1871 and 1895 to insist that the aged move into the workhouse as a way to put pressure on relatives to provide care, thus reducing the number of people on relief (Webb and Webb, 1929:351).

22. See Coll (1969:9). However, there is evidence that the Speenhamland system was unjustly blamed for many of the economic ills of the era (Blaug, 1963; 1964). Other major factors contributing to unemployment and low wages were the end of the Napoleonic wars and the spread of the threshing machine (Oxley, 1974:114).

23. While this explanation fits the data for the English case better than does the Piven and Cloward thesis (1971), it still does not explain all the evidence. For example, the liberalization implicit in the policy change associated with the Gilbert Act of 1782 is not adequately accounted for by the Piven and Cloward thesis or our modification of that thesis.

24. The teachings of St. Paul, St. Augustine, and St. Francis on the virtues of voluntary poverty were frequently cited by church canonists when discussing relief policy (de Schweinitz, 1943:17).

25. See Polanyi (1944:55, 68-76). However, capitalism was starting to emerge. This was reflected in the sharp increase in the portion of production that was carried out by wage earners hired by capitalists (Dobb 1963:18).

CHAPTER 4

AGING POLICY IN AMERICA PRIOR TO 1900

THE FOCUS in this chapter will be on the evolution of American policy toward the elderly poor from the seventeenth to the nineteenth centuries. In the United States as in England the public policy which most directly affected the elderly was relief policy. During the seventeenth and particularly the early eighteenth centuries, old-age relief policy was more restrictive in England than in the American colonies; but by the middle of the nineteenth century, old-age relief policy had become more restrictive in the United States than in England.

This trend raises two major questions: (1) Why did relief policy in the United States become more restrictive over this two-hundred-year period? and (2) Why did relief policy become more restrictive in the United States than in England by the middle of the nineteenth century? In answering the first question, the analysis will for the most part parallel that for the corresponding period in England. The second question requires more than an analysis that emphasizes the role of an emerging market economy and capitalist economic structures. Thus, the analysis will be extended to take into consideration differences between the environment in England and the United States. Environmental differences between the two nations include social and cultural factors (such as norms and values) as well as physical factors. These environmental differences had a profound influence on the ways in which English ideas about poor relief were adapted and the direction in which they evolved in the New World.

POOR RELIEF IN COLONIAL AMERICA

Although during the early part of the seventeenth century the colonial population tended to be quite young, the proportion of elderly had begun to rise by the end of the century. At the end of the seventeenth century approximately 6 percent of the population was over age sixty and approximately 2 percent was over age sixty-five.[1]

It might seem that poor relief would rarely have been necessary for the elderly in colonial America. Not only was the population young, it was rural with 90 percent living on farms (Fischer, 1978:102). Many of the elderly had a farm to pass on to their children. In rural areas it was common for the elderly to be cared for in old age by one of their children (often the youngest) who in return was given the homestead and some land (Fischer, 1978:53-54). Those who owned a substantial farm typically had at least some economic protection in old age, but many, particularly laborers in the towns, did not have significant economic assets to pass along to their children.[2]

Many of the early American colonists brought with them English ideas about how to deal with poverty, particularly those embodied in the Elizabethan Poor Law of 1601 and the Law of Settlement and Removal of 1662. However, the policies which evolved were a product of English ideas about poverty and an environment that was very different from that of England. The population in England was much older than that of the United States in the seventeenth century (Laslett, 1976:99). In addition, there was more land, and a more equitable distribution of wealth in the colonies than in England (Main, 1965:8-11).

Many of the colonists found themselves in small isolated frontier communities. In these areas, those in need could only rely upon neighborly mutual aid (Bradford, 1962). During the early years, this isolation and insecurity contributed to the suppression of certain aspects of Protestant individualism (Fischer, 1978:109-110). It also contributed to community solidarity, a sense of social responsibility, and a willingness to provide for needy persons who were members of the local community (Trattner, 1974:17).

The early colonial settlements were willing to provide for their own elderly poor in a way that was generally adequate, given the

standard of living available to the nonelderly working population,
yet they were often unwilling to care for poor outsiders.[3] This reluctance was particularly problematic for those elderly persons who
were displaced by natural disasters or frontier hostilities with the
French and native Americans.[4] An older person, particularly one
who was in some way disabled or showing signs of the infirmities of
old age, was not a good risk. Such persons might end up dependent
on the community without having first made a sufficient contribution to justify such support.[5] As early as 1636, an ordinance was
passed in Boston, requiring that anyone entertaining an outsider for
more than two weeks, secure official permission which could be denied if it seemed likely that the person would become dependent on
public support.[6]

During the seventeenth century, the colonies all passed statutes
for dealing with the poor. It was common for the statutes to be based
on the Elizabethan Poor Law of 1601 and tailored to fit the specific
needs of the colony (Coll, 1969:19). Some colonies omitted certain
sections that had little applicability, such as those dealing with charitable trusts or those requiring towns to build almshouses (Riesenfeld, 1955:175-223). Most statutes specified that poor relief was to
be organized at the level of the local community and to be paid for
by a local poor tax. Many also included residency requirements that
made it possible to deny support to the indigent who had not lived in
the community for a specified length of time.[7]

Communities also established statutes based on the English Law
of Settlement and Removal of 1662. These statutes called for such
procedures as "warning out" and "passing on" to deal with the problem of indigents from outside the community (Jernegan, 1931:193;
Parkhurst, 1937:446). If newcomers seemed likely to become dependent on the community, they were told to leave (warned away) by
the selectman or constable (Trattner, 1974:19-20). A related procedure was "passing on" in which the constable from one town would
escort the person to the constable in the next town. This process continued until the person was delivered back to his town of legal residence.[8]

Not only were colonists unwilling to provide relief for indigent
nonresidents, they were also reluctant to provide for residents of
questionable moral character. Those who had led a corrupt life were

held resonsponsible for their poverty and could be refused relief (Rothman, 1971:5). The lower the person's long-term social standing in the community, the more likely they were to be considered shiftless rogues worthy of little if any relief.[9]

A variety of procedures had evolved during the colonial period to provide care for the elderly poor. As in the English case, the elderly poor tended to get lumped together with other categories of the impotent poor — the blind, the disabled, and those with mental disorders (Pumphrey and Pumphrey, 1961:63). Although various statutes would specify that the community was responsible for providing for its poor, the term "poor" was never clearly defined (Rothman, 1971:4).

The colonists differed from their seventeenth and eighteenth century English counterparts in that they did not attribute any special value to institutionalization.[10] Typically, relief was administered in such a way that the lives of relief recipients were minimally disrupted (Rothman, 1971:30). It was common for an elderly widow who had her own home, or a place in the home of one of her children, to receive relief in the form of a small pension (Mohl, 1973:7). Another frequent practice was to reduce or eliminate taxes for those experiencing serious economic problems (Trattner, 1974:19). When an elderly person became debilitated and there were no close relatives, communities many times paid a neighbor or another member of the community to provide the necessary care (Parkhurst, 1937:446). One of the most controversial approaches to relief was to auction off the poor to the lowest bidder (Coll, 1969:21-22). This tended to minimize the cost to local taxpayers, but it had unfortunate consequences for the living conditions endured by relief recipients.

In some communities, particularly the large seaport towns, almshouses were constructed. This was typically the relief alternative of last resort.[11] If the relief recipient required more care than could be given by a neighbor or had serious physical (or mental) health problems, then the almshouse alternative was more likely. However, unlike the English, for colonial Americans the institutional alternative was infrequently used and it was not in any way a preferred alternative.

In many New England towns, laws were passed making those who brought servants into the community economically responsible for them in their old age (Trattner, 1974:21). Nevertheless, it would appear there was considerable difficulty in enforcing such statutes. Some slaves were sold off or freed before they became a burden. Other old slaves were sent to live in a hut in the woods. If they were fortunate enough to have relative in the area willing to help with the provision of food, these slaves could survive for a time. It seems reasonable to conclude that while there were exceptions, elderly slaves in general were not well provided for, particularly when they were no longer capable of work (Fischer, 1978:64-66).

By the end of the eighteenth century, there was growth in the size of towns and a subtle, but important, shift in attitude toward the poor. In smaller communities the poor had originally been viewed as neighbors or peers who had fallen on hard times and deserved support. Now the poor were coming to be viewed as a lower class made up of rogues, vagabonds, and other disreputable types who were personally responsible for their economic condition.

NINETEENTH CENTURY RELIEF POLICY

During the early part of the nineteenth century there was a sharp increase in the number of people on relief and a corresponding increase in the poor tax. One of the most important factors contributing to this increase was the severe depression from 1815 to 1821 brought on by the Napoleonic wars (Coll, 1969:21).

As was the case in England, this increase in the poor tax burden led to a series of studies on pauperism. An outcome of a major English study of pauperism was the enactment of the English Poor Law Reform of 1834 (Rothman, 1971:157). Many erroneously thought that the English had decided to eliminate all relief to persons outside of institutions (Coll, 1969:29). The English "reform" was used to support the decision in the United States to put a heavier emphasis on institutionalization.

One of the most important studies of pauperism in the United States was in an 1824 study of poor relief throughout New York state conducted by John Yates.[12] The Yates Report concluded that an overly generous relief system was contributing to idleness, crime, and other forms of social pathology. Yates recommended public assistance be forbidden to any able-bodied person between the ages of 18 and 50. Another recommendation was that relief to the elderly, the blind, and other such needy groups should be given only in institutions, not in their own homes (Schneider, 1938:228). A third recommendation was that the administrative unit for poor relief should be the county, not the town.[13]

In response to this report, the state of New York enacted the County Poorhouse Act (1824) which called for the construction of at least one almshouse in each county in the state (Schneider, 1938:235-246). The extent of the shift from outdoor relief (relief to persons living in their own homes) to indoor relief (relief in an institution) did vary from state to state and from one community to another, but there was a definite shift in policy toward the almshouse alternative (Mohl, 1973:8-9; Rothman, 1971:180-205).

This movement toward the almshouse for dealing with relief of the elderly poor and other needy groups was not confined to poor relief. It must be seen as part of a more general movement at that time toward institutionalization for dealing with criminals and the mentally ill as well as the poor (Rothman, 1971). During the colonial period, almshouses were for the most part confined to the large port towns, yet by the middle of the nineteenth century every town of any size had an almshouse (Rothman, 1971:30-31, 1984; Coll, 1969:22). By the end of the Civil War, 80 percent of those receiving long-term relief in Massachusetts were in institutions (Rothman, 1971:183). In some states, particularly in the South, the proportion was lower. In others, such as Maryland, it may have been higher (Coll, 1969:30-32).

In Boston between 1825 and 1860 one-fourth to a one-third of relief expenditures went to outdoor relief and the remainder to indoor relief (Coll, 1969:31). In New York state during this same period outdoor relief accounted for between one-third and one-half of relief expenditures. During periods of financial panic and depression such as the panic of 1857, the proportion receiving outdoor relief increased considerably (Coll, 1969:29-30). From this evidence it is clear that although more public money was being spent on relief in institutions than on outdoor relief, a substantial fraction of relief expenditures still went to people living in their own homes.[14]

While a significant proportion of the population, including many elderly persons, continued to receive outdoor relief, the tendency to emphasize indoor relief or institutionalization continued for the rest of the century (Rothman, 1971:205). Even as early as 1848 30 percent of those in the Blockley Almshouse in Philadelphia were elderly (Klebaner, 1952:211). By the end of the century, most of the almshouses had become heavily populated with the elderly.

By the middle of the nineteenth century, indoor relief predominated in the United States while outdoor relief predominated in England.[15] Although policy in England was now more restrictive than it had been during the Elizabethan era, it was less restrictive than in the United States. Conversely, America originally had less restrictive policies during the earlier colonial period and became more restrictive in the Jacksonian era. Why did the institutional response to relief that was advocated both in England and the United States come to differ so greatly?

Various theories have been offered to account for the dramatic shift toward institutionalization during the Jacksonian era. On suggested by Adrew Scull is that it was a response to the imperatives of the developing capitalist market economy (Scull, 1977:15-40). A market economy produces structural pressures to get as much work from labor as possible at as low a wage as possible. If certain categories of deviants and dependents are isolated in institutions, this frees a greater proportion of the labor force to fully participate in the work force and allows them to support their families on lower wages.[16] At the time, it was assumed that a greater emphasis on the almshouse alternative would also make the administration of poor relief more efficient and economical. And indeed, the grim conditions of almshouses discouraged all but the most needy from seeking assistance or refusing work (Furniss, 1965:107; Scull, 1977:26).

Market imperatives can be used to account for the trend toward institutional care in both England and the United States. But this approach does not adequately explain why the mid-nineteenth century institutionalization was more common in the United States than in England, particularly in light of the fact that England had a much more fully developed capitalist economy. A Weberian approach that considers the influence of the Protestant ideology may help to explain this difference.[17]

The individualism and work ethic of the Protestant ideology was present in both England and the New World, but the environmental contexts were very different. In England there was less opportunity for the poor to significantly improve their lot through individual effort and initiative. In colonial America there was an abundance of land, a high demand for labor, and a more fluid social structure (Rothman, 1971:156-159). Given the opportunities for social mobility, poor people in the United States were held more responsible for their poverty. To remain poor in America where so many opportunities existed suggested the person was very lazy or unusually inept.[18] Thus, the abundant land and the fluidity of the American social structure contributed to a harsher stand towards the poor than was found in England.

During the period between the Civil War and the end of the century, public attitudes towards the elderly poor became less sympathetic and public policy less generous (Achenbaum, 1978:51-54; Feagin, 1974:34-37). These shifts were largely a function of the social Darwinism of Herbert Spencer which had become far more popular in the United States than in England (Duncan, 1908:128).[19] Social Darwinists not only vehemently opposed all forms of public relief to the poor but also went so far as to oppose private charity (Trattner, 1974:81). The social Darwinists were callous in the public policies they suggested for all categories of the poor, including the elderly poor. Relief to the elderly poor, so they believed, would undermine the incentive for the nonaged to work hard and be thrifty.[20]

The scientific charity movement which was influenced by social Darwinism was another important English relief policy that was replicated in the United States (Feagin, 1975:54). The first American Charity Organization Society (COS) was established in 1877.[21] The COS leaders emphasized that they would not be giving out any relief funds. Instead, the COS would organize charity in a scientific manner and serve as a clearinghouse for persons seeking relief. The role of the COS was to screen applicants and, where appropriate, refer them on to other relief granting agencies.

Organizing referral agencies did not in and of itself restrict relief policy. Far more detrimental was the perception of relief as a necessary evil (Lowell, 1884:89). The mission of the scientific charity movement was to encourage people to be self-sufficient and to make do with as little relief as possible. They sought to substitute counseling and moral uplift for the direct distribution of relief funds.[22] The destitute elderly who decided to forgo relief so as to avoid the stigma of becoming public dependents were praised for their choice.[23] By the turn of the century, there were 138 COS organizations around the nation.[24] While the movement did not seem to change what was already a very restrictive attitude toward relief, it was one factor that reinforced a continuation of stringent relief policies.

The other major policy development during the post Civil War era was the growing importance of Civil War Veterans' pensions. The first Civil War pension legislation (1861) restricted benefits to the disabled, but subsequent legislation provided benefits to all soldiers and their dependents who had served in the Union army (Olson, 1982:41). One authority estimates that by the end of the century nearly two-thirds of the elderly population was benefiting from these pensions (Tishler, 1971:89). In some years between 1880 and World War I, these veterans pensions accounted for more than 40 percent of the federal budget, and by 1900 these pensions had become in effect an old-age assistance program (Fischer, 1978:170).

One limitation of the Civil War pension was that they were not expressly designed to care for the poor. Consequently, some who received these pensions were financially much better off than many who were being taxed to support the program (Glasson, 1918:238-239). In addition, the restrictive benefits excluded many blacks, immigrants, or other poor whites who had not served in the Union army (Fischer, 1978:170).

During the closing years of the nineteenth century, there was some discussion of a need to develop a federal pension system similar to that introduced by Germany in 1889. Ironically, although the federal government was administering what amounted to the largest old-age pension system in the world in the form of military pensions, by in large the United States was opposed to any national social security program. In fact, the Civil War veterans' pension system itself may have contributed to the substantial lag between the time the United States and various European nations introduced a national social security system (Fischer, 1978:169).

CONCLUSION

Between the seventeenth and the nineteenth centuries old-age relief policy in America became increasingly restrictive. One indication of this was the trend toward greater emphasis on the almshouse
as opposed to "outdoor relief" and other noninstutitional alternatives. This trend can be accounted for, in part, by the emerging
market economy and the ideological concomitants of this change.
Another important factor was the influx of immigrants who did not
share a common ethnic background with those who had come
during the colonial era. Environmental factors such as the abundance of land and the physical dangers associated with frontier life
also had a major impact on the way in which English ideas about
poor relief were adapted and how these policies evolved over the
years. These differences led to an even stronger commitment to an
ideology of individualism than in England.

NOTES

1. Age structure estimates for this era are limited and there may have
   been marked demographic differences between communities. These
   estimates for New Rochelle, New York in 1698 may have overestima-
   ted the size of the elderly population (Fischer, 1978:272). For instance, the more extensive eighteenth century evidence shows that in
   1773 the proportion age 60 and over in six New Hampshire towns
   ranged for 2.0 percent to 5.5 percent (Wells, 1975:72).
2. One estimate is that one-fifth of whites were laborers without significant property holdings. The same authority estimates that in the late
   eighteenth century this "permanent proletariat" may have been as
   high as 30 percent of the population if blacks are also considered
   (Main, 1965:271-272).
3. See Rothman (1971:5), Trattner (1974:19-26), and Fischer
   (1978:61). In 1720, for example, a law was enacted in New Jersey
   that instructed justices of the peace to search arriving ships for "old
   persons" as well as "maimed, lunatic, or any vagabond and vagrant
   persons," and to send such persons away so as to reduce pauperism in
   the colony (Leiby, 1967:7).
4. During King Philip's War (1675-1677) there was an influx of "impoverished refugees" from frontier settlements to towns such as Boston,

New York, and Newport. In 1675 alone, more than 500 of these refugees arrived in Newport (Tràttner, 1974:21-22).

5. In Plymouth Colony the two major reasons people were refused inhabitance were: (1) incompatibility in religious beliefs and (2) likelihood of early public dependency, a factor that was particularly problematic for the aged (Kelso, 1922:35-36).

6. See Trattner (1974:19). Three years later an ordinance was passed which required that a townsman provide security (post bond) for any such person (Betten, 1973:2-5).

7. In 1642 Plymouth Colony established the first residency requirement for relief eligibility (Trattner, 1974:20).

8. In 1822 some 1,800 people were subject to the process of "passing on" in the state of New York (Coll, 1969:20).

9. The workhouse was far more common in eighteenth century England than in the United States (Rothman, 1971:31).

10. See Rothman (1971:30). In 1696 the town of New York rented a house for sick paupers and in 1736 the town's first almshouse was constructed. By 1772 there were some 425 paupers in the facility (Mohl, 1971:43-45).

11. Fischer argues that "old age seems actually to have intensified the contempt visited upon a poor man." For instance, in some cases poor widows were driven out of the community by neighbors who feared increases in the poor taxes (Fischer, 1978:60-63).

12. For a thorough discussion of the Yates Report, see Schneider (1938).

13. By viewing the poor as members of a lower class rather than as neighbors who had fallen on hard times, the distinctions between classes intensified.

14. By the end of the Civil War the number of long-term relief recipients in the almshouse was much greater than the number on outdoor relief, but if we take into consideration those persons receiving casual relief on a very short-term basis, then the total number of outdoor relief recipients was greater (Rothman, 1971:183).

15. In England in 1950 approximately 11 percent of those receiving relief were in institutions (Rose, 1966:607). While in the United States a majority (by the end of the Civil War, 80 percent) were in institutions (Coll, 1969:29; Rothman, 1971:183).

16. Scull (1977:128-129) argues that in the nineteenth century the working and lower classes found the care of aged and incapacitated relatives an intolerable burden, given the problems they were having providing for their own subsistence.

17. By the early nineteenth century the laissez-faire ideology of classical

economists such as Adam Smith and David Ricardo was reinforcing the earlier Protestant ethic ideology described by Weber (1958). Poor relief was viewed by those classical economists as a violation of a person's "natural right" to accumulate wealth.

18. This view can also be linked to the Enlightenment. The Enlightenment resulted from the growth of science as reflected in the work of Newton and the thinking of philosophers such as John Locke. Persons in this tradition argued that everyone possesses reason and can use this reason to understand the universe. The perspective also put an emphasis on equality among people and the belief that it was possible to solve social problems such as poverty. But, as Trattner (1974:50) points out, it led many to the conclusion that the poor themselves were responsible for their poverty.

19. See Hofstadter (1944:18-19). Social Darwinism provided a "scientific" basis for many tenents of laissez-faire ideology, including the view that the only remedy for poverty is individual self-help (Bremner, 1956:19).

20. While Darwin (1936:501) briefly discusses the application of his ideas to the poor, it was Herbert Spencer who coined the phrases "survival of the fittest." Social Darwinism combined laissez-faire economics with the doctrine of survival of the fittest.

21. The COS movement originated in London in 1869 (Coll, 1969:44).

22. The motto of the COS was "not alms but a friend." The reference here is to the corps of middle-class volunteers or "friendly visitors" who provided sympathy, hope, encouragement and supposedly help with such problems as indolence, intemperance, and improvidence (Trattner, 1974:87).

23. The COS considered its approach scientific in part because of the thorough investigation of the applicant's financial situation. Relief, if given, was to take need into consideration. Also, it was to be more efficient by avoiding fraud and duplication of benefits from different agencies (Trattner, 1974:84-85).

24. By the turn of the century there were 138 COS organizations around the country (Trattner, 1974:84).

CHAPTER 5

PRIVATE PENSIONS: LINKING WORK AND RETIREMENT

IN THE following two chapters, we examine the social control features of the two major retirement income programs in the United States: social security and private pensions. In this chapter, the development of the private pension system will be examined as it relates to the relations of control within the workplace. In the following chapter, working within the conceptual framework of the welfare state developed by neo-Marxists, we analyze the ways in which the social security system reproduces current inequalities in income distribution and power relations.[1]

In December 1980, the United States House Select Committee on Aging (1980) released a report entitled, "Retirement: The Broken Promise" which stated that in contrast to the image of America's elderly as enjoying a financially secure and leisurely retirement, there was increasing pauperization of the elderly and a failure of private and government support programs to effectively provide income maintenance for the elderly during retirement.

In this chapter, we argue, as others have (e.g. Graebner, 1980) that private pensions were introduced to facilitate the termination of elderly workers through the institutionalization of retirement. However, we develop this insight by locating the phenomenon of private pensions within the context of three larger features of a capitalist po-

By Avery Gordon, Department of Sociology, Boston College.

litical economy: the exercise of control over workers at the point of production; the legitimation of capitalist social relations; and profit maximization. The point we stress is that the outcome of the introduction of pensions for older workers reflects aims specific to a particular segment of the work force, the elderly, and the broader requisites of maintaining a capitalist economy.

Second, we argue that the private pension system fails to provide an adequate system of income maintenance. We show how the private pension system produces a class-stratified elderly population because of the direct relationship between income, job tenure and labor market location during working years and pension receipt during nonworking years.

Third, we examine alternative pension systems and the methods by which the elderly can contest or gain greater control over their pension rights.

Within the political economy perspective, the study of private pensions and the elderly has been underdeveloped, if not neglected. Where interest has arisen in private pensions, two principal areas have received the most attention. The first area of interest has been in the large stock of pension capital which has accumulated from the steady rise in pension plans since the 1950s. Here, attention has been focused on the potential this stock of capital provides for socializing ownership either through Employee Stock Ownership Plans (Woodworth, 1981), as in the United States, wage-earner funds (Meidner, 1981), as in Sweden, or through other collectivist methods. Similarly, social investment of pension equity through union and/or stockholder control has become an increasingly interesting area, particularly since pension fund assets remain the largest source of standing capital in the United States (Rivkin and Barber, 1978; Barber, 1982; Lowry, 1982). The second focus is more conceptual in nature and views pensions as promoting the three imperatives of capitalism: control over the workers, capital accumulation, and profit maximization (O'Connor, 1973; Gough, 1979).

Both of these approaches, while stimulating important insights, are unsatisfactory as a basis for understanding pensions as a method of labor control. The first approach is essentially an alternative strategy for the distribution and control of pension capital and provides little insight into the nature of benefit provision, although it does develop a cogent analysis of the relationship between capital formation and broad labor policies. We will discuss this strategy later and its significance for labor's control over investment capital and the possibilities this strategy offers for providing key services to the elderly during their nonworking years.

The second approach is more relevant for understanding state intervention in the maintenance of the labor force than for understanding the use of pensions as a method for simultaneously controlling labor costs and ensuring a system of normative integration. It is a view which can explain the government's role in providing wage supplements where firms are unable to provide sufficient wages for the necessary reproduction of the labor force. However, private pensions are not social wages, they are deferred wages provided by employers principally in the monopoly sector of the economy where wages are generally sufficient to ensure the maintenance of the work force. In contrast to these perspectives, pensions can be more appropriately viewed as one mechanism whereby the control over labor is secured.

CONCEPTUALIZING CONTROL: THE CAPITALIST LABOR PROCESS

The fundamental problem of the capitalist labor process is the transformation of labor power into labor. The capitalist, or firm, purchases not the entire laborer, as in slavery, nor labor services, as in feudalism, but labor power — or the capacity to work. This labor power exhibits a unique characteristic: it is a commodity capable of producing commodities, the value of which is greater than the value of itself. This capacity to labor must not only be realized in the production process, but it must also produce a surplus in order for the firm to accumulate, compete and survive financially by securing high-profit rates. The production and extraction of surplus value is essential to meet capital's accumulation and competition imperatives. It is the securing of surplus value which provides the link between the realization of labor power and profit accumulation (Marx, 1974).

The process by which surplus is secured entails control over the entire array of activities necessary for production, such as control over investments, distribution of profits and other aspects of financing or money capital; control over the process of production, or the technical labor process; and control over labor power or human capital. But why is control necessary? Why is it necessary to subordinate labor and separate the worker from the various aspects of the production process (Marx, 1974; Gartman, 1979)?

First, control is inherent in the wage-labor relationship. The firm, in purchasing labor power, or the capacity to work over an agreed amount of time, purchases only the *possibility* of actual labor. Management has an interest in controlling the labor process in order to transform labor power into commodities and surplus value. Second, control must be wrested from workers because the greater their control over production, the more they are capable of resisting increased exploitation or other actions which threaten their interests. Because the worker has no logical or inherent interest in perpetuating his own exploitation, it becomes essential for the capitalist to control the labor process (Braverman, 1974:58).

However, systems of control can and have taken different forms. Capital accumulation requires control over the labor process — how this control occurs will and has varied according to historical situations, differences in workplaces and sectors of the economy, and differences among types of workers. In contrast to the argument made by Braverman and other similar Marxist theorists (e.g. Clawson, 1980), explicit domination through deskilling and fragmentation of the work process, epitomized by Taylorism and Fordism, is not the most efficient method to obtain profits because it tends to produce crises, discontent and contestation at the workplace.[2] To secure profits, it is also necessary to secure the cooperation and consent of workers (Burawoy, 1978, 1979). Cooperation is essential if workers are to internalize the goals of production and to see a congruence, rather than opposition, of interest between themselves and management. It is precisely the process of obscuring the exploitive nature of capitalism that makes labor control a dynamic process.

In contrast to more explicit and direct relations of control within the workplace, bureaucratic control relies on a structure of consent and legitimation. Cooperative relations are established through specific mechanisms which help to secure workers' attachment to the firm and thus help to obscure the more exploitive aspects of the workplace (Edwards, 1979; Herman, 1982).[3] The bureaucratic mode of control is characterized by three main features. First, management hierarchies, formal organizational rules, and personnel departments all tend to diffuse the center of power and impersonalize control. In the case of elderly workers, the fact that termination is rationalized as retirement is a clear example of how bureaucratic decisions displace or obscure the coercive nature of control.

Second, bureaucratic control relies on positive incentives rather than negative punishments in order to maximize productivity of workers. Pensions, for instance, have been presented to workers as a reward for long and committed service. Even with the legal definition of pensions as deferred wages, the current rules regarding pension coverage and receipt ensure that the pension is used as a positive sanction for compliance with the rules of the corporation.

And, third, bureaucratic control fragments workers and promotes competition among workers themselves (Gordon, Edwards and Reich, 1982). The use of rules and hierarchies within the firm based on skill and seniority pits old against young and skilled against unskilled. Particularly in the case of seniority hierarchies, younger workers perceive their interests as opposed to those of more tenured workers. This entire process obscures the fact that younger workers will inevitably become older workers. In this case, pensions are by far a more flexible means of controlling labor than the technical labor process.[4]

The bureaucratic mode of control is located primarily in the monopoly sector of the economy, as are the majority of pension plans (Olson, 1982; Edwards, 1979; President's Commission on Pension Policy, 1980). Monopoly firms which tend to consist of highly unionized smokestake industries, unlike competitive sector firms, can concentrate on securing long-range profits. Insulated from extreme market competition, these firms can invest in the bureaucratic structures mentioned above which ensure not simply technical efficiency but reproductive efficiency (Gordon, 1976). Expenditures for the continuation of control provide a mechanism whereby explicit domination is obscured and consent established.[5]

THE HISTORY OF PENSIONS AND THE CONTROL OF LABOR

The shift from simple hierarchical control to bureaucratic control affected older workers in many ways, including the introduction of retirement and retirement systems designed to facilitate the flow of workers out of the labor force. In addition to providing a useful mechanism for the release of older workers from the work force, pensions simultaneously reduced wage costs and created a considerable stock of capital available for investment by corporations or financial institutions. In order to place the following discussion in context, it is important to note that prior to the turn of the century, the number of private pension plans in effect was minimal.

While credit goes to the American Express Company for initiating the first pension plan in 1875, the establishment of pension plans did not reach a number of any relative importance until the period between 1910 and 1920. In 1897, there was one pension plan in effect; in 1900, 12; in 1920, 270; and in 1930, 720 (Fisher, 1978:166). The Depression years saw the bankruptcy of many pension plans, and attention quickly focused on the Social Security Act and other New Deal legislation. It was not until the post-1942 expansion of pension plans, particularly with the introduction of collectively bargained multiemployer plans in the late 1940s and 1950s, that employer-sponsored pension plans came to resemble their current counterparts.

Thus, while we can identify the reasons for the establishment of pensions and the functions pensions serve for facilitating the control of labor, their significance for a substantial majority of the working and non-working population was minimal. Although pensions provided some financial security for a small number of individuals who actually received them, they did very little to improve the financial security of the majority of the elderly during retirement.

The paucity of pension plans reveals much about the absence of a humanitarian or social welfare aspect of retirment. Retirement more often than not ushered in a period of dependency for the elderly, rather than independence or security. However, old-age dependency was not considered a major social problem requiring public attention until the hardship years of the Depression. Even then, the scope of the economic crisis required massive state intervention on behalf of old and young alike. It was not until the 1930s that old-age dependency was seriously addressed as a social problem requiring fundamentally new solutions (Achenbaum, 1978). Up until this time, there was little agreement on the extent to which old-age poverty constituted a significant social problem. The estimates regarding the number of elderly persons financially dependent ranged from less than 1 percent to 60 percent of the elderly population (Achenbaum, 1978). Where state-run programs did exist to provide old-age benefits, they varied enormously. By 1931, 18 states had legislated old-age pension laws, yet the requirements for eligibility and the quality of benefits lacked uniformity (Achenbaum 1978:122-3). The family was considered ultimately responsible for the economic plight of the elderly and the privatization of the elderly's care only highlighted the extent to which society wished to keep hidden the real manifestations of retirement.

If retirement proved less a reward for an active life of work and more a punishment for having reached a certain chronological age, what benefits did firms acquire in releasing older workers from the world of work? In order to answer this question, we need to focus on the drive for increased labor productivity which was perhaps the key characteristic of corporate policy towards labor from the turn of the century until the mid-1930s.

While profit maximization through increased labor productivity is an essential feature of capitalist production, the highly competitive nature of early twentieth century capitalism prevented firms from focusing on long-range profit plans. A focus on long-range profits provides capital with more varied methods for maximizing profit and, as mentioned previously, allows firms to invest in bureaucratic control methods which help obscure overt attempts to increase productivity. Prior to the development of bureaucratic control, however, increased productivity was secured principally through alterations in the technical labor process, such as mechanization or new technology, and increasing the pace or speed of work (Braverman, 1974; Edwards, 1979).

The transition from simple machine production to Henry Ford's assembly-line production entailed qualitative differences in levels of skills, the division of labor and the pace of work.[6] Similarly, once the assembly line removed control over production pace from the workers on the shop floor, it was relatively simple to institute speedups characteristic of Frederick Taylor's so-called "scientific" method of management (Palliox, 1976).[7] Inherent in this process was the deskilling jobs by which the worker is stripped of knowledge and control over the labor process.[8] Taylorism and Fordism, or scientific management more generally, with its stopwatches and time clocks, marked a new era in the production process which was focused on improving efficiency through the use of new technology (Palmer, 1975).

In their attempt to establish industrial discipline or strict control over the labor process, scientific managers, themselves a product of a division of labor which separated knowledge and skill of the work process from execution, confronted a cohort of elderly workers whose work habits and work culture were rooted in pre-industrial craft production (Gutman, 1976; Thompson, 1968). Craft production entailed worker control over the labor process, the pace of which was ordered by master craftsmen. The time-honored hierarchies and work rules, self-determined by the crafts, provided a sharp contrast to the increasing alienation and deskilling of workers wrought by capitalist control over the labor process (Montgomery, 1980).

For the elderly, then, the whole meaning of efficiency acquired new significance. Efficiency meant adjusting not simply to a faster pace of work but to new technology and a new work ethos rooted in management control and its corresponding alienation. There were three aspects of the "thrust for efficiency," all of which were designed to increase control over the labor process, reduce wage costs and secure higher profits. First, the increased speed or pace of work associated with the new technology and production quotas undermined workers' traditional control over the pace of work and forced them to work at higher speeds for the same wages. Older workers, finding it difficult to maintain the pace at which production was carried out, were considered inefficient and were replaced by younger more energetic workers. The cases of the printers (Graebner, 1980), machinists (Montgomery, 1980) and steel workers (Stone, 1975) illustrate this process.[8]

By fragmenting the work process in an assembly line fashion, workers were deskilled and the older more skilled craftsman became obsolete. The desire on the part of management to minimize labor costs led to the termination of older skilled workers in favor of hiring younger unskilled labor — labor who brought to the workplace no pre-defined work habits or cultural orientations. The more work became separated from knowledge and skill, the cheaper the labor force could be acquired and the easier control could be exercised upon them (Braverman, 1974).

The third feature of the new industrial policy was a variation of the prevalent nineteenth century theme of selection of the fittest. The metaphor of industrial discipline required a work force selected to meet the criteria of stamina, energy and strength. The older worker, considered more fragile and less capable of turning the wheels of industrial machinery, was cast aside in favor of a young virile labor force.[10] However, the outright firing of older workers was a difficult public posture for corporations to assume, particularly outside of large urban areas. The establishment of retirement and pensions plans provided one answer to the problem of removing older workers from the work force.

The systematic establishment of retirement radically altered the nature of the work cycle which characterized both pre-modern production and non-industrial production. Industrial technology had changed the pace and character of work by substituting a work week in which workers integrated work and leisure for regulated hours and days of work (Gutman, 1977). This new work life assumed that at a certain point in time, the older worker was inefficient and a cost burden to the firm. With the passage of the Social Security Act, the precise determination of the work life was established at age 65.[11] At the same time, retirement, the formal disengagement of older workers, and the pension, could combine the desire for productivity and reduce labor costs. Retirement provided a boundary, an end to work, and the pension both an incentive and reward for acceptance of the limits imposed.

The logic of the pension was clear. A portion of the worker's wage was set aside, reducing immediate labor costs and creating equity that assisted future capital accumulation. When the worker was retired, the pension might be offered.[12] The firm could, in this way, control the flow of labor, hiring it at a lower rate with the promise of future benefits and at the same time release older workers who, because of their tenure, were generally at the higher ends of the pay scale. The pension also offered flexibility. While it could be used to control the flow of labor by shifting older workers out of the work force, it could also be used to reduce labor turnover by encouraging employees to remain in the firm (Graebner, 1980).

Simultaneously, the pension legitimizes the firm's control of labor and encourages workers to perceive the completion of their working years, not as a state of unemployment, but as a condition of positive withdrawal from the labor force. The introduction of Social Security played a similar role. In order to alleviate the massive unemployment which characterized the economic crisis of the Depression, the state redefined elderly unemployment as retirement and provided the elderly with a monetary benefit for their exclusion from the labor force. Thus, the federal government used the concept of retirement to obscure the labor market control of the elderly (Lubove, 1968; Fisher, 1978:Graebner, 1980; Haber and Cohen, 1960). The pension, like Social Security benefits, diffuses insecurity about the end of work by promising an income during retirement. Indeed, one of the compelling arguments which has been made by employers since 1910 is that pensions further enhance efficiency by eliminating worker insecurity about their future.

Finally, pensions foster a spirit of cooperation within the firm because workers recognize they now rely on the corporation for subsistence during nonworking years.[13] In this way, the pension provides the owners and managers with a mechanism for controlling both employed and unemployed or retired workers. In addition, by providing elderly workers with an income, however meager, during retirement, the elderly's purchasing power and demand for goods and services will not radically change. The Social Security system exhibits the same functions as pensions, except on a much broader scale. Social Security is, of course, much more successful at both creating jobs for younger workers at the expense of older workers and providing disposable income so that underconsumption crises do not develop (Sclar, 1980).[14]

Eventually, the development of a complex system of bureaucratic control reduced the significance of the pension and retirement as the primary mechanism for control of older workers. In combination with the pension, other inter-organizational methods of control allowed the firm to satisfy needs for both technical and social efficiency (Graebner, 1980). Retirement established an artificial end to work, a period of unemployment which was woven into the fabric of American society through the provision initially of pensions and later Social Security. The growth of state intervention with the enactment of Social Security and other public-welfare-oriented support programs definitively established the boundaries of the elderly's work life.

CONTEMPORARY PENSION POLICY

In the previous section, pensions were viewed as one method of controlling labor though bureaucratic means. However, despite the significance and growth of private pension coverage since the 1960s, only 45 percent of private sector employees are covered by a pension plan (President's Commission on Pension Policy, 1980:26).[15] Of these individuals, only a small percentage actually receive a pension upon retirement. It is estimated that in 1979, of the 24.6 million elderly persons in the United States, 19 million (77%) received *no* pension benefits whatsoever (U.S. House Select Committee on Aging, 1980:118). Various legislative efforts, beginning in 1958 and culminating in the 1974 Employment Retirement Income Security Act (ERISA), have established regulations and requirements governing coverage and receipt of pension benefits, as well as funding, disclosure and tax regulations (Schmitt, 1979). While ERISA (Public Law 93-406, 1974) has eliminated some of the flagrant violations that surrounded private pension plans prior to the 1970s, the reward which the pension represents is meager.

In 1979, 31 million workers were covered by a pension plan; 48 percent of pension plan participants were female and 52 percent were male. The likelihood of being covered by a pension plan is contingent upon many factors, including pre-retirement earnings. In 1979, 78 percent of workers earning $25,000 or more were covered by a pension plan, while 10 percent of those earning less than $5,000 were covered. Eighty percent of all individuals earning between $20,000 and $50,000 a year were covered by a private retirement program (President's Commission on Pension Policy, 1980:27). In addition to earnings, race and employment status have a signficant effect on the likelihood of being covered by a pension plan.

Perhaps the most important determinant of pension coverage is labor market location. As mentioned previously, pensions are primarily located in the monopoly sector of the economy which is heavily unionized and characterized by relatively high wages and secure employment patterns. The focus on long-range profits (and monopoly firms' higher profit rates) makes the pension a feasible instrument for controlling labor and accumulating capital. Conversely, the competitive sector is not insulated from extreme market competition and is forced to seek short-term profits by adjusting to market fluctuations. The financial instability of firms in this sector makes the cost of maintaining pension plans very high. The competitive sector is characterized, in contrast to the monopoly sector, by high job turnover, low wages, greater part-time employees, lower levels of unionization, and a predominantly labor-intensive work force concentrated with females and minorities (Gordon, Edwards and Reich, 1982).

The characteristics of those persons not covered by pension plans reveals the importance of labor markets. In 1978, 38 million private sector workers were not covered by a pension plan. Of these workers not enrolled in a pension plan:

- 91% were not unionized
- 30% worked part-time
- 78% were in firms with fewer than 100 employees
- 84% were in firms with fewer than 500 employees
- 60% worked in trade and service industries
- 47% were either service or clerical workers
- 93% earned less than $20,000 in 1978
  (U.S. House of Representatives Select Committee on Aging, 1980:128)

The lack of pension coverage in competitive sector industries like trade and service explains the low levels of representation of women, blacks, low wage earners and part-time workers in pension plans. Despite the forecasted growth of this sector both in terms of size and its share of the work force, it is unlikely pension coverage will concomitantly expand. Pension coverage for full-time workers increased only 2 percent from 1972 to 1979 and is not expected to exceed the level of 50 percent (U.S. House of Representatives Select Committee on Aging, 1980:120).

Even given the relatively low numbers of persons covered by pension plans, participation in a pension plan does not guarantee receipt of a pension benefit. Workers covered under a pension plan must meet eligibility requirements regarding length of service before they are vested or attain a nonforfeitable right to their pension benefit. In 1979, only 38 percent of workers between the ages of 25 and 64 were vested in a pension plan (President's Commission on Pension Policy, 1980:31). In 1979, some 23 percent of those persons 65 years of age and older received benefits from a private pension (Olson, 1982:81). The distribution of these benefits favors white married couples, while the group with the lowest likelihood of receiving a pension were single black women of whom only 4 percent received pension benefits in 1979 (Olson, 1982:82).

Vesting requirements, set up by ERISA (Public Law 93-406, 1974), were designed to encourage worker attachment to the firm through continuous service. While there are different systems for meeting vesting requirements, most plans require ten years of continuous service before a worker is entitled to a nonforfeitable right to the pension annuity.[16] These vesting requirements, however, do not reflect the amount of time most workers spend at one job. The median job tenure for men is 4.5 years and 2.6 years for women (U.S. House of Representatives Select Committee on Aging, 1980:122). In addition, pension credits are typically not portable from one employer to another, and, where multiemployer plans provide for limited portability, only vested pensions are transferable. The cost advantages for the firm are obvious. While each worker contributes to the pension fund by deferring a present wage for a future benefit, only a small percentage of workers actually receive a benefit. The lack of portability further ensures that corporations need only maintain a very small proportion of the pension fund assets in a liquid form. The firm accumulates capital from all plan participants and funds the pension plan in part through benefits forfeited by those not meeting vesting standards.

Thus, the corporation defers workers' wages for the promise of a future benefit which it often does not provide. Where workers receive pension benfits, they are often inadequate. It should be noted that the adequacy of pension benefits is a complex issue. First, any discussion of the overall social adequacy of retirement income standards must involve a discussion of the combined effects of employer-sponsored pensions and Social Security benefits. Comparative analysis of the adequacy of the U.S. retirement income system with those of other industrialized countries requires in addition a comparison of the differing objectives which underlay their tiered systems. It is, however, clear that where older persons are in receipt of both Social Security benefits and pension annuities, their standard of living during retirement is higher than those subsisting on Social Security alone. The additional income from employment further positively alters the retirement income standards for the elderly (U.S. House of Representatives Select Committee on Aging, 1980; President's Commission on Pension Policy, 1980; Schulz, 1974).[17] The quality of the pension annuity workers receive essentially depends on the following five factors: (1) earnings, (2) length of service, (3) type of firm, (4) integration with Social Security, and (5) the level of inflation.

Since most pension plans are based on some formula combining the workers' average earnings either shortly before retirement (five years) or a career average, the higher a worker's earnings, the greater the pension benefit. The replacement rate for earnings, however, is highly dependent upon length of service. The Bankers Trust Company's Study of Corporate Pension Plans (1980) indicates that the average monthly benefit for a worker with 30 years of service and an average final salary of $15,000 in a large plan was $202. Similarly, in a defined benefit plan, the replacement rate is dependent upon the length of service. Where a plan provides for a replacement rate of 1 percent of final average wages for each year of service, the adequacy of the final benefit is contingent upon the number of years worked. If a worker only works 15 years, he receives 15 percent of his final wage, whereas if a worker is employed for 40 years, he will receive 40 percent of his final wage. Thus, the amount of time a worker spends continuously at a job can have a significant affect on his pension benefit.

Labor market location of workers also affects their length of service, pre-retirement earnings and thus the level of wage replacement the pension provides, Monopoly sector firms typically have both higher wage rates and higher job tenure rates. In 1979, for instance, at age 65, a worker enrolled in the Amalgamated Clothing Worker's plan who had 30 years of service would receive an annuity of $1,890, whereas a worker covered under the United Auto Workers plan with the same work history would receive a benefit of $3,960 (Olson, 1982:84).

These benefit levels, however, are contingent upon a worker being enrolled in a pension plan which is not integrated with Social Security. Currently, approximately 62 percent of large pension plans and 84 percent of small plans are integrated (U.S. House of Representatives Select Committee on Aging, 1980:130). An integrated pension plan is one in which the employer can offset or deduct the pension benefit by the employee's Social Security benefit. In some cases, the employee benefit can be reduced by as much as 83 percent. The effect of integrated pension plans is to allow the corporation to provide greater benefits to higher paid employees and virtually eliminate pension benefits for lower paid workers.

While the tax advantages corporations receive preclude them from engaging in discriminatory behavior towards highly paid workers, the effect of integration procedures outlined by ERISA is precisely the opposite. Integration works as follows. An employer can contribute on behalf of an employee up to 7 percent of compensation above the integration level, which is currently the Social Security wage base, and provide no contributions below the integration level. The current Social Security wage base is $29,700; thus, any employee whose earnings fall below $29,700 can have their pension benefits eliminated if they are enrolled in an integrated pension plan. This constitutes a significant portion of the working population: In 1981, 94 percent of all workers earned less than $25,900, the 1980 Social Security wage base (U.S. House of Representatives Select Committee on Aging, 1980:131). The class nature of integration is reflected in Table 1, where the integrated plan shifts the same contribution significantly to higher wage earners.

Integrated pension plans provide a mechanism for corporations to simultaneously reduce the costs of their pension plans and offset the cost of employer contributions to the Social Security program. They shift the contributions towards higher paid managerial person-

TABLE 1

EFFECT OF INTEGRATION ON CONSTANT EMPLOYER CONTRIBUTION

(Defined contribution plan in 1980, total contribution of $5,474)

Salary of Employee	Non-Integrated (3.421% of salary)	Integrated (7% above $25,900)
$ 10,000	$ 342	$ 0
$ 20,000	$ 684	$ 0
$ 20,000	$1,027	$ 287
$100,000	$3,421	$5,187
Total Employer Contribution	$5,474	$5,474

U.S. House Select Committee on Aging, "Retirement: The Broken Promise." Comm. Pub. No. 96-267, Ninety-Sixth Congress, Washington, D.C.: U. S. Government Printing Office, 1980 (130).

nel, thus reducing the amount of benefits paid to lower workers and provide firms with a mechanism for shifting the costs of Social Security contributions which favor low income workers. For the low income worker, the effect of integration is disastrous. The integrated plan not only reduces or eliminates the pension benefit but counteracts any positive ramifications of increases in Social Security benefits.

Finally, pension benefits, unlike Social Security benefits, are often not protected from increasing rates of inflation which erode the value of the benefit over time. Where benefits are adjusted to meet inflation, no uniform or automatic cost-of-living increases are provided.[18] The effect of inflation on pensions or other fixed annuities is dramatic. "If inflation averages only 5 percent a year, the value of the initial retirement benefit is cut at the end of five years by 23 percent; at the end of ten years by 40 percent; and after 15 years — the average lifetime of retired employees — 54 percent" (U.S. House of Representatives Select Committee on Aging, 1980:126).[19]

The reward for industrial discipline in the form of the pension proves more illusory than real. Less than half of the work force is covered by a pension, yet the stock of pension capital is close to $800 billion (Barber, 1982). This $800 billion represents the deferred wages of workers, yet yet many never receive a benefit because of vesting, length of service requirements, and the integration provisions of ERISA. Integrated plans in particular, clearly reveal the class nature of the pension system, shifting contributions and benefits towards highly paid managerial personnel and away from low-income workers. The Social Security retirement test in combination with an integrated pension plan has an even more insidious effect on the income status of the elderly. The relationship between pre-retirement earnings and pension benefits further serves to reproduce and maintain class division. Indeed, the increasing pauperization of the elderly indicates the extent to which pension controls labor inelasticity through working and nonworking years.[20]

Having described some of the problems with the private pension system, in the following section we examine two alternative strategies for confronting two distinct, yet related problems associated with private pensions. The first proposal, an example of a mandatory pension system, is primarily designed to deal with social adequacy issues for elderly retirees. The second is a strategy for labor control over pension capital which ultimately seeks ownership of ths stock of capital. The integration of these two goals — social adequacy and the exercise of control rights over pension fund assets — offers the possibility for both increasing retirement income standards for the elderly and redistributing both ownership and control of the equity generated by the growth of pension plans.

ALTERNATIVES

The 1980 federal budget, which included major reductions in social programs and a forceful attack on the Social Security system, mobilized the elderly in a manner not seen since the movements of the 1930s (Pratt, 1976; Fisher, 1978). While the formal organizations of the elderly have grown in influence in recent years, the birth of various grass roots organizations suggest a new phase of elderly activism. This movement, however, has been largely defensive, focusing on efforts to prevent further encroachments to programs essential to the elderly's survival. Solutions to the larger problem of inequality in capitalist society have been phrased in terms of a problem specific to the elderly. The problem of inequality has been translated into the dual problem of providing adequate income to the current cohort of retirees while at the same time ensuring the solvency of the retirement income system for future retirees, forcing the elderly to perceive their interests as opposed to the young and middle-aged. Consequently, solutions to the problem of maintaining the balance between current needs have ranged from modified improvements to existing program to the total dismantling of the Social Security system. Similarly, the response to the problem generated by private pension systems specifically has been fragmented and primarily unsuccessful.

In order to move beyond proposals and programs which perpetuate current inequalities, strategies need to be developed which have far-reaching goals. Such strategies need to ensure social adequacy, redistribution of wealth, and the exercise of the ownership rights which are vested in pension plan participants. In the following pages, one mandatory pension system is examined which has been proposed and seriously studied for its potential to meet these goals. In addition, another element of a revitalized pension system, namely, control over pension fund assets and the use of those assets, is reviewed.

The recommendation of a national pension system is not unprecedented. The President's Commission on Pension Policy (1980), which undertook perhaps the most extensive study of retirement income programs in the history of the United States, recommended the establishment of a new pension system designed to improve the adequacy of pension provision in the United States. The commission recommended the establishment of a Mandatory Universal Pension System (MUPS), the goal of which is to increase the replacement rate of pre-retirement earnings and to provide, in conjuction with Social Security and individual savings, a basic minimum level of retirement income.[21]

The MUPS would require all workers be provided a pension that would be funded by a minimum employer contribution of 3 percent of payroll. Eligibility for coverage under a MUPS is identical to the current ERISA regulations: a worker must be 25 years of age, have one year of service, and complete 1,000 hours of employment per year. Pension benefits would be immediately vested, portable, and transferable throughout a working career. The portability system is to be administered by the firm, through traditional trusts or insurance means, or transferred to a central portability clearinghouse administered by the Social Security Administration. Integration of a MUPS plan would be prohibited, and additional modifications to ERISA would alleviate clear abuses in existing integration rules for pension plans providing benefits greater than the MUPS level. Since the MUPS is designed as a minimum universal pension system, all existing plans would be modified to meet the MUPS criteria, but firms may provide more extensive pension coverage if desired.

The major provisions of the MUPS — universal coverage, immediate vesting and the prohibition against integration — address the most pressing problems associated with private pensions, namely, the problem of coverage and adequacy of benefits.[22] The MUPS promises to provide pension coverage and benefits to those people currently not covered and to increase the benefits for those persons whose benefits are currently below the expected MUPS level. However, the increased cost to employers of the program may encourage higher unemployment despite the generous tax deductions employers are provided under the plan. A tax credit of 46 percent of the 3 percent contribution for small businesses is suggested.[23] In addition, the increased cost to the employer may be passed on to the workers in the form of lower wages and/or the elimination of collectively bargained plans which currently provide higher benefit levels than the MUPS would provide.

A comparison with the Swedish pension system is instructive here. Where the MUPS provides for a wage-related income program to supplement Social Security, also a wage-related retirement program, the Swedish national pension system provides a basic pension (AFP) available to all Swedish citizens and a series of supplementary wage-related pensions bargained through the major trade union federations (Lagerstrom, 1976). While the MUPS system entails the notion of a tiered retirement income system, it is qualitatively different from the Swedish tiered system. In Sweden, the first tier is a basic pension, not wage related, whereas the second tier is wage related and thus increases the basic benefit by an amount relevant to pre-retirement earnings. The combination of a MUP system and the current Social Security program still does not provide, as the Swedish system does, an old-age income benefit; it only provides a wage-related benefit for which the redistributional effects are minimal.[24]

While both a national pension system, such as in Sweden, and a mandatory pension system, such as the MUPS, improve the replacement rate for pre-retirement earnings and insure a higher level of social adequacy for the elderly during retirement, they do not transform the class structure apparent in a capitalist society. Since the goals of both systems are to provide both a minimum benefit *and* higher replacement of pre-retirement earnings, they do not change the distribution of wealth, except insofar as the lower level of the income scale is raised. Within the context of a capitalist economy, the attachment of old-age benefits to pre-retirement earnings reproduces during retirement the same class structure which characterizes the elderly's pre-retirement years.

From the point of view of "gradational" notions of class (Wright, 1979a; Ossowski, 1963), specifically those which focus on income hierarchies, a wage-related pension system does not alter existing class arrangements. If there are inequalities in the income structure, then pension systems which base provision on that same income structure are likely to reproduce those same inequalities during retirement.[25] From the point of view of relational theories of class, the elderly do not, within either of the two systems mentioned, enhance their functional control over corporations. Within the workplace itself, in the United States retirees are not legally considered employees or members of bargaining units, and employers are not required to bargain with retirees over increases or changes in pension benefit provision. While it may be politically premature to suggest that the elderly should be able to exercise control over their former workplace in matters relating to the labor process, it is not unreasonable to suggest that retirees should have some control vis-à-vis their pension benefits.

The control over pension benefits for retirees entails a twofold process of empowerment. First, retirees could be recognized as members of bargaining units and their right to negotiate increases in their pension benefits firmly established. This would require overturning the 1971 Supreme Court decision, *Allied Chemical and Alkali Workers of America, Local Union No. 1* vs. *Pittsburgh Plate Glass Company* to allow retirees to bargain over their pension benefits. Also necessary would be an increased involvement of elderly workers in the affairs of their unions. Second, *both* workers and retirees could be accorded the right to share in the control of the capital that is generated through the establishment of pension plans and the investment decisions made regarding the use of that capital.

In addition to the advantages that pensions provide for controlling labor, pensions play a role in the accumulation of capital necessary for the continued existence of capitalism. While the growth of pension fund assets has increased dramatically — between 1945 and 1980, pension fund assets increased from less than $5 billion to over $700 billion (Olson, 1982; Barber, 1982) — control over these funds, as well as decisions regarding their use, has remained concentrated in the hands of corporations and financial institutions.

The size and power of these assets has furthered the concentration of monopoly capital and strengthened the power of financial institutions (Olson, 1982).[26] The overlapping relationshp between corporations and financial institutions, combined with ERISA's regulations regarding fiscal responsibility for pension plan funds, ensures that workers have little control over their deferred wages which comprise pension capital.[27] Further, the use of pension equity has not been directed to socially useful projects which enhance either workers in general or elderly pensioners specifically. In addition to assisting capital flight and the disinvestment of American industry (Bluestone, 1982; Rivkin and Barber, 1978), pension capital has been invested in firms with anti-union policies, firms who violate equal opportunity and health and safety regulations, and firms who invest in South Africa.[28]

There are two questions which emerge in discussing alternative strategies for pension funds in the United States. The first is how to link the ownership of pension equity which legally belongs to the workers with control over the use and direction of these funds. Second, given the establishment of formal mechanisms for the control of pension fund assets, what investment policies should be pursued to ensure that socially useful outcomes result from the use of this capital?

The proposals which have emerged thus far to enhance worker control over pension fund assets have primarily been of three kinds. First, worker representation on retirement boards which govern state and local pension plans must be strengthened. Currently, state and local employees have some degree of representation on retirement boards in 75 percent of the pension plans in effect (Olson, 1982:106). Secondly, there must be a strenghtening of union control over pension fund assets through joint union-management control combined with extensive training and education for representatives. The UAW, for instance, jointly manages Chrysler's pension funds and has also established a training program for the union's trustees (Barber, 1982). Thirdly, workers must use voting rights attached to stock ownership to pressure corporations to either modify existing policies or actively pursue other policies (Lowry, 1982; Schwartz, 1982).

While all of these proposals hold much promise for restructuring control over pension fund assets, little attention has been paid to the role of the retired worker. While greater union involvement in pension fund control might establish a role for elderly workers, the retired workers' relationship to the union and corporation is tenuous, particularly if the legal definition of retirees is not modified. The use of voting rights to disrupt existing corporate strategies is relevant to those elderly who either own stock or are in unions where the union is a large holder of stock. Here, again, a limited role is provided for the retired worker. These proposals require the addition of formal mechanisms for enhancing the autonomy and control of the retired worker as well as older and younger workers.

The demand for increased worker control over pension fund assets has emerged in tandem with social investment strategies. Social investment has as its objective the use of pensions or other assets in a socially useful capacity. The ideas for the use of this capital which have emerged are both innovative and promising. The use of pension fund assets for providing low-income housing, improved health care delivery, day care, energy assistance, and revitalization of abandoned factories all enhance the quality of life for the community. But socially useful investment raises two major questions: (1) for whom is the investment useful, and (2) are investment decisions governed by capitalist criteria of market efficiency in addition to the social good?

The extent to which the decision making process regarding the use of the capital is democratized or controlled by workers will determine who may benefit from social investment strategies. For the elderly and the retired, it is not clear they hold a formal position of control which would enable them to exercise a direct influence over the use of this capital. Particularly in the case of the unions, who have been increasingly interested in pursuing control over pension fund assets, the lack of democratization within the union itself raises important questions about the representativeness of decision. The AFL-CIO, for instance, has released a report developing proposals for an economic revitalization program which uses pension fund assets in order to both encourage growth and enhance union control over the allocation of resources (Barber, 1982). While partial labor control over capital allocation is a significant step towards ensuring socially beneficial outcomes, what role is being established for the elderly and retirees? The specific mechanisms by which the elderly can control the outcomes of these policies are not made clear.

Related to the question of beneficiaries of social investment strategies is the question of the criteria which guide the choice of investments. Lowry (1982) has suggested that investments can produce socially useful outcomes and economic rewards for investors. However, investment within a capitalist economy is guided by the criteria of market efficiency and the goal of assisting in capital accumulation. Social investments can only be transformative of capitalism if ownership is socialized such that the formation of capital does not lead to its concentration *and* control over those ownership rights are directly exercised.

CONCLUSION

The establishment of formal mechanisms for the democratization of control, then, is essential in order to guarantee outcomes that benefit both young and old. While the advocates of social investment have made elderly services a priority, the elderly, particularly retirees, must be given a formal active role in this process if their interests are to be included and if negative stereotypes regarding the passivity of the elderly are to be overcome.

NOTES

1. The discussion of these two programs is separated here for the sake of clarity, although these two programs are obviously interrelated. It is important to understand the relationship between private pensions and Social Security, particularly since they both perform functions necessary for the reproduction of capitalist social relations. However, for analytic purposes, private pensions and Social Security occupy different immediate arenas of control. Pensions are essentially a privatized form of wage deferrals, while the Social Security system represents a public form of income maintenance. The private pension system has as its immediate reference point the social relations of control embedded in production relations and the control of labor, while the Social Security program principally reflects relations of control whose immediate reference is the arena of state relations.

2. Braverman's analysis exaggerates the extent to which Taylorism was a successful strategy. Taylorism, in fact, engendered considerable worker resistance and this resistance was one of the factors which led to the development of Fordist methods of control. See Davis (1975) and Stark (1980) on worker resistance to Taylorism. However, Fordist forms of control have led to increasing worker alienation and declines in productivity, one cause for the current economic crisis. The current economic crisis is one manifestation of the crisis of control in the firm and has led to the recent expansion of new work arrangements or work humanization schemes. See Gordon, Herman, and Schervish (forthcoming) for the development of this argument.

3. Bureaucratic or hegemonic control does not imply, however, the disappearance of deskilled or routinized work. It simply facilitates worker acceptance of their subordinate position by creating, as Burawoy (1979) notes, an industrial citizenry (see Herman, 1982).

4. The analysis made by Leutz (1978) is interesting in this regard. His application of a Marxist analysis of the labor process to the capacities of the elderly to perform work tasks is an important counterargument to studies which consider work capacity outside of the context of the specific imperatives of the capitalist production process. But, this kind of analysis neglects the political dimensions of the labor process — that control over labor can be secured through a range of methods, but that the most efficient forms of control are those which obscure or mute the politics of production. Our point is simply that the technical labor process is a less flexible means of controlling labor than hegemonic or bureaucratic means.

5. See O'Connor (1973) for his analysis of the distinctions and relationships between the monopoly, competitive and state sectors.

6. Although we treat Fordism and Taylorism very similar here, there is at least one significant difference. Fordism, through the introduction of assembly production, reorganized the entire technical organization of production, rooting control and the division of labor in the technology itself. Taylorism, on the other hand, focused on specifying the fragmentaion of tasks which had already been developed (see Coriat, 1980; Palliox, 1976; Braverman, 1974; Edwards, 1978; Burawoy, 1978; Herman, 1982).

7. Graebner's argument that the trade unions traded a shorter working day for consenting to speedups is relevant only to the period preceding expanded machine production and the assembly line (i.e. Fordism). Indeed, Fordism forced unions to relinquish their right to bargain over job control issues for securing of higher wages. In this regard, the unions traded their ability to bargain over fundamental interests and perhaps the interests of most importance to the elderly.

8. This is similar to Marglin's argument that the factory resulted not from the natural development of productive technology but rather facilitated the coordination and control of labor. Both Marglin (1974) and Clawson (1980) provide convincing evidence which suggests that factory production preceeded technological developments and not the other way around. As Gorz (1973:62) notes, "Capitalist technology and the capitalist division of labor were developed not because of their productive efficiency *in itself* but because of their efficiency in the context of alienated and forced labor."

9. See also Zimbalist (1979).

10. See Fisher (1978) and Achenbaum (1978) for a description of the broader social phenomenon of the "cult of youth" prevalent in the 1920s.

11. The debates surrounding the initial formation of the Social Security Act regarding age eligibility reveal the lack of substantive rationales for selecting age 65 (see Cohen, 1957).

12. It was not until the passage of the Employment Retirement Income Security Act (ERISA) that regulations standardizing eligibility and benefit provision were established.

13. Graebner makes the argument that union pension plans achieved the same integrative function by attempting to secure worker loyalty to the union rather than the firm. The unions recognized that older workers, facing job loss and diminished opportunities for re-employment, would react more conservatively during labor disputes. During the 1930s, for

instance, the pension was used by management to secure the commitment of older workers against younger more militant workers, creating division within the union between young and old (Graebner, 1980).

14. This is the catch, of course. Both Social Security and pensions have significantly improved the standard of living for the elderly, but through restrictive means (i.e. through an agreement to leave the labor force and through forced saving during working years).

15. In this regard, the almost universal application of Social Security makes both its beneficial and labor control features more significant than those of private pensions.

16. There are three types of vesting standards: (1) cliff vesting which requires 10 years of continuous service before 100 percent vesting is achieved; (2) graded vesting which allows partial vesting after the first or second year of service and full vesting after 15 years: (3) 50 percent vesting when age and service equal 45 and 10 percent vesting per year until 100 percent is reached.

17. The increase in the standard of living of the elderly over the past fifty years is an important part of this debate but one which often acts as a barrier to understanding that both pensions and Social Security represent the accumulated savings of workers and not gratuities. Thus, the implication that is often inherent in arguments that compare the elderly's standing of living across generations is that the improvement generationally minimizes the inherent inequalities and control features of both programs.

18. Federal employees do receive cost-of-living adjustments under the civil service retirement system but are not covered under Social Security.

19. The 1980 inflation rate was 14 percent, making these figures somewhat modest estimates of the current impact of inflation on pensions or other fixed-income benefits.

20. While the poverty rate for the elderly declined from 1959 to 1974, since then the poverty rate has remained stable but is currently increasing. The U.S. House Select Committee on Aging (1980:1) estimates that "almost one out of three older men and two out of every three older women live on annual incomes of less than $3,999." Indeed, in 1979, the poverty rate among the elderly reached 15 percent, reflecting a 10 percent increase in the actual numbers of the elderly poor. For women, the statistics are more alarming — it is estimated that over 70 percent of the elderly poor are women (U.S. House Select Committee on Aging, 1980).

21. The rate of replacement of pre-retirement disposable income is the measure most often used to determine income adequacy during retire-

ment. See Schulz (1974) for comparisons of the U.S pension replacement rates with other industrialized countries. When discussing pensions, the replacement rate alone is not always a clear indication of income adequacy, since other sources of provision, such as Social Security, increase the level of retirement income overall. As we discuss below, the replacement rate does not capture the need for redistribution of income and thus is a somewhat uncritical measure of adequacy.

22. It should be noted that the President's Commissionon Pension Policy Final Report (1980) is over 2,000 pages long and contains detailed and sophisticated analyses of the impact of the MUPS system by itself and in conjunction with other retirement-income programs. Any attempt to discuss the general implications of the MUPS system must inevitably neglect the complexities of the real impact of the commission's recommendations. Our purpose here, however, is to reflect broadly on the benefits which such a system could provide for the elderly within a political economy perspective, rather than produce a detailed analysis of this particular proposal.

23. The commission estimates a job loss of 0.2 percent with the introduction of MUPS (President's Commission on Pension Policy, 1980:1159).

24. Of course, the strength of Swedish unions and their high level of unionization among both blue- and white-collar workers provides Swedish workers with substantial supplementary pensions. The structure and adequacy of the Swedish pension system is rooted in the powerful and unique role Swedish labor plays (see Martin, 1977). The United States, by contrast, has a weak labor movement and low levels of unionization, particularly among white-collar workers, who have, in Sweden, been at the forefront of expanding the terrain of collectively bargained issues. A MUPS-type pension system in this regard may be more compatible with the political realities of American labor than a Swedish-type pension system which ultimately relies on the power of organized labor to secure significant benefit levels.

25. See O'Connor (1973) and Gough (1979) for the distribution effects of Social Security, which, despite public misconception, does not favor the low income.

26. The accumulation of such substantial stocks of capital is confined to a relatively small number of firms, fostering concentration. The management of these funds by financial institutions, in addition to their ownership of stock, has both strengthened the relationship between financial institutions and monopoly corporations and given the financial institutions disproportionate control over the corporation's investment policies.

27. ERISA's regulations are on the one hand quite vague in that they mandate "pruduent" means. At the same time, the managers of pension trusts are personally liable for the payment of benefits and thus the solvency of the trust fund, encouraging corporations to defer responsibility for the plans to larger financial institutions.

28. See Olson (1982:113) for her summary of the 1979 Corporate Data Exchange Study of the investment practices of some of the largest pension trusts.

CHAPTER 6

SOCIAL SECURITY AND DISENGAGEMENT
FROM THE MARKETPLACE

A S THE historical accounts of old-age policies in England and colonial America suggested, relief has been used in various ways to reinforce labor participation. At times, public assistance has been introduced and expanded to curtail social unrest in periods of economic downturn, and, on other occasions, particularly in America, relief policies have been made more harsh during already hard times. In most cases, old persons were not the target of relief policies but were nonetheless subjected to the prevailing rules. Due to certain values prevalent in colonial America, such as Calvinism, individualism, and self-reliance, public-assistance programs were viewed as exceptions to a market definition of community and carried stringent eligibility requirements.[1] Eligible individuals who did not collect assistance were often praised for their fortitude, and by the mid-nineteenth century, social participation within the community was literally dependent upon economic participation (Trattner, 1974; Scull, 1977). As the needs of capitalist expansion changed, so did the state's assistance policies alter. Just as almshouses complemented the rise of industrialization and factories, so did Social Security represent a response to monopoly capitalist needs at a later point.

With rapid industrialization and the introduction of the factory in the nineteenth century came an emphasis upon hierarchical controls and increased discipline of the labor force. Almshouses or indoor relief (relief in institutions) became the preferred mode of dealing with the unemployed and the poor. If individuals did not participate in the work force, they were excluded from the community. As was noted in Chapter 4, the existence of almshouses reinforced the imperative of developing capitalism to extract surplus labor value by isolating deviants and thereby freeing up family members to work harder and putting the fear of God into those who might want to avoid work (Scull, 1977). Together, entrepreneurial/hierarchical controls in factories and their alternative mode of control — indoor relief — accommodated the needs of capital to exercise control over workers, legitimize capitalist relations, accumulate capital, and maximize profits. Combinations of these particular work force and government controls were prevalent from roughly 1830 to 1890 (Edwards, 1979).

By 1890 some corporate sectors were beginning a transition toward monopoly and their interests were beginning to differ from those of competitive sector industries. Labor unrest was widespread at the turn of the century as workers rebelled against Taylorism, then Fordism (technical control), and against high unemployment rates for older workers. High overhead costs or capital outlay in large monopolized industries led to an emphasis being placed on stability and ability to anticipate long-term returns. Monopoly sector industries eventually struck a bargain with labor in renegotiating their respective areas of control and in establishing a bureaucratic mode of control within the workplace (Herman, 1982). Social Security legislation was part of the bargain struck and represented overt state involvement in supplementing the monopoly sector's need for rationalization and predictability. Social Security is itself a complementary bureaucratic form of social control.

It is important to note that the battle over Social Security legislation was a long and protracted one. While managers of monopolized industries wanted government help in their labor troubles, many business persons in the competitive sector bitterly opposed the legislation and firmly believed that the threat of old-age dependency was necessary as an incentive to work and as a character builder (Lubove, 1968:117). Such persons emphasized volunteerism, charity, and privatized solutions to social problems. Thus, the eventual product was a response to economic and political crises and represented a fragile, reluctant, and minimal political solution.

The form Social Security took spoke to its purpose in reinforcing the economic system. As was noted in Chapter 2, O'Connor (1973; 1981) argues that the capitalist state must involve itself in two primary and occasionally contradictory purposes: accumulation (the creation or reproduction of conditions necessary for the private accumulation of capital) and legitimation (the maintenance of conditions for social harmony which usually involve concealing or justifying the accumulation functions of state policies). Because monopoly sector growth is a primary determinant of the material progress that underpins the state's ability to promote social harmony, it is in the capitalist state's interest to reinforce the monopoly sector(s) by subsidizing costs (Griffen, Devine and Wallace, 1981; Gough, 1975). This is done through such policies as corporate tax loopholes and job training programs. Social Security legislation, in responding to monopoly sector needs, served many accumulation and legitimation functions that will be inferred throughout this chapter. It might be useful to specifically identify some of the major ones here.

By lopping off the elderly from the work force and tying Social Security eligibility to work history, for example, Social Security modified the reproduction of labor and assured future reproduction of labor. Without retiring, one could not receive Social Security; without a work record, one could not receive Social Security. Social Security provided a means for maintaining the nonworking and destitute old population and thereby transformed "social dynamite" to "social junk" (Spitzer, 1975). Surplus labor was both created and mollified. As we shall see in the discussion of the causes for Social Security legislation, it also helped perpetuate the class system by stabilizing the relations of production, ritualizing management-labor negotiations, and transforming class issues into political ones. Not incidentally, these changes solidified capitalist control over workers, maximization of profits, and the additional accumulation of capital.

This overview of Social Security and its close relationship with bureaucratic control within the workplace and the accumulation-legitimation functions of the state reflects a political economy emphasis on structural relationships. The functional perspective will be used in exploring additional purposes of Social Security in maintaining social order, and the labeling view of social control, in analyzing some of its effects on the lives of individual old persons. As functionalist theorists concede, some social policies can involve dysfunctions, and we shall suggest some of the dysfunctions of Social Security when applying the labeling perspective. And finally, we shall examine where Social Security is at today and relate its present situation to the causes, purposes, and effects of the legislation. Also of interest will be the changing needs of capitalists and how these impact the parameters of public debate.

CAUSES FOR THE LEGISLATION

The political economy explanation for why Social Security legislation passed rests on several arguments. First, the nature of business organization had changed dramatically by 1885, and the profile of the ideal employee was consequently altered. Second, unemployment was beginning to be viewed as something separate from poverty, and the locus of responsibility was shifted among the American public from presumed individual culpability to system flaws. Third, private sector efforts to deal with unemployment and poverty were woefully unsuccessful. A boundary dispute over where private and public solutions to problems should begin and end was eventually fought over the form of Social Security rather than over its necessity. Underpinning these observations is the argument that retirement as an institution preceded Social Security, not vice versa, and thus the government was the tail that appeared to be wagging the dog but was in fact subsidizing the needs of business.

Prior to the late nineteenth century, the dominant business form was the small-scale entrepreneurial unit. Laissez-faire was the prevailing philosophy within these businesses, and it was assumed that voluntary retirement left to individual discretion would add up to a rational policy.[2] Between 1890 and 1920 changes occurred to undermine this approach. Specifically, corporate units became the dominant mode, shorter workdays and national markets made for competitive conditions, and unemployment rose.[3] Concurrently, some firms were attempting to monopolize industries, and laborers' efforts to unionize escalated.

As unemployment became a serious problem, concern grew over

the potential existence of a permanent and dangerous pool of unemployed people — people who might call the entire economic system
into question. Employers, scientific managers, economists, and physicians began to stress the benefits of employing younger or "more
efficient" workers at the same time that articles increasingly depicted
older persons as worn out and unfit for the wear and tear of industrialization (Achenbaum, 1974). Removal of older workers from the
labor force was to be the panacea for widespread unemployment
(Graebner, 1980:13). Two arguments were prevalent. First, young
workers were portrayed as more productive than older ones. Second, since some kind of investment was now required in training
managers, a return had to be guaranteed by holding out potential
promotions for those who remained with a company. Long-term
costs, so it was argued, could then be reduced.

Along with the new corporation and competitive conditions came
an emphasis upon production efficiency. It is important to note that
from a radical political economy perspective, all references made to
production efficiency during this period must be interpreted within
the context of owners and managers attempting to extract surplus labor value from workers. Marglin (1974) contends that the fine division of labor along with increased reliance on machinery that
occurred during this period were not entirely due to machines technical superiority, as is usually presumed.[4] Often, workers were
brought into a hierarchical factory setting prior to the development
of machines, and their output was not always improved by machines. Introduction of factories thus reflected a need among capitalists to strengthen their control over the labor process when
confronted with a rapidly organizing working class.

Another point of importance is that the process initiated with
Taylorism of subdividing skills into tasks and then into abilities was
originally targeted at reducing the control of highly skilled older
workers. Their knowledge and control of all aspects of a craft were
perceived as a threat to management's need to pace work output and
thus profits. There is considerable evidence that the process of subdividing work, not characteristics associated with aging itself, led to
the dislocation and downward mobility of older working-class
Americans. This finding is contrary to early twentieth century
charges that older workers were inherently "unfit." Rather, those job

features that most undercut the older worker's accumulated experience, the repetition of narrowly defined abilities, were exactly what were being instituted.[5]

Employers during the late nineteenth and early twentieth centuries not only wanted to control the pace of production but also the "stock and flow" of labor (Myles, 1981a:15). By the 1920s the pace of production was set by technical (machine) controls as well as the already in-place hierarchical arrangements within factories (Braverman, 1974; Edwards, 1979). Speedups were commonplace, and labor was sufficiently deskilled to make laborers — the old and the young — interchangeable operatives, not craft workers. Union resistance to workplace controls intensified during the 1920s, particularly in industries such as steel and automobile, where management's efforts to monopolize were occurring and machine-pacing was widespread.

Retirement was an increasingly relied upon corporate method for controlling the stock and flow of labor. Forced retirement thus had several purposes: to relieve unemployment, remove potentially disruptive older laborers from the workplace, and allow for a rise in the extraction of surplus labor value. While these changes were occurring, union leaders were besieged by members to simultaneously guarantee employment, control the rate of production, and permit some security for old age (Graebner, 1980).

Various management strategies were employed to effect unemployment rates, removal of older workers, and increased profits. The most widespread approach was corporate discrimination against older workers. Many were simply dismissed from their jobs, and the need for individual savings and ingenuity in facing old age was stressed (Fischer, 1978). A second approach was company provision of private pensions. These were never widespread, and even as late as 1932, only 15 percent of the American labor force was covered (Lubove, 1968:128-130). Also, the vast majority of the pension programs were discretionary and involved no legal obligations from employers. Union pension funds and homes for retired members comprised a third strategy, but these were even less available than employer-sponsored pensions.

Considerable debate surfaced regarding how to solve the recently created problem of old-age dependency. While many almshouse residents had been old people by the end of the nineteenth century, by 1930 unemployed and poor elders were highly visible within the community itself. Most Americans recognized that the capacity for older Americans to support themselves had been undermined by the transition to wage labor, the cheapening of skills, and increased family mobility in pursuit of jobs. Voluntary thrift was impractical under these conditions. Businesses tended to stonewall in an effort to keep control of pension programs within their domains, but, because their efforts on behalf of older workers were so meager and coupled with dismissal policies, collectivism of some type was increasingly seen as the only way to subsidize the old (Lubove, 1965:116).

It is important to point out several key aspects of the eventual solution — Social Security. First, it was part of a "social bargain" between management and labor within monopolized industries, although others were potential beneficiaries as well. Second, Social Security represented a "social expense" that the state provided in order to facilitate capitalist growth, legitimize capitalist relations of production, and foster social harmony. Forced retirement was already a reality for many older workers by 1935. The questions left unanswered by corporations were how adequately and in what way these outcasts' retirements were to be financed and how union activities could be tamed. Social Security helped shift certain labor unrests from the workplace to the state. Third, the purposes and form of Social Security legislation guaranteed some future political vulnerability. We shall briefly discuss each of these characteristics of Social Security.

As has been suggested throughout our discussion, monopoly sector management was facing a two-pronged goal by the 1930s: eliminating older workers (reconstituting the labor force) and reducing labor disruptions (Braverman, 1974; Edwards, 1979). The dependency of the state upon economic growth within the monopoly sector of the economy led to it helping forge the eventual solutions to these goals.

One solution reached during the 1930s was that in return for future guaranteed raises in real wages, monopoly sector workers acknowledged managements' prerogatives in the work process, the firm, and the economy. What this meant was that unions would now restrict their terrain of struggle to distributional issues, and management would not be challenged on matters relating to production goals and control of the labor process.[6] Unions would merely negotiate over wages and benefit levels, that is, over the distribution of profits, not their extraction through surplus labor value.

Bureaucratization, legitimation of unions, and introduction of some due process procedures were also part of this bargain. The federal government in establishing labor negotiation guidelines facilitated this solution and shifted much of the burden of future class negotiations to itself (Wolfe, 1977). As part of due process and bureaucratic formalities, workers would now have acknowledged grievance and seniority protections against arbitrary dismissal. Management received stability, predictability, and rationalization of the workplace, in addition to uncontested control of the work process.

Labor, in losing control of the labor process, was only a short step away from losing control of the "stock and flow" of labor as well. Mandatory retirement was a logical extention of the new seniority system (Graebner, 1980), and with its acceptance by unions, management had complete control over the "stock and flow" of labor (Myles, 1981a:19). Management was thus able to foster normative integration of younger workers to the firm through implied promotional opportunities.

According to Myles (1981a), the price demanded by labor for all of these concessions within the workplace was the welfare state, or more accurately its first component: Social Security. When workers lost control of the labor process, conditions became even more intolerable for older workers. It was thus in labor's interest to promote retirement, retirement pensions, and deferred wages to pay for them. Pressures for a government solution to this plight of older workers heightened because the corporate sector response to the pension issue had been so inadequate.

The state fulfilled its accumulation and legitimation functions during the 1930s by trying to rationalize or stabilize a faltering economy. One way it did this was the already discussed step of implementing collective bargaining between management and labor. The second means was to provide for the unemployed old and the disabled through Social Security legislation. The state thus created an atmosphere for corporate investment and growth while extending the bureaucratic control of the workplace into the government by assuming responsibility for those lopped off by the new seniority system. It is in this sense that Social Security represented a "social expense." It was a state-subsidized solution for human fallout left behind by corporations in their drive for monopolies of markets, surplus labor value, increased profits, and hegemonic and bureaucratic control over the labor process and force.

Together, management and labor's "social bargain" and Social Security legislation placed older Americans outside the work force. In tying benefits to earning history, Social Security helped recreate the class system in old age, and in legitimizing the elimination of older workers from the workplace, it helped splinter the working class. Organized labor was thus very much involved in the systematic dismissal of older workers. In hindsight, the one defense of labor that can be made is that the existence of Social Security has made additional reforms (such as health insurance and Social Security benefit increases) easier to obtain. Today, class conflicts frequently find expression over the terms of these programs.

A final point about Social Security passage is that because it represented a resolution to a capitalist crisis more than a welfare philosophy to protect the well-being of citizens, the form that it took guaranteed rapid reduction in unemployment but no long-term stability.[7] Unlike many other societies that have established old-age benefits based on a genuine pension fund and a principle of social adequacy,[8] America opted for a pay-as-you-go strategy and launched a welfare system that would be substantially financed by government borrowing (Gough, 1975:71) and subject to repeated ideological assaults.

Not only has the pay-as-you-go approach required political negotiation of Social Security's financing, but it has prevented any large buildup of funds which might have transferred sizable economic power from the private to the public sector (Myles, 1918b). We shall explore the ramifications of these facts in a later discussion of the current assault on Social Security, the changed needs of capitalists today, causes for the elimination of mandatory retirement, and the possibility that older Americans will be forced into rather than out of the future labor market. For purposes of the present discussion, Social Security legislation can best be thought of as the vehicle by which older Americans were officially forced from a producer to a consumer role within the economy. Indeed, this, in addition to reducing unemployment and reconstituting the labor force, was one of its key functions in stabilizing the social order.

THE FUNCTIONS OF SOCIAL SECURITY

The functions of Social Security for stabilizing the social order and thus social control were many. Some functions were deliberate; others were latent or unanticipated consequences. From a functionalist perspective it can be argued that the elderly became a new official category of deviants with passage of Social Security, a group deliberately created so that the system and other employee groups would benefit. This stabilization process occurred in several intended ways: unemployment was reduced, old people were to support the economy through consumption, they were to serve as both positive and negative role models for others, and the political steam they had gathered in working for change was to be diffused. Less obvious consequences of this process were solidification of age norms and the creation of numerous administrators, caretakers, and experts who were to make their livings, their profits, and their reputations off of the elderly.

If social control theorists are correct in saying that the worker role is the primary means by which individuals are integrated within a society, then legitimized retirement made possible by Social Security must be seen as a blessing for younger workers at the expense of older ones. Not only does work serve as a major source of identity for Americans, but it is also promoted as the basis for social and self worth. These attitudes were reportedly even more prevalent in the 1930s (Piven and Cloward, 1977:60-64). With rapid industrialization and rationalization of the work process, sizable economic disruption was wrought by the turn of the twentieth century, and the workability of the economic system was called into question by many Americans. The "rational" disposal of old people eventually made possible by Social Security helped reduce this questioning.

Along with retirement as a panacea for economic crises came the belief among many corporate managers that increased consumption was necessry (Graebner, 1980:15). Advertising was increasingly relied upon to promote economic growth, and certain subpopulations were targeted as major consumers. The Townsend Plan put forth during the 1930s acknowledged this new corporate emphasis in suggesting that older Americans receive $200 a month on the condition that all of the money be spent by the month's end. This noble attempt to capitalize on the new corporate ethos lost out to the significantly more meager Social Security package.

The problem with this relegation of old people to a consumer role is that it automatically meant a reduction in status (Palmore and Manton, 1973). No matter how necessary advertising attempts to make the roles of consumer groups — be they housewives, old people, or today's teenagers — these groups do not have as much social power as middle-aged producers. While this fact has proven unfortunate for the elderly, it nonetheless helps underpin the social order.

By withholding maximum prestige from the consumer role, citizens get a better understanding of what is valued — namely, the worker role. And this imposition of boundaries, as functionalists say, reinforces moral meanings, the economic system, and the distribution of ownership which underpins the system. Any successful pressure on individuals to produce within the present structure is ultimately reinforcement for the status quo. It is in this sense that old people joined women on the sidelines of the workplace and became a negative referent for those still toiling away at their jobs.

Retirement generated a second role function for old people, one which was closely associated with their consumption role. Just as women have been traditionally packaged through stereotypes as a "soft" and more civilized underbelly of a hard-driving and individualistic system (Lifton, 1965), so were old people portrayed as the great humanizers of a raw and ruthless industrialization process.

As rapid change occurred, passive attributes were ascribed to the elderly, such as an ability to advise and guide the young against the "temptations" and "allurements" of an increasingly unpredictable society (Achenbaum, 1978:17). At the same time that old people were systematically denied participation in the major goals of America (i.e. expansion and commercialization), they were promoted as stabilizers and counter balances to these processes (Graebner, 1980:11).

Clearly, this designation served two purposes in advancing social order. First, by declaring some use of old people for the greater cause of "progress," the elderly could be mollified in their relegation to the economic sidelines. They could perhaps take some pride in this new role and consequently not strive to reclaim their producer positions.[9] Nascent unrest could thus be deterred from developing into a genuinely disruptive force. Second, those who were engaged in the harsh exigencies of capital's growth and change, such as exposing workers to grim working conditions and low wages, could rest assured that American culture was based on more virtuous principles than exploitation and higher profits at any costs. The "ideal" culture of nondiscrimination and equal opportunity for all could be maintained in the face of a competitive and survivalist material culture.

The difficulty for any group which is set up to epitomize the more virtuous side of humankind is twofold. An obvious drawback is rationalized exclusion from the ballpark in which the real game of power is being played. Another problem is that the stereotype is invariably double-edged. There is a short step between "this is your use" and "this is all you are good for." To the extent that a group's purpose is to act as a conservative (and face-saving) force against the actions of others, the conservative image itself is frequently employed as a justification for ridicule and further inappropriateness for participation in the "real" world.

Women, for example, have been popularly depicted as more religious than men (their better halves) and as nurturant; the first has elicited sarcasm and charges of conservativism, while the second has rendered them "inappropriate" for the heartless world of business. Old people who as a group were willfully assigned to the role of stabilizer and conservative influence have since been mocked as a basically conservative group. Evidence to the contrary has not significantly altered this image (Glenn, 1978). What began as a positive group role to serve the needs of the larger society has had negative results for the lives of many older individuals.

The last intended function of Social Security was the erosion of old people as a political force. From 1885 to 1935, old people and/or issues of concern to them, such as poverty, pensions, and health insurance, remained on the political agenda with varying degrees of intensity (Lubove, 1968:137). After Social Security passed, the elderly "movement" declined into what Pratt (1976) calls the "dismal years." There is little doubt that large-scale changes at the turn of the century began to undermine political cohesion and the confidence of political leaders. By the 1930s these conditions were very serious indeed, and political leaders finally responded to pension protesters with Social Security. Old people were politically defused and socially contained for several reasons.

First, Social Security legislation dealt with old people's immediate grievance — the need for income maintenance in the face of massive unemployment and basically nonexistent private pensions. Second, it channeled their anger into legitimate and less disruptive or contagious forms of protest. In the future old people would put lobbyists in Washington rather than take to the streets as they had been doing. Nothing so rattles advocates of order and the status quo as unpredictable and nonorderly protesters.

By substituting a skimpy Social Security for the more expansive Townsend Plan, the government could undermine popular support for the elderly's cause. Now that it appeared that the moral, if not the monetary, demands of old people had been met, future protests could be discredited. Essentially, a protest movement was conciliated and disarmed,[10] the malcontent elderly were politically integrated, and American's old became an officially regulated subpopulation. Thus, old people were successfully coopted and controlled politically and insulated economically and socially.

Although all of these strategies reduced the elderly's political efficacy for many years, the major reason for their demise was their loss of the worker role. As Piven and Cloward (1977:20-21) point out, most major protests arise when patterns of everyday life and institutions such as work are disrupted. Because the elderly as a group lost connection with the workplace and were assigned no substitute institutional positions, they had virtually no forum for becoming a political aggregate until senior centers, old-age associations, and mass communication techniques became widespread.

And it still remains to be seen how politically effective these political vehicles will be in protecting Social Security benefits and eligibility requirements. While one goal of the current assault on Social Security may be to force old people back into the labor market, at present they are not sufficiently integrated within the productive force to use this as the stage for protest and disruption. If all employed older persons withheld their services in protest against any Social Security cuts and/or union members of all ages participated in a protest, these actions would unquestionably be more disruptive, and thus effective, than efforts among unemployed older persons.

Thus far we have limited our discussion to some obvious functions of Social Security in preserving social order and imposing controls on America's old. There were two additional yet interrelated social control mechanisms triggered by this legislation: age norms and the proliferation of an aging enterprise whose members advise, tend, and make their livings off of the old. We shall only briefly outline these issues here, but each is elaborated in later discussions.

The most serious impact of Social Security legislation upon age norms was its implied designation of when old age begins. Employers increasingly used age 65 as the cutoff point for mandatory retirement, and people began to associate receipt of Social Security with being "old" (Cohen, 1957). Whereas older Americans once blended into the population through their occupations and family ties, they now constituted an officially segregated group. Individual choice about when and how to terminate work gave way to bureaucratic policies. Along with these policies and age norms came a lot of problems for older Americans and many individuals to help solve these socially generated problems.

One function of mandatory retirement policies within corporations and organizations was to bureaucratize the termination of older workers and thus enhance personnel planning. System needs had priority over individual needs, and increased efficiency was the goal. Within the larger society, gerontologists appeared to study old people's problems, and eventually nursing home entrepreneurs surfaced to take the bureaucratic model even further.[11] With Social Security, family members became accustomed to independence from their older members and vice versa, but when people lived to be very old or became infirm, demand arose for a new institution — the nursing home. This was a logical extension of America's increasing reliance upon a bureaucratic and distancing response to old people's needs.

Gerontologists for their part served an important function in solidifying the institution of retirement and age norms. They devised theories of aging which either stressed the virtues of retirement for society or took retirement for granted and emphasized old people's need to look within themselves for ways to adjust to their reduced economic and social circumstances (Marshall and Tindale, 1978:165; Decker, 1975).

Just as corporations argued for rationalizing the personnel process through planned exits of older employees, one theory of aging argued that society benefited from the disengagement (including retirement) of older members by being able to fill the social void ahead of time which would be caused by their deaths (Cumming and Henry, 1961). This theory in its result, if not its intent, represented a justification for social death prior to physical death. All of the aging theories, in rarely pointing out the class aspects of Social Security and in emphasizing individual adjustment, have contributed to the selling of retirement as a commodity to the American public.[12]

Gerontologists are merely one group of experts among many who now manage and control the lives of old people. Social workers, psychiatrists, nursing home operators, legislators, and Social Security administrators supplement the ranks. Unquestionably, their existence has helped deflate unemployment rates over the years.

If it is true, as Hughes (1964) argues, that the degree to which a group is subjected to caretakers reflects their social distance from the community, America's old are in a more socially constrained and stigmatized position today than prior to passage of Social Security. As we have seen, this legislation served many functions in preserving the social order, including reducing unemployment and legitimizing discrimination against America's old. What was deemed functional for the system was not necessarily functional for individual old persons. We now turn to the subject of how the official segregation of the elderly and their relegation to a deviant status — transitions made possible by Social Security — can impact individual old persons in their everyday lives.

EFFECTS OF SOCIAL SECURITY

What we only inferred we can now state: Social Security launched a process by which a primary deviation, old age, became a secondary deviation — one with definite role expectations, not the least of which was exit from the labor force. Older persons' roles, unlike those of most, were heavily defined in terms of "should-nots" rather than "shoulds." Whether one calls the elderly a "negatively privileged status group" (Neuwirth, 1969), a deviant group, a disvalued group or "discreditable persons" (Goffman, 1963), there is no question that an ascribed status (age) became a master status as a result of Social Security. Because this transition centered around a loss of the producer role, it always implied disability and thus moral deficiency (Miller, 1979). As Clinard (1974) notes, disability connotes an incapacity to perform role expectations and is very much in keeping with the medical model of social control.

One of the prices nonproducers must pay in America is to agree to put themselves under the management of others — be they spouses, welfare officials, administrators, or psychiatrists — and this is precisely what happened to the old in accepting Social Security. As Parsons (1953) suggested in his famous paradigm, people in the sick role are exempt from normal social responsibilities, *but* they are expected to seek competent help and to cooperate; and, at the same time, being ill is socially defined as sufficiently undesirable so as to push individuals toward reentry into their roles. Their special treatment from others is conditioned on the premise that they will do all that is possible to get out of this special status and continue to "pull their weight(s)."

In a similar way, old people have been allowed to abandon their obligation to produce but under specific conditions. They frequently do not control the timing of their role exits, the pension amounts available, nor the economic and social costs of the exits. Nor can they avoid coming under the auspice of numerous bureaucrats who certify their eligibility for Social Security, Medicare, housing, social services, and sometimes their claims to legal competency and sanity.

Several problems and some ironies have resulted from the social creation of old age as secondary deviance. One problem is that in order for secondary deviance to be effective, negative stereotypes must be pervasive throughtout a society (Lemert, 1967:42-43). And official labeling and segregation of a group only tend to reinforce the stereotypes. Second, as labeling theorists point out, negative stereotypes often lead to negative self-concepts and self-loathing among victims of the stereotype. Individuals with negative self-concepts, in turn, frequently impose harsh expectations and evaluations on those who are similarly labeled.

An irony of the labeling phenomenon is that secondary deviance can sometimes carry a "secondary gain" for targets. A secondary gain is a reward or satisfaction experienced as a result of the labeling process. There is evidence today that older Americans now view retirement as a secondary gain of labor market discrimination which has been directed their way. It is likely that they will fight current efforts to redefine them as "normal" and thus eligible for the workplace. After decades of having retirement sold to them and hearing that they should accept being rather than doing, old people may resist attempts to redefine their proper place within American life.

The official relegation of the old to the economic and social sidelines has been accompanied by pervasive negative stereotypes. We have already referred to assumptions of conservatism and disability among the old, and other aspects of the stereotype are discussed at length in later chapters. Some of the most prevalent images, in addition to disability and conservatism, have included a presumed loss of creativity, sexual dysfunction, rigidity, and nonproductivity (McTavish, 1971). The images are reflected in Americans' humor (Palmore, 1971). Media presentations also tend to reinforce these stereotype characteristics, but an even more relied upon control device is to not present any image at all.

These problems associated with secondary deviancy, as well as others, are elaborated throughout the book. What is of most interest is that while the needs of capitalism once dictated a definition of old people as deviants, the needs of capitalism now call for their redefintion as "normals." Whereas systemitized retirement policies were once deemed the most efficient and profit-oriented mode possible, individual merit is now the preferred basis for retirement within some corporations.

SOCIAL SECURITY TODAY

Four trends have contributed to this situation. First, American corporations have lost their competitive edge in world markets (despite monopolized national markets in some cases), and some managers now believe that bureaucratic modes of decision making (e.g. mandatory retirement) are sloppy and not cost-effective (Graebner, 1980:16). Second, the existence of such "social expenses" as Medicare means that employer-paid fringe benefits for older workers can cost less than those required by younger workers. There is some indication that the government may force employers to make fringe benefits available to older workers as an alternative to Medicare, but at present this is an unresolved issue (U.S. Senate Special Committee on Aging, 1982:20). The government's motive is to reduce Medicare costs, while employers' motive is to curtail their employee costs.

Third, reduced birth rates along with technological changes, such as computer dependency, have resulted in current labor shortages in certain sectors of the economy and projections for more sizable ones in the future (Trausch, 1981:36). Instead of relying upon advertising and consumption to generate profits, business now shows signs of increasing its rate of exploitation. Rate of exploitation refers to the ratio of productivity to labor costs and is directly related to extraction of surplus labor value. Supply-side and monetarist economic policies testify to this transition as well as verbal and legislative attacks on unions and the "social bargain" of guaranteed increases in real wages (Gough, 1975:91). By expanding the labor supply through increased unemployment rates and/or the addition of older workers, managers can more successfully play off employee groups and drive wages down. The present debate on Social Security and proposed increases in eligibility ages are part of an attempt to redefine old people as producers. A business community that protrayed older workers as decrepit and inefficient at the turn of the century is beginning to say, "the negatives are a myth" (Trausch, 1981:36).

A fourth trend contributing to a redefintion of elders as "normal" is the slowdown in economic growth that has occurred within the past five years and managers' growing desire to control and invest private pension funds.[13] The "pay-as-you-go" method of financing Social Security precluded the federal government having available a sizable pension fund for investment purposes. Indeed, two reasons why Social Security was not set up as a genuine pension fund were to assure a quick (five years) start-up time for Social Security payments and to deny the federal government sufficient monies to alter capital priorities through investment of public monies.

Today, a number of corporate managers and their political allies are trying to encourage the development and expansion of private pension programs by attempting to undermine confidence in Social Security. In other words, Social Security is a pawn in a class struggle between private capital accumulation on the one hand and labor's attempts to hold onto its reward for having foregone wages and control of the labor process in accepting Social Security. The continuation of a market definition of community in gaining public attention, by the absence of serious media evaluations of their arguments or their real motives, and by the application of market analogies to Social Security.

As Myles (1981b:20) points out, by market (or capital accumulation) standards, Social Security is subversive and "out of control." Over the past fifty years, Social Security has become a "citizen's wage" as opposed to a market wage; it has mildly redistributed income toward the poor within generations; it has been paid on the basis of need, not just contribution; and it has attached income claims to individuals, not just to their capital (Myles, 1981b:20). Despite critics attempts to apply market criteria in discussion of Social Security, such as declaring the program "actuarially unsound" because current funds do not match anticipated outlays, these criteria are inappropriate. Social Security was established with the knowledge that the ratio of producers to beneficiaries would decrease drastically as the system matured and the understanding that financing formulae might have to be revised (Shannon, 1982:19). The "soundness" of Social Security is a political matter and depends upon the American people's willingness to subsidize their old-age fund with a fraction of the magnanimity they demonstrate in subsidizing their "defense fund" (Myles, 1981b:5). For example, proposed federal budget allocations for Social Security in 1984 are $178.2 billion as opposed to $245.3 billion earmarked for military spending (Oliphant, 1983:1,14).

What then are some of the arguments that are currently being leveled by some corporate sectors against Social Security? Coupled with the charge that Social Security is headed toward "bankruptcy" have been assertions that Social Security represents a demographic burden, that it constitutes a bad investment for younger generations, and that it will lead to intergenerational "class" warfare.[14]

The argument that Social Security represents a demographic burden refers to the fact that in 1940 the ratio of workers to recipients was 16 to 1 and today it is 3.3 to 1 (Shannon, 1982:19). As has been noted, this shift was anticipated by the program's designers and is irrelevant in and of itself (Cohen, 1957). Furthermore, when critics speak of the "dependency burden" of producers to nonproducters, they invariably include only the elderly as nonproducers. A more accurate way of presenting this ratio is to include both children and old persons as dependents.[15] While the proportion of old persons is expected to rise in the twenty-first century, the proportion of young persons is expected to decline due to lowered fertility rates. Although it is true that public expenditures on the old are greater than those for the young, private expenditures on children are extremely high. Thus, as families have fewer children, they presumably will have more taxable income.

Also implied in these references to the dependency ratio is the idea that smaller future cohorts will involve lower levels of production and thus a reduced taxable economic base. In reality, women will probably comprise an increasing proportion of the labor force, particularly as family size declines, and smaller cohorts do not necessarily infer lowered productivity. Just as today's young workers are "undercapitalized" in the work force because of their large numbers, so might less numerous young workers in the future be handsomely capitalized (Myles, 1981b). Indeed, some respected economists are predicting high productivity levels from fewer workers in the future and forced leisure — not only for elders but for all workers.[16]

The assertion that Social Security represents a bad buy for young generations also has limitations. This argument is based on the premise that the rate of return from Social Security will be lower than that provided by private pensions (2%- 5%) (Feldstein, 1977:92). As has been mentioned elsewhere, the history of private pensions is abysmal, less than 50 percent of workers are covered by such programs, and vestment and nonmobility stipulations separate many potential beneficiaries from their "benefits." Also, while Social Security benefits have been adjusted for inflation and are available to a worker's survivor, many private pensions are calculated in fixed dollars and/or are not transferable to survivors.

It is in fact impossible to know what the future rates of return will be for Social Security as opposed to private pensions since the rate of growth in real wages will be contingent upon fertility, mortality, and marriage rates, and Social Security benefit amounts will additionally depend upon wage and price changes, what constitutes a typical job history in the future, and levels of taxation. The criticism of Social Security as a "bad buy" serves two purposes. It reflects positively on private pensions as an alternative program for workers, and it infers that both workers and the economy would benefit from workers' investment in the private sector. For reasons already noted, these suggestions are highly debatable. What is not open for speculation is the fact that if most workers opted to start or join private pension programs, corporate managers and financiers would have enormous capital funds available for investment and additional capital accumulation.

The idea that Social Security will lead to intergenerational "class" warfare involves a misuse of the concept of class and is not really an argument at all. Social Security has already splintered workers by separating older workers from the labor force and turning them into consumers rather producers. As a part of the "social bargain" between management and labor struck during the 1930s, Social Security also facilitated the economic gulf between workers within the monopoly and competitive sectors.[17] If workers allow their interests to be further splintered, it will be due to their susceptibility to the image of old persons as a new leisure class that is presented by some critics of Social Security. Any such intragroup splintering or conflict would not constitute "class" warfare but rather group warfare since capitalists and workers comprise the major groups worthy of a "class" label. This type of labor infighting if it developed would nonetheless speak to a formidable degree of ideological control by capital. It would seem that only in America is talk of such an intergenerational "class" warfare possible. Many Western European countries have a higher percent of old persons than the United States, all spend a higher proportion of their budgets on this group, and all take the position that solutions will be found as problems arrive. What these countries share is a belief that old-age security is a "right," not a privilege to be redefended, and that community extends beyond the marketplace.[18]

The question that remains is how these assaults on Social Security are to be reconciled with older Americans' adamant defense of Social Security. While Social Security helped transform the elderly from "social dynamite" to "social junk" in the 1930s, any undermining of the program may have a reverse effect today. An unavoidable irony is that post-1935 efforts to socialize older Americans into acceptance of retirement have largely succeeded. As stigmatizing and uncomfortable as this process has been for older Americans, nonlabor force participation and the leisure time it provides have become secondary gains for many. Parsons (1953), in his discussion of the sick role, pointed out the risk of certain privileges associated with the role, such as being excused from other role responsibilities, becoming secondary gains.

Labor may have lost control of the work process and the work force in the 1930s, but for those who live long enough a legitimized escape exists: state-subsidized retirement. Even in the absence of mandatory retirement (Peterson, 1982:12) today, only 4 million of the 25 million persons age 65 and over work at all. It seems that most older Americans want the right to work but not to work. As charges of age discrimination persist, it appears that employers want the threat of hiring older workers but do not in fact want to hire them, at least not yet nor in large numbers. Under proposed increases in the age for Social Security eligibility, older Americans will have to live longer in order to escape from workplace control or fend for themselves longer if forcibly expunged sooner. Private pensions may not benefit from proposed revisions in Social Security but neither will old persons in any major way. As has become evident in our discussions of relief and income security throughout American history, when the going gets rough, Americans can get a lot rougher.[19] Social Security today shows signs of becoming more "exceptional" rather than less so.

CONCLUSION

Social Security, as part of a bargain struck between management and labor and under the auspices of the federal government, facilitated the government in fulfilling both its capital formation and legitimation functions. Managers of monopoly sector corporations wanted increased predictability, rationalization, and bureaucratization within the work process and work force. Forced retirement of older and more skilled workers was one aspect of reconstituting the labor force and defusing workers' power. With Social Security the federal government provided a "social expense" in assuming responsibility and bureaucratic control of the recently expunged older worker.

As we have seen in our application of a functional analysis, Social Security served many purposes in preserving the status quo — it reduced unemployment, diffused elderly protest, and relegated elders to consumer roles, to name just a few. With Social Security, "old people" as we know them were literally created, they became a "problem" group, and they experienced secondary deviance. Today, as the needs of capital are once again shifting, both old persons and Social Security are political targets for redefinition.

NOTES

1. Williamson, Evans, and Powell (1982:146-188) elaborate on this exceptionalism and market definition of community.
2. Much of the information in this discussion of the period 1890-1920 is drawn from Graebner (1980), a painstaking analysis of how and why retirement policies evolved in the United States and a work that is not of the neo-Marxian school of thought. Some of Graebner's arguments are supplemented and recast throughout our discussion.
3. Some of the reasons for this labor activity are discussed in Chapter 2 on "Social Control of the Elderly."
4. Gough (1979) elaborates on this idea.
5. Leutz (1978:60-61) points out that even marginal mental and manual declines become significant within an industrial system, such as Taylorism, where skills are reduced to narrow abilities and performance standards are set almost at the limit of human function. Older workers are best able to offset any declines with age when they can draw upon their experience by substituting known short cuts in one part of the job for difficulties experienced in another area. Variety in tasks is critical for compensatory strategies to be devised, and variety in tasks (skills) was the target of Taylorism as well as more recent labor process controls. Leutz further notes that working-class older

persons have been most devalued by this deskilling of labor, since many managerial positions — even middle-level ones — allow some discretion in task peformance.

6. See Myles (1981a) for development of this idea.
7. By "rapid" we mean in comparison to the time that would have been required to establish a genuine pension system, rather than one set up on the pay-as-you-go basis of current workers funding retirees. Retirees received the first Social Security benefits in 1940.
8. Williamson, Evans, and Powell (1982:174) discuss the concept of social adequacy to mean indicators of pension quality. These include the level at which pensions maintain the income of the elderly relative to other groups, whether payments are contingent upon previous earnings, and the extent to which the government makes contributions to pensions from general tax revenues.
9. Wood (1971) cites the 1953 Havinghurst and Albrecht public opinion study which revealed evidence of this competitive aspect of labor discrimination against the elderly. The authors concluded: "We want them to do what they want to do as long as they are not too strenuous and too competitive with middle-aged people. . . ."
10. This process of defusing a protest movement is discussed in Piven and Cloward (1977:28-32) and Achenbaum (1980:470-488).
11. Myles (1980) makes a good argument for why nursing homes represent a logical extension of a rationalized labor force.
12. Graebner (1980:15) refers to retirement as a commodity that was marketed just as any other commodity would be.
13. Much of this discussion of Social Security and its critics is informed by Myles's (1981b) excellent analysis.
14. See Feldstein (1977:90) and Davis and van derOever (1981) for examples of these types of accusations.
15. See Myles (1981b) for development of this reasoning.
16. Wassily Leontief, 1973 Nobel prize winner for economics, is one such person. See Curtis (1983) for his comments on this subject.
17. See Edwards (1979) for an excellent discussion of this class splintering between monopoly and competitive industry workers and its relationship to other social divisions, such as gender and racial discrimination.
18. See U.S. Senate Special Committee on Aging (1981) for a good overview of European public pensions of the elderly.
19. Various proposed policies being bantered about suggest this trend (e.g. efforts to extend the age for Social Security eligibility, to have old persons pay more of their health costs, to place liens on nursing

home residents' homes, and to make social services in the future only available to old persons without families). This last suggestion arose in several sessions of the 1982 meetings of the Gerontological Society of America in Boston. For accounts of the other policy recommendations, see Special Committee on Aging, United States Senate (1982) and Shribman (1983:19).

CHAPTER 7

THE POLITICAL ECONOMY OF HEALTH CARE POLICY

A S THE United States moved from an industrial to a post-industrial society, economic and bureaucratic imperatives forced changes in the structure of the family and the role of government. These changes had direct implications for the design of health policies and, within these policies, how the needs of the elderly would be met. The adherence to the Jacksonian notion of laissez-faire capitalism and limited government intervention has meant that strong, consistent government assistance for the elderly has not been forthcoming (Rossman and Burnside, 1975:86).

Indifference towards the aged in part persists because of the emphasis in American culture on individualism and independence. As a result, financial responsibility for the elderly continues to be a conflicted and unresolved issue. The ambivalence of American society to care for its elderly members suggests that any movement towards increasing the government's involvement in the financing of health services is unlikely to have been generated by a sense of equity and justice, but rather as a means to promote capital accumulation and maintain social control (Battistella and Rundall, 1978:18).[1] The legitimacy of such an interpretation gains credence as Americans have witnessed a progressive restructuring of health care from a humanitarian social service to a purely economic and bureaucratic activity (Battistella and Rundall, 1978:20).[2] The effect of such shifts, particularly over the last quarter of a century, has been to increasingly repress and alienate the most vulnerable members of our society.

Pressure for reform, although sustained, has never been particularly successful because of some basic tenets inherent in American culture. The Protestant work ethic has rationalized minimal government involvement in health care by assuming that industrious members of society can acquire sufficient capital to freely purchase any goods or service, including health care (Cottrel, 1966:91). Social Darwinism is subtly used to account for the existence of the illness by attributing such conditions to the innate qualities of the individual, not industrialization and the resulting alienation (Mechanic, 1978:254). An exception in American history are the blind, the handicapped and the permanently disabled who, while not held to blame for their present condition, given the sparest of resources, may as well have been (Stevens and Stevens, 1974).

Although it is comforting to deny the existence of market imperatives in health care, the fact is that they do exist and they perform significant social control functions, particularly with respect to the poor and the elderly. The forces of capitalism are such that unless the elderly can impact upon the power institutions within the state to improve their monetary position, no major health reforms which truly meet their needs will be promoted, and no amount of incentives to encourage families to care for their elderly members will be effective (Cottrel, 1966:97).[3]

Families have been put in an untenable position, attempting to both meet the needs of elderly parents and grandparents while devoting increasing amounts of time to the production process. Sociologists are generally agreed that the capitalist imperative to expand production has been realized only by sacrificing maintenance functions of the family as basic as housecleaning, child-rearing and the care of its elderly members.[4] So, although the family is ill equipped to provide such services, the government has done little to encourage or support home health care.

The first vestiges of health reform occurred at the turn of the century, with a series of measures prompted by the release of the Flexner Report. The Flexner Report cited severe inadequacies in the numbers of physicians needed in the United States and also questioned the quality of American medical training. The quality issue was quickly seized by medicine as an opportunity to establish a monopoly of services, which they have maintained until this day (Feldstein, P., 1977:238).[5] There is ample evidence that because financial remuneration for the care of the elderly is limited, few physicians treat this population.[6] Despite the apparent unwillingness of physicians to provide medical care to the aged, medical societies have repeatedly stalled efforts by other qualified professionals, such as geriatric nurse practitioners, to independently and less expensively manage the elderly's medical care.

But the social control issue of how the provider-consumer relationship will be negotiated does not simply end with who will be legitimately recognized as a provider. Barbara and John Ehrenreich (1978:62) characterize the transmission of ideological messages by physicians to their patients as the most frequent, yet most difficult to document, form of cooperative social control. The esteem generated by the medical profession is unequalled, and the concomitant power this has provided medicine has been exercised repeatedly not only with individual patients but within the entire health delivery system.

Motivated by a humane concern that availability of medical care was limited for the poor and the elderly, the federal government became interested in the issue of equal access. Equal access to health care continued to predominate the attention of legislators, providers and consumers alike for the better part of this century. The events of the last fifty years surrounding this issue may be briefly summarized as pitting the medical establishment against the working class in as yet an unresolved struggle to determine whether medical care for the elderly is an entitlement or a form of welfare. Congress, serving as the arena for fifteen years of this debate, reached a climactic moment in 1965 when it finally passed, and President Johnson signed, Medicare and Medicaid enacting legislation. The inability of Congress to resolve the welfare/entitlement question is reflected in the administration of Medicare as an entitlement through Social Security, and Medicaid as a welfare program.

It was hoped by more liberal supporters that Medicare and Medicaid would be a stepping stone to broad-based government support of elderly health care. However, rising expenditures quickly put an end to such assumptions. The effort to contain health costs began almost immediately after Medicare and Medicaid were both enacted. Now, the confidence that equity in access can be assured by eliminating financial barriers to the elderly has been seriously questioned.

Health care costs have been rising twice as fast as any other index in the GNP and are already hitting 12 percent. This continued rapid growth is related to higher medical prices (54%), population growth (10.5%), and quality increases (34.9%) (Carels, Neuhauser and Statson, 1980:6). The effects of population growth may become even more ominous as present death-rate data indicates that by the year 2000, the elderly population would have increased by 32 million, or 35 percent (U.S. Department of Health, Education and Welfare, 1978a).

The consequence of a general deterioration of the economy and spiraling health care costs has been to drive more and more of our elderly citizens into poverty.[7] In testimony before the U.S. House of Representatives Select Committee on Aging (1978a), Thomas Luken noted that although persons over 65 account for only one-tenth of the population, they account for 29 percent of all Americans earning incomes below $3,200. Mr. Luken faulted "stingy" benefit levels for federal programs and inflation for the growing destitution of our senior citizens. In fact, the combination of increased medical costs, population growth and inflation has led to a situation where, although expenditures for Medicare have increased, the actual federal contribution per elderly person has declined.[8]

In the face of growing expenditures for the care of the elderly and the alleged inability of the government to meet these needs, the remedies that have been forwarded have not advocated the obvious — that is, a major restructuring of the health care industry. In fact, there is every reason to believe that the United States will maintain its unfortunate distinction as the only industrialized country in the world without national health insurance. Instead, solutions are promoted which tinker with a cumbersome array of rules, regulations and market incentives, none of which hangs together with any coherence but all of which maintain the hegemony of the health care triumvirate — physicians, hospital administrators, and third-party insurers.

The Reagan administration, whose allegiance to such forces is clear and unmistakable, has chosen not to challenge the powers that be. Instead, this administration seeks to expand their power through pro-competition models.[9] The Reagan administration proports that pro-competition models will properly align relationships and services, thereby ridding the system of inefficiency and waste and ultimately lowering the cost of health care. But if these models fail to make an appreciable difference, there are still the dramatic cuts made in the Medicare/Medicaid budget by limiting eligibility and benefits or increasing cost sharing.[10] Quite simply, the elderly continue to be easy targets for restraint in a health delivery system dominated by a profit imperative and sustained by the power of a select group of providers.

Ginzberg (1977:6) draws upon Tallyrand's analogy that a war is too serious to be left to the generals, in noting that health reform is too serious to be left to physicians. Yet, in instances where planning for elderly health services includes a variety of experts (as was the case with the 1981 White House Conference on Aging), the proposed solutions are equally narrow. The emphasis of the conference on supporting the family's ability to care for its elderly members is a necessary and noble gesture. Unfortunately, what the well-meaning participants overlooked was that the push for financial support will be moot in the absence of available members to provide the necessary care. Given the increasing economic demands on the family, especially women, there is every reason to believe that family members will be less, not more available. Equally naive is the proposal that private industry, foundations and charities can fill the void left by government in providing elderly related services. One participant candidly acknowledged that being at the conference was being like an ostrich (Kaplan, 1982:128).

Realistically, progressive solutions cannot be offered in a society which advances medical science and technology at the expense of the fundamental health needs of all Americans, especially the elderly. Government policies that value market and bureaucratic imperatives above social needs will unquestionably seriously disrupt all health programs. Such a philosophy presupposes that the aged, or others acting in their behalf, have the power to harness new capital made available through expansion and direct it towards elderly services. A more likely scenario is that as profit incentives become more pronounced, the elderly will be subordinated to other more lucrative health care markets (Cottrel, 1966). Turning outwards the state offers little encouragement, at least in the Reagan administration, which has chosen to dismantle programs that are already barely adequate. A review of the history of government's and industry's response to providing geriatric health services may illustrate why, as a society, our elderly have been and continue to be so grossly underserved.

HISTORY OF HEALTH CARE POLICY AND THE AGED

There are basically three reasons why government becomes involved in formulating health care policies (Steiner, 1971). If external costs beyond the consumer or producer inhibits the private market from providing a needed good or service, the government can directly subsidize the necessary service. Examples of this form of government involvement include federally financed biomedical research projects or public health immunization programs. Back in the 1940s, the American Geriatric Society and the Gerontological Society were able to convince the government that funding for research on aging was essential. Through their pressure (between 1937 and 1950), the National Institute of Health developed six divisions to research chronic conditions primarily afflicting the elderly. It was by means of this initial research that imperfections in the market, specifically the effects of entry problems upon the elderly, began to be identified.

Problems of entry for the elderly stemmed from the overwhelming numbers of aged citizens who, because of their economic position, could no longer purchase health services. The costs of health care was becoming increasingly prohibitive as the country, and the health care industry itself, became more industrialized. The professionalization of medicine (which gained prominence after the release of the Flexner Report in the 1920's) not only insured physicians would be educated in the scientific method but also marked the stiffening of statutes allowing the practice of medicine and, as a consequence, escalated the cost of medical care. Radical critics such as Ehrenreich (1971) and Illich (1976) argue persuasively that although such measures may have advanced the medical profession, they did so by strengthening the social control physicians had in American society and promoting dependency on a medical system of questionable therapeutic value. Whether the product physicians' proposed to deliver was necessary and beneficial will not be argued here, although critiques like Illich's would claim that in fact medicine is dangerous to one's health. The point is that the product or service offered by this new breed of sophisticated medical men was perceived as critical to maintaining one's health and it was significantly more expensive. Those most adversely affected by the advancement of medical science were the poor and the elderly who could no longer afford the cost of high-priced medical care.

The condition had now been created for the second form of government intervention: correcting market imperfections. Costs had now severely limited entry to the medical marketplace. Structurally, the market wasn't performing adequately to meet the needs of two overlapping populations — the poor and the elderly. The attention of the government became refocused from quality to the issue of access.

Major change in the health care system was repeatedly stalemated by the struggle between professional monopolists (primarily physicians who controlled most of the delivery), corporate rationalizers (representing the insurance and hospital industry), and members of the community (Alford, 1980:450). Only with the devastating economic plight of the Depression would the government be capable of instituting minimal protection for the needy. By the end of 1934, 28 states and 2 territories had passed old-age assistance laws (Stevens and Stevens, 1974:6). The passage of the Social Security Act in 1935 finally recognized that the needs of the elderly poor for cash income was a matter of right, rather than of charity (Sundquist, 1968:294).

Although the passage of the Social Security Act was heralded as insuring financial protection for Americans in times of need, health care was not among its various provisions. Roosevelt wanted to integrate health with income security benefits, but the American Medical Association adamantly opposed the inclusion of health benefits and threatened the passage of the entire Social Security Act. In fact, the American Medical Association has opposed all national health insurance since 1939. The influence of the AMA was sufficient to dissuade Roosevelt from including any provisions for national health insurance.

Unlike his predecessor, President Truman was not intimidated by the AMA, and he submitted his own national health insurance plan founded on a financing, not a welfare model. To defeat the Truman proposal, the AMA in 1949 spent a record $1.5 million to promote their position that the poor and the elderly were receiving adequate care (Harris, 1966:29). Findings by sociologists from the National Institute of Health refuted the perceptions of the AMA and so did the direct experience of the American public, who, by in large, supported the measure. Nonetheless, Congress yielded to intense lobbying pressure from the AMA and voted down the Truman proposal.

The last effort to secure comprehensive health care insurance was led by Senator Wagner in the late 1940s. The Murray-Dingell-Wagner bill would have provided health insurance for all Americans. Benefits were to be comprehensive and included hospital, physician and dental care. Financing would have been through a payroll tax, and the entire program was to be administered by the federal government. The tactic taken by the AMA to defeat the Murray-Dingell-Wagner bill was to equate such proposals with socialized medicine (Sundquist, 1968:290). Senator Wagner's efforts to deny such allegations were ineffective and, subsequently, that marked the last time a national health insurance proposal would be introduced until the 1970s.

Beginning in the 1950s, measures for health care reform became incremental in their approach, targetting those in most desperate need and turning to a welfare, not a financing model. After World War II, private health insurance for the elderly had become two to three times as much as it was for the general population. Forced to retire at age sixty-five, unable to pay for private insurance on a limited budget, and faced with the rising physician fees and hospital charges, more and more elderly were forced to seek treatment in the grossly inadequate public health care sector.[11] The Social Security Amendments of 1950 partially compensated the public sector and relieved some of the burden of providing care to the indigent. These amendments expanded federal public assistance grants-in-aid by including vendor payments for providers of medical services and hospital care. However, the administration of public health services still rested with the states and there was considerable state to state variation.[12]

The 1950s was a relatively complacent era for social reform.

Congressmen had become more subdued owing to the fact that several ardent supporters of national health insurance failed to win reelection. By 1956 the Democratic platform no longer endorsed health insurance proposals, and the Republicans even went so far as to embrace the socialized medicine rhetoric of the AMA. The present financing system, woefully inadequate in meeting the health care needs of the elderly, was still not sufficiently hideous to warrant reform.

Bills introduced by Democratic Senators Murray of Montana, Humphrey of Minnesota and Representative Dingell, to provide sixty days of hospitalization for the elderly, were quietly defeated. So, too, was an Eisenhower proposal designed by the first Secretary of Health, Education and Welfare, Oveta Culp Hobby, which would have boosted the development of private health insurance companies through a reinsurance mechanism. But the lack of enthusiasm for health insurance did not deter Congress from sponsoring legislation which acknowledged the deteriorating conditions of the elderly. Senator Charles Potter of Michigan proposed a national commission to research the needs of the aged; Senator John F. Kennedy proposed state grants to support elderly programs; and President Eisenhower in March of 1956 established the first Federal Council on Aging (Sundquist, 1968:295).

Efforts towards health care reform were reinstituted when, in 1958, Representative Aime Forand of Rhode Island introduced a bill which would have provided the elderly with limited hospital and medical insurance financed through Social Security taxes. The AMA, quiet throughout most of the fifties, began an intense lobbying crusade. A coalition was formed which included the AMA, the American Dental Association, the American Hospital Association, and the American Nursing Home Association. By the time it was over, the campaign waged by the AMA and its associates against health insurance for the elderly would cost an estimated $50 million (Harris, 1966:29).

The overkill tactics of the AMA began to backfire and acted instead to galvanize the proponents of Forand's bill. Organized labor joined with the American Nurses Association, the National Medical Association (whose members were black physicians), and various groups representing the elderly to support the Forand legislation.

Their efforts, although significant, were not enough to secure passage and the Forand bill died. But the growing popular support for such a measure did not go unnoticed by members of Congress.

Representative Wilbur Mills of Arkansas, who was then chairman of the powerful House Ways and Means Committee, proposed a bill based upon recommendations by the AMA: that the eligibility be based upon a means test enabling the elderly who were not collecting welfare to qualify for medical benefits. The Kerr-Mills bill was very comprehensive and was financed through tax revenues with state matching funds calculated according to a formula.[13] The passage of Kerr-Mills signified recognition, at least by the federal government, that the health care market was not operating optimally. The question then became the degree to which the federal government in the future should intervene to correct market imperfections. That debate became one of the key issues in the Nixon-Kennedy presidential campaign and obviously continues to this day.

Kennedy realized early in his presidency that to counteract the strong lobbying efforts of the AMA (which had spent more than any other lobbying group), the elderly had to be well organized. Kennedy turned to Representative Forand, now retired from Congress, and asked him to chair the National Council for Senior Citizens. By 1961, the council, with a membership of over one million, had distributed a record seven million pieces of literature informing the public about Medicare (Sundquist, 1968:309). Not to be outdone, the AMA stepped up its propaganda efforts with poster, literature, and nationwide speaking programs warning the public that the proposed Medicare legislation was an insidious form of socialized medicine. A Gallup poll indicated that 67 percent of Americans favored Medicare, and anticipation heightened that the time was finally right for passage of Kennedy's Medicare plan.

Unfortunately, a totally unanticipated twist occurred as a result of Kennedy's behavior at a rally of Medicare supporters in New York City. On nationwide television, the image projected by the president was frivolous. In contrast to Kennedy, Doctor Edward Annis of the AMA pleaded with the public in a subdued, reassuring manner to oppose Medicare. The manipulation of the television media was a complete and immediate success. From that moment on, Kennedy never again gained the momentum he needed for passage of his Medicare plan.[14]

The tide again shifted in 1964 after a Democratic landslide gave the Democrats two more additional seats on the powerful Ways and Means Committee. The landslide was credited to the grass roots efforts by the elderly and labor to elect officials who would support Medicare legislation. The chairman of the House Ways and Means Committee, a shrewd political operative, decided to capitalize on this clear mandate from the public. In 1964, Chairman Mills promised President Johnson that health insurance for the elderly would be his top priority, and in one year Mills delivered on his promise.

What Mills did was use a combination of brilliant statesmanship and sheer power to forge a compromise measure and then muscle it through Congress. Mills constructed the Medicare/Medicaid plan out of three separate proposals. From the Anderson-King bill, Mills took institutional benefits. Labelled Medicare Part A, it was financed through Social Security funds. Medicare Part B, which included physician coverage, was a combination of the Herlong-Curtis (Eldercare) bill supported by the AMA and the Byrnes bill. Medicare Part B was financed through premiums and general revenues. Two other important differences were that Medicare Part A reimbursed hospitals on a cost basis and was administered through intermediaries, while Medicare Part B reimbursed physicians on a fee-for-service basis and was administered through carriers. Medicaid, a welfare, not an entitlement program like Medicare, was designed to meet the medical needs of those people on categorical cash assistance and the medically needy. It was financed by joint federal-state matching funds with the federal government picking up 50-83 percent depending upon the state's per capita income. There are nine mandatory services, including hospital, nursing home and physician benefits, as well as six optional services. Thus, the insistence of physicians and hospital administrators that their right to professional autonomy must be maintained was endorsed by fee-for-service or cost-base reimbursement. What no one anticipated was that the "blank check" given to physicians and hospitals would blow the lid off health care costs, starting an inflationary spiral which may bankrupt the entire system.

The history of Medicare and Medicaid has been reviewed to illustrate that its enactment hinged not on the will and the needs of the
people but rather the power of special interests. It also could be persuasively argued that the eventual passage was a product not of hu-
manitarianism but a subtle form of social control to placate the
electorate with a marginal reform measure which would eventually
lead to even greater degrees of abuse and manipulation of elderly
Americans (Piven and Cloward, 1971).

The politics evident throughout this process did not stir the ideals
of democracy. Actions in Congress were dictated almost exclusively
by the lobbying power of the AMA and its associates. The issue was
used by politicians for their own political advantage only when it became obvious that the elderly were becoming a constituency to be
reckoned with and had little to do with the merits of the Medicare
plan. No doubt, because special-interest groups directed the design
of Medicare and Medicaid, there were substantial flaws that would
insure enormous profits for the capitalists in the health care market.
The tragedy was that the consequences of this profiteering and the
magnitude of its dire effects would not be realized for several years.

CONTEMPORARY PROBLEMS: LIMITED ACCESS AND EXCESS COST

Not long after the passage of Medicare and Medicaid, attention
was redirected to cost containment. In a similar way to previous
health policies, the federal government received some ambivalent
assistance from the health care industry in developing programs to
slow-rising health care costs. The proposals can be generally characterized as promoting either market incentives or as regulating restraint. While policy makers were desperately attempting to contain
costs, there came the growing realization that Medicare, essentially
an acute care program, was falling far short of meeting the needs of
the elderly. Additionally, the social and medical needs of the aged,
although clearly intertwined were fragmented into innumerable social service and health agencies making comprehensive treatment for
the elderly nearly impossible to implement.

To provide a general idea of the scope of elderly programs and agencies which provide health care services to the elderly, in addition to Medicare and Medicaid (which are administered through the Health Care Financing Administration), consider the following:

1. Federal grants provide mental health services to the elderly poor and are administered by the National Institute of Mental Health.
2. Federally insured loans are available for the rehabilitation and supply of nursing homes and are administered through Housing and Urban Development or the Veterans Administration.
3. Homemaker services to the needy are provided by Medicaid; home care money is available through the Administration on Aging program; home health services for the disabled are available through the Developmentally Disabled Assistance program; and hot meals at home are administered through the Food Stamp program.

Contending with these multiple bureaucracies, all with their differing rules and regulations, locations and personnel, acts as an additional hindrance to the elderly who, more often than not, have to negotiate these services on their own.[15]

Proponents of Medicare and Medicaid argue that although there are some areas where the elderly are still inadequately served, the steady decline in morbidity and mortality is directly attributable to the enactment of Medicare and Medicaid. It seems illogical to credit Medicare with improved mortality when in 1965 Medicare paid for 50 percent of an elderly person's total health care, while in 1978 it paid for only 38 percent. In addition, back in 1965, Medicare paid for 66 percent of all physician's bills, but by 1978 it paid only 50 percent (Pegals, 1980a:164). Clearly, the elderly are less well off now than they were back in 1965. The present situation is exacerbated by government cutbacks in coverage and increases in the percentage of the charges doctors pass on to their elderly patients.

Effective January 1, 1985, the Medicare deductible for hospital care is to be increased to $400. The co-insurance will increase to $100 per day for days 61 to 90. After using 150 "life-time reserve days," patients will pay the entire bill. For psychiatric hospitalization, coverage is for 190 days with an initial deductible and daily cost sharing (Braverman, 1982:83). For skilled nursing care the first 20 days are covered; from day 21 to 100 Medicare covers $50.00 per day, and after 100 days the patient pays the entire cost. Home care coverage may shortly change, so that the number of home visits by a registered nurse covered by Medicare will be determined solely by the patient's diagnosis (termed DRG — diagnostic related grouping).

In Medicare Part B the elderly pay a monthly premium of $15.50 and a $75 deductible (both slated for an increase). Medicare pays 80 percent of what it determines are "reasonable" physician charges. In the last few years, physicians have increased their charges far and above what Medicare has determined is "reasonable." So, rather than covering 80 percent of the physician's actual bill, Medicare may only cover 40-60 percent of the charges, leaving the elderly to pick up the difference.

This year, for the first time since 1965, mortality rates for people over 65 have not declined. In the future, it is entirely possible that the mortality rate will gradually rise as a result of the cuts in Medicare and Medicaid as well as the drastic cuts in preventative programs for the elderly — programs like meals-on-wheels, elderly day care and fuel allowances — which act to protect vulnerable seniors from costly debilative conditions. To sum it up, economic hard times put an even greater strain on older Americans, who are additionally victimized by the state and health care providers.

The purported purpose of a government-funded financing mechanism was to provide equal access to medical treatment. While the continued effectiveness of Medicare in this regard is questionable, consideration also must be given to what impact, if any, the social reform aspects of the Medicare/Medicaid plans have had in improving the overall quality of life for our aged. One study, for example, has found that the mortality rate of elderly males was inversely correlated to the amount of personal health expenditures (Friedman, 1976).

Certainly, one of the ideals of the Medicare/Medicaid legislation was to lift more elderly out of abject poverty. Theoretically, income differentials would be shortened by financing through payroll deductions and general revenues. Since no means test is required for Medicare, on the surface it would appear to be a fair and equitable plan — at least in terms of eligibility. But it is precisely because there is no differentiation between coverage and available income that gross inequities exist in the Medicare plan.

At least two-thirds of the elderly have purchased private supplemental policies to augment their Medicare coverage. The costs of these policies has increased seven-fold by 1978 to a total of $3.8 billion (Pegals, 1980a:164). It is estimated that the cost of supplemental medical insurance deters approximately 460,000 elderly (comprised primarily of the poor, blacks, and those living in rural areas) from purchasing this added protection (National Center for Health Statistics, 1977:113). Thousands of Americans are not even eligible for Medicare coverage because they must have paid into the Social Security system. Once in the program, the poor elderly, who are not eligible for Medicaid coverage and yet can't afford supplemental policies, are the ones most adversely affected by Medicare's flat-deductible design. The more affluent elderly have their out-of-pocket expenses picked up by supplemental insurance, the poor by Medicaid or simply by the hospital's bad-debt provisions, while the elderly, falling in the middle, must still personally finance the bulk of their medical expenses.

Wide differences exist between Medicare and Medicaid coverage in rural versus urban areas, or different regions in the country. Reasonable charges for physician's fees are calculated by taking the seventy-fifth percentile of actual physician charges in a specified geographical area. Physicians anticipated they could increase their reimbursement the subsequent year by increasing their present charges. This behavior by physicians generated such a rapid rise in costs that in 1972 a provision was added to Medicare which only allowed for a certain percentage increase each year. However, the effect was *not* to slow the escalation of physicians's fees but rather to pass these increases onto the elderly patient. Medicare physician fee coverage has deteriorated to such a degree that now Medicare only covers about 28 percent of all physician charges (Davis and Shoen, 1978:100).

The "reasonable" reimbursement mechanism deters physicians from practicing in rural areas where physician's charges have historically been less than those of their counterparts in the cities. Rural elderly were in such dire need of medical care that in 1977, a Rural Health bill was passed with a provision to reimburse nurse practitioners and physicians who practiced in rural communities. Although the Rural Health bill enabled needy citizens to get medical treatment by qualified personnel who deserved reimbursement, as yet no effort has been made to rectify the discriminating nature of the Medicare reimbursement formula as it relates to physicians. Consequently, by 1975, office visits to a physician ranged from $10 in rural Mississippi to $50 in urban Georgia (Davis and Shoen, 1978:115).

These wide differences are not restricted to urban and rural sectors. The greatest differences occur among the states, who are responsible for the administration of Medicaid. Medicare and Medicaid comprise a substantial portion of each state's budget, making these programs a frequent target for cuts. Some states are tightening eligibility for Medicaid, which, unlike Medicare, is based upon a means test. There are not deductibles or co-insurance in Medicaid because of the presumption of indigence, but there are optional services that each state is not mandated to provide. When a service such as vision care is dropped from Medicaid, elderly are faced with seeking an alternate, more costly form of treatment. In Georgia, Medicaid no longer covers vision care, and one-half of the elderly receive eye care at an emergency room (covered by Medicare) or a public clinic (Hall, 1974).[16]

The dispersion of federal Medicaid dollars is skewed with California and New York taking 33 percent of the total, or five states taking slightly over 50 percent. These differences are evidenced in the actual delivery of services, where in Texas only one-fourth of the elderly in poverty are covered by Medicaid, while in Massachusetts over 100 percent of this same population is covered. The unfortunate irony is that precisely where the incidence of illness and disability is the highest (the South and rural areas), the least is spent on medical care.

It is easy to conclude that Medicare and Medicaid have been totally unsuccessful in decreasing income differentials. If anything, the bureaucracy of both programs, coupled with the complex rules and regulations, has meant that states ill prepared to manage programs of this magnitude (which are generally the states with the highest incidences of poverty and morbidity) have the least resources to adequately implement Medicare and Medicaid. Even within the states, perverse reimbursement mechanisms provide disincentives for physicians to practice in underserved rural areas because the financial reward is substantially higher in the oversupplied areas.

The effect of Medicare's flat-rate deductibles has been to place the greatest burden on the elderly too poor to purchase supplemental insurance, yet not poor enough to qualify for Medicaid. The financial burden shouldered by most Medicare beneficiaries will intensify if a proposal by the Reagan administration to increase deductibles and co-insurance is approved. The rationale for such action is economic — the logic being that by charging more up front, out-of-pocket expenses, the elderly Americans will be less apt to excessively use the medical system. Of course, this reasoning completely overlooks the fact that in 1976 39 percent of the aged had chronic conditions and about one in six had the chance of being hospitalized during a year (U.S. Department of Health, Education and Welfare, 1978a). Furthermore, between 12 percent and 17 percent of the elderly have levels of disability so acute that they require total assistance (Institute of Medicine, 1977). It would appear there is not a preponderance of evidence to suggest that vast numbers of elderly have some discretionary power regarding their medical treatment.

Medicare and Medicaid were originally designed to give the elderly and the poor purchasing power in any health care market they chose. That is, the elderly, with their Medicare card, theoretically could obtain medical treatment from any physician or any hospital they desire. Granted, the flexibility of selecting a physician was restricted to those physicians who would agree to accept Medicare reimbursement rates, but there has always been relatively free entry to acute care settings.

Back in the 1970s, MediCal (Medicare of California) decided that to maximize Medicare/Medicaid dollars for ambulatory treatment, they would ask ambulatory centers to bid for the care of Medicare/Medicaid clients. Clients were then directed to seek their treatment in those centers with the lowest bids. Care was given by less costly providers, such as nurse practitioners, which in and of itself wasn't bad, but these providers had to follow a case load normally carried by three people, with the sparsest of ancillary services, clerical help and examining areas. The situation deteriorated to such an extent that Senator Edward Kennedy, after visiting one of these centers, coined the term "health care ghetto" to describe the disgraceful conditions. The disastrous experience of MediCal forestalled any similar strategies until recently.

Under a new proposal forwarded by the Boston teaching hospitals, each hospital would receive a prospectively negotiated fixed budget for providing care to a specified Medicare/Medicaid population. The recipients of Medicare/Medicaid benefits would subsequently lose their option of freedom of choice and be assigned to a hospital clinic for treatment. In the absence of freedom of choice, it is inescapable that the elderly will fall victims to a delivery system where savings may now be realized without any concern for alienating the elderly consumer. The "health care ghettos" that perished in California in the 1970s may now be revitalized in Massachusetts in the 1980s.

Perverse and restrictive reimbursement mechanisms are not confined to physician's fees; they also exist in home health care. The Medicare requirements for home health care are so stiff that the use of home health care has been severely limited. Up until 1980, patients had to be in the hospital for at least three days before they could even be eligible for home health reimbursement. All patients receiving home health care must be homebound, that is, totally incapable of leaving their house except for medically related appointments. New regulations will equate the number of allowable home visits to a patient's medical diagnosis (DRG) without any consideration given to complicating social or nursing conditions.

Some movement has been made towards providing greater financial incentives for home health care. However, these incentives will have to be extraordinarily powerful given the amount of capital investment in the nursing home industry.[17] Presently, there are approximately 1.3 million elderly in nursing homes with an estimated 1.5 times that number who are disabled or chronically ill in the community (Congressional Budget Office, 1977a). Medicaid, which pays for over 50 percent of all nursing home expenditures, pays in full the daily cost of nursing home care (Medicaid/Medicare Management Institute, 1979). To qualify for Medicaid, most elderly "spend down" their available savings. In other words, to become eligible for nursing home benefits, Medicaid forces the elderly to exhaust most of their savings.

Although Medicaid reimburses nursing homes on a flat-rate per-day basis, Medicare reimburses on a cost-plus basis. With Medicare, profits are maximized by inflating the actual costs. By this defrauding of the government, patients are eventually hurt as these added costs are passed on in the form of higher deductibles and coinsurance. With Medicaid, the profits are maximized by providing as little as possible. Up until this point, regulations to prevent rampant fraud and patient neglect have been largely ineffective, leading some to recommend removing the incentives that presently exist to divert resources towards profits and away from patients by having nursing home care entirely owned and supported by the government (Pegals, 1980a:124). But realistically radical restructuring of the nursing home industry is just as unlikely as enacting national health insurance.

Another inhibiting factor to the zealous implementation of home-based treatment was briefly raised in the beginning of this chapter — it is the role of the family. Even if a family had the financial resources to hire a registered nurse or home health aide to provide home care services, would there be enough nurses or home health aides to meet the demand? The financial remuneration for registered nurses, licensed practical nurses and nurses' aides has always been significantly lower than their female equivalents in other industries. The shortage of health care personnel who provide nursing services has been linked to their low wages relative to other women workers (Aiken and Blendon, 1981). Thus, given the market's inability to reasonably compensate nurses, it is entirely possible that the demand for nursing personnel will exceed the supply, placing an even greater burden on families.

Exactly where and how the long-term health care needs of the elderly will be met will be largely decided by issues of cost. The increase in the numbers of elderly who are disabled has led to estimates that by 1985 the cost of providing long-term care will be $50 billion (Ginzberg, 1977:171). These issues regarding the cost and utilization of long-term care by the elderly will be covered in greater detail in the next chapter.

CONCLUSION

Over the years, the government's involvement in health care policies has shifted from concerns about quality and access to that of cost containment. Fundamentally, the dilemma faced by government is how it will attempt to resolve the contradictory forces of growing demand, limited resources and escalating health care costs. Solutions offered by policymakers and medical economists either promote competition and the free market or government regulation. Regulation has been criticized as cumbersome, not cost effective, and nearly impossible to implement in a democracy where such high value is placed upon the freedom of the individual and medicine to choose and control their treatment or work. Others view pro-competition schemes as incongruous to the existing health care market where physicians have a monopoly, hospitals a monopsony and the ordinary rules of supply and demand simply cannot operate unfettered.

In the end, given America's pluralist society, it may well be that all the parties with competing economic interests — the elderly, the American taxpayer, and the health care elites — may have to make sacrifices. If, however, the constraints or expectations placed upon each group are not equitable and reasonable, the alternative is a deepening of class differences and even greater degrees of social control. To date, federal and state governments have systematically reduced their commitments to provide health care to the elderly (Iglehart, 1982:840) and avoided aggressively restraining the tremendous flow of capital to medicine and health insurers, whose power and control clearly have dictated the direction of health policies and escalated costs (Ginzberg, 1982:84-85). Hopefully, in the future, interests will be more evenly balanced and the original humanitarian ideals of health care policies will not become antiquated in an era overwhelming shaped by cost containment.

NOTES

1. Authors such as Barbara and John Ehrenreich (1971), Vincente Navarro (1976), and Ivan Illich (1976) have written penetrating radi-

cal critiques of the health care industry. For a succinct quarterly reference on the functioning of the health care market, refer to Standard and Poor's Health Industrial Surveys.

2. Medical economists have noted that perverse market relations enable physicians to determine their own demand (Newhouse and Phelps, 1976; Redish, 1978). Physician's capacity to target their incomes has been attributed to the mechanism of third-party reimbursement which shields the consumer from actual cost (Evans, 1974; Sloan and Feldman, 1978).

3. The elderly have recently developed political-action coalitions (PACS), such as the National Association of Retired Persons and the Grey Panthers, to promote their interests on Capitol Hill. Although some question the strength of these coalitions, Sundquist (1968) credits the power of the elderly, in conjunction with labor and health groups such as the American Nurses Association, as being instrumental in countering the attempts by the American Medical Association and the American Hospital Association to defeat Medicare.

4. Most older persons live at home with 83 percent of the men in a family setting and 58 percent of the women. Almost two-and-one-half times as many women (42%) live alone as compared to men (17%) (U.S. Department of Health, Education and Welfare, 1978a).

5. Studies (Richard and Miedema, 1977; McCormick, 1976) have supported the clinical efficacy of nurse practitioners, and others point out that nurse practitioners provide high-quality services at significant economic savings to the underserved elderly (Eastaugh, 1981; National Commission on the Cost of Medical Care, 1978). However, statutory restrictions upon nurse practitioners enacted through legislation sponsored by state medical societies, and limits on reimbursement by third-party insurers to physicians, inhibits the full use of nurse practitioners in caring for the elderly.

6. The apparent avoidance of the elderly by physicians is amply documented in a supporting paper to the U.S. Senate Special Committee on Aging (1975).

7. About 15 percent of the elderly were below the poverty line in 1976. For widows living alone, only 12.9 percent of them had an income greater than $8,000, while for couples, 50.5 percent had incomes greater than $8,000 (U.S. Department of Health, Education and Welfare, 1978a).

8. In 1976, two-thirds of the government's health expenditures were spent on the elderly, with Medicare and Medicaid costing $15 billion and $5.6 billion, respectively (U.S. Department of Health, Educa-

tion and Welfare, 1978a). However, Medicare only met 38 percent of all health care expenses incurred by the elderly and Medicaid only 26 percent, making total payments by the aged for physicians' services twice as high in 1975 as it was when Medicare and Medicaid were first enacted (Davis and Schoen, 1978).

9. Ginzberg (1982:81) cites noted economists Arrow (1963) and Pauly (1978) in drawing his conclusion that pro-competition models will not work in health care as two preconditions for a competitive market — free entrance into the industry and the inability of producers to affect prices — never existed. Nevertheless, economists advocating pro-competition models, such as Enthoven (1980), P. Feldstein (1981), Havighurst (1978), McClure (1981) and Iglehart (1981), are finding their views increasingly embraced by the Reagan administration. Bills submitted in the Ninety-Seventh Congress by Hatch (S.139) and Durenberger, Boren, Heinz (S.433) are both designed to encourage competition in the health insurance industry and are strongly supported by the Reagan administration.

10. In fiscal year 1984, the initial budget proposal issued by the Office of Management and Budget would seek substantial cuts in health and social programs. The administration is reportedly working on additional cuts in Medicare and Medicaid which would include an increase in patient cost sharing (Bauknecht, 1983). These increases will occur despite the fact that 10 percent of the elderly's personal income is spent on health care (U.S. Department of Health, Education and Welfare, 1978a).

11. Stevens and Stevens (1974:22) note that at the time the 1950 Social Security Amendments are under consideration by the Congress, the maximum possible federal contribution to OAA (Old-Age Assistance) and AB (Aid to the Blind) was $30 of the first $50 a month spent by the state.

12. By 1960, ten states made no vendor payments for medical services at all, and of those which did they ranged from 19 cents a month in Montana to $43.93 in Wisconsin (Stevens and Stevens, 1974:26).

13. A major flaw of the Kerr-Mills legislation was that 90 percent of the federal dollars only went to four or five of the participating states.

14. For a detailed account of how the use of the media ruined Kennedy's public support of Medicare and reinforced public confidence in the AMA, see Sorenson (1965:343).

15. A detailed review of all the programs for the elderly, and an analysis of the impact of the proposed 1980 federal budget, is available in an information paper prepared by the staff on the United States Senate

Special Committee on Aging (1979).

16. Physicians have attempted to sustain a monopoly of vision services by limiting Medicare reimbusement to opthalmologists providing expensive secondary and tertiary eye care, thus excluding the less expensive, preventative and more utilized services of the optometrist (Soroka and Newcomb, 1981:82-83).

17. Callahan (1981:183) notes that particularly with Medicare, where cost reimbursement is used, and when no limits are placed on the financial returns from real estate appreciation, nursing homes have become ideal investment opportunities.

CHAPTER 8

LONG-TERM CARE: PROFITS, REGULATION, AND COST CONTAINMENT

GOVERNMENT intervention in the provision of long-term care began to expand in the early twentieth century. Growing industrialization had fragmented families, and traditional caretakers and active members of the work force were unavailable to tend to their debilitated family members. Initially, in pockets of the private sector, some welfare and health programs were made available for employees and their families. But even these few programs were forced to close at the outset of the Great Depression. At the same time, mortality shifted from infections to chronic disease placing new demands on health delivery (Starr, 1982:336). Yet, despite the growing demand, few of the fledgling health insurance carriers were willing to risk expanding coverage beyond acute care. Partial relief came in the firm of the 1955 Social Security Act. Two components of the Social Security Act — Old Age and Survivor's Insurance (OASI) and Old-Age Assistance (OAA) — indirectly provided a dependable source of payment for nursing home care (Birnbaum, 1981:10). However, on the whole, the role of government remained quite limited. Even as late as 1960, private sources accounted for upwards of 80 percent of all national health expenditures on nursing home care (Birnbaum, 1981:11).

By the mid-1960s, social reforms in health care policy included additional services for long-term care. Specifically, Medicare legislation provided funds for home care services, and Medicaid included coverage for nursing home care. Unfortunately, in future years, this added revenue would have little effect in mitigating the dehumanizing conditions in nursing homes.

Nursing homes continue to be characterized as total institutions, stripping the elderly of their humanity and devoid of warmth and compassion (Jules, 1963; Gubrium, 1975). Reports of deteriorating conditions prompted federal and state authorities to conduct formal investigations of nursing homes in the mid-1970s (U.S. Department of Health, Education and Welfare, 1975; U.S. Senate, Special Committee on Aging, 1974; Moreland Commission, 1976). These studies uniformly concluded that only 40 percent of all nursing homes met minimum federal quality standards. For example, investigators found that 37 percent of nursing home patients who were taking cardiovascular drugs, and one-third of the patients who were being treated for diabetes, had no diagnosis in their chart warranting either medical intervention (Moos, 1977:43).

One of the most well-known exposes on the widespread fraud and deplorable conditions of nursing homes was the 1974 publication of Mary Adelaide Mendelson's *Tender Loving Greed*. Mrs. Mendelson portrayed nursing home administrators as singularly interested in maximizing profits even if it meant virtually starving patients (Mendelson, 1974:40). To many people's shock and dismay, in a hearing before the Long-Term Care Senate Subcommittee, a special prosecutor from New York corroborated Mrs. Mendelson's findings. In fact, the fraud in the nursing home industry had become so extensive that every one of the first seventy nursing homes audited by the special prosecutor was overcharging the government (Hapgood, 1978:361).

Over the years, little headway has been made in preventing Medicaid fraud by the nursing home industry. In 1980 alone, nursing home operators represented 15 percent of the more than three thousand pending Medicaid fraud investigations and 37 percent of these who eventually went to jail (Halamandaris, 1983:114). In testimony to House Select Committee on Aging in May 1980, the FBI reported that virtually every ancillary service they contacted offered kickbacks to nursing home operators (Halamandaris, 1983:113).

The exploitation of the elderly is hardly limited to the profit-maximizing behavior of nursing home operators. Recently, 7 percent of all the skilled nursing facilities (SNF's) nationwide were found by the Health Care Financing Administration's Medicare/ Medicaid Certification System to be deficient in caring for patients with dignity, consideration and respect (Doty and Sullivan, 1983:224). There are continuing reports in the literature of excessive medication and oversedation of nursing home patients (Spasoff 1978:281-291: U.S. Department of Health Education and Welfare, 1978b:3). The perpetuation of such abuses is viewed by many as the fault of individual staff and nursing home administrators. Certainly, there is widespread agreement that nursing home staff are not well trained, their numbers inadequate, and their turnover exceptionally high. Additionally, physician involvement is limited and the management expertise of administrators is questionable (Reif and Estes, 1982:147; Report of the Joint AMA/ANA Task Force, 1983:62). But to simply blame these individuals ignores the broad structural issues which have had a pervasive effect on the quality of nursing home care.

Part of the problem is that monitoring is fragmented between local, state, and federal agencies. The Department of Health and Human Services alone has twenty-seven programs that provide long-term care resources (White Houses Conference on Aging, 1981:87). Responsibility for quality control is spread among state and local health departments, Professional Standards Review Organizations (PSRO's), professional societies, and advocacy groups (Callahan and Wallack, 1981: 225). An example of the confusion and inconsistency generated by such fragmentation is illustrated by the ombudsman program. In 1978, amendments to the Older Americans Act mandated that each state establish a long-term care ombudsman program. Presently, less than half (twenty-two) of the states guarantee the ombudsman access to nursing homes (Doty and Sullivan, 1983:232). Regulations developed by Secretary Harris of the Department of Health, Education and Welfare under the Carter administration guaranteed ombudsmen twenty-four-hour access to nursing homes. However, these regulations have been withdrawn under the Reagan administration (Demkovich, 1982).

Regulations, when they do exist, tend to be excessive and extremely time consuming (Bowker, 1982:80). To insure recertification by Medicaid officials, staff must spend inordinate amounts of time documenting care in the patient's chart, time that could be much better spent providing direct care. Some authors even question whether regulations can ever reasonably safeguard human rights (Caldwell and Kapp, 1981). Even on the state level, vague and confusing provisions in the present law has limited the effectiveness of a "Bill of Rights" for nursing home patients (Silfren, 1980).

Because of these inadequate and counterproductive bureaucratic policies, amendments were added to the Older Americans' Act in 1981 which reinforced the need to coordinate long-term care services. Thus far, coordination continues to be problematic, with policy formulation and fiscal responsibility divided between the Administrations of Aging and Social Security (Koff, 1982:5; Hospitals, 1982). As a result, benefits are maldistributed, costs are rising, and programs continue to promote institutionalization (Callahan and Wallack, 1981:3). Blurred lines of accountability, stiff regulations, and dwindling financial resources make operating a nursing home, even for an innovative nursing home operator, quite difficult (Grimaldi, 1982:3). As shall be discussed, there is every indication, based upon demographic and cost projections, that such problems will be exacerbated in the future.

INCREASING DEMAND AND INCREASING COSTS

Not many Americans prepare, either financially or emotionally, for the possibility that they may spend their remaining years in a nursing home. Yet presently, for Americans over 65 there is a 20-40 percent chance that they will enter a nursing home, and, of those who do, most will die there as well (Kane and Kane, 1982:8; Moos, 1977:8). Those entering nursing homes can expect to stay a little over two years, and during that time many will never receive visitors (Moos, 1977:8). Of the 10 percent who have living spouses, the non-institutionalized spouse will have to divest themselves of all but $2,000 so that the spouse requiring continued long-term care will qualify for Medicaid (Kane and Kane, 1982:15). In such cases, the price for long-term care is literally pauperization, and it would appear that in the near future more Americans than ever before will be confronting these grim prospects.

The percentage of Americans over 65 is expected to increase from 11 percent in 1981, to 13 percent in 1990 and 18 percent by 2030 (U.S. Department of Health and Human Services, 1981). Although the average rate of increase for those over 65 is approximately 2.6 percent per year, the demand for nursing home beds is increasing at a rate of 3 percent a year (Gibson, Waldo, and Levit, 1983:20). In nursing home care alone, a total of $27 billion was spent in 1982, up from $24 billion in 1981 — an increase of 13 percent (Gibson, Waldo, and Levit, 1983:6). In 1982, Medicaid, which finances more long-term care than Medicare, spent almost one-half of its entire $34 billion budget on long-term care (Gibson, Waldo, and Levit, 1983:25).

Recent policy changes have contributed to increased demand in long-term care. Deinstitutionalization of psychiatric patients is thought to account for a 30 percent increase in nursing home utilization (Pollack, 1977; Bassuk and Gerson, 1978). In the early 1970s, Medicaid coverage for intermediate care facilities expanded to include another traditionally institutionalized population, the mentally retarded (Freeland and Schendler, 1983:29). Unfortunately, a sequalae to the rapid influx of the chronically ill psychiatric patient and the mentally retarded into long-term care facilities has been an increase in the incidents of abuse and theft directed against the more vulnerable elderly residents (Bowker, 1982:80).

Not all Americans requiring long-term care are institutionalized. In fact, for every person in a nursing home, three equally impaired individuals are in the community. The growing use of home care is evident in Medicare expenditures for home care services, which have doubled ($60 million to $1.3 billion) since 1968 (Gibson, Waldo, and Levit, 1983:25). The increase in demand is partly due to state and federal programs to minimize hospital utilization and cost. The most widely recognized method of controlling hospital costs are prospective reimbursement programs which pay the hospital prospectively for a fixed rate. Except in states with waivers, the fixed rate for Medicare patients is determined by the patients' diagnosis and related demographic factors and is termed "DRG" (diagnostic-related grouping). If the hospital discharges the patient in less time than is paid for by the DRG, the hospital gets to keep the difference. The incentive is to discharge early or, in some cases, prematurely.

The extent of medical complications which have arisen from the practice has yet to be determined, but anecedotal reports thus far suggest that premature discharge is a serious problem, particularly for the elderly.

Because Medicare and Medicaid spent approximately $48 billion for hospital care in 1982, cost containment activities have primarily focused on the hospital sector (Gibson, Waldo, and Levit, 1983:25). However, given that nursing home care is growing at a rate even faster than that of hospitals (17% versus 12%), it seems reasonable to assume that the interest in cost containment will soon shift. Already, in the Omnibus Budget Reconciliation Act of 1981 (OBRA), the federal share of Medicaid, the largest payer of nursing home service, was reduced by 3 percent in 1982 and 4 percent in 1983 (Gibson, Waldo and Levit, 1983:26). The states, now faced with an even larger burden for long-term care and under enormous fiscal pressures, are attempting to develop programs that will control the costs of long-term care either by stiffening regulations or promoting competition.

Increases in the costs of providing nursing home care are due to a combination of inflation (53%), the growth in the number of patient days or demand (20%) and growth in the intensity of services (13%) (Freeland and Schendler, 1983:9). It is against these increases that the states must attempt to develop a policy for long-term care which offers low cost, high quality, and free access. Such a balance is difficult to attain and, characteristically, those states where the quality of care is high have runaway costs, while those states where Medicaid reimbursement is excessively low have a shortage of nursing home beds (Birnbaum, 1981:4). Because states have such flexibility in deciding eligibility critiera, benefits, and reimbursement rates, there is a wide variation in the cost, quality and access of long-term care.

Presently, there are 10 states which account for almost 70 percent of the entire Medicaid budget for long-term care (Birnbaum, 1981:19). Among the states, the percentage of public patients in intermediate care facilities (ICF's) compared to skilled care facilities (SNF's) ranges from 11 percent to 98 percent (Birnbaum, 1981:17). Nevada, for instance, has completely dropped ICF coverage for patients with tuberculosis (Buchanan, 1981:26). In Virginia, when the reimbursement rate for SNF's increased by only 6 percent, there was a loss of 216 SNF beds. Conversely, the increase for ICF's was 13 percent and there was an increase of 1,345 ICF beds (Buchanan, 1981:72). Because of such trends, it is widely believed that inadequate reimbursement is the primary reason substandard care continues to exist in nursing homes (U.S. Senate Special Committee on Aging, 1974:105). Consequently, many attribute the spiraling costs and shortages in long-term care to government, not market failure, and strongly favor solutions to promote competitiveness in the nursing home industry (Grimaldi, 1982:116).

Based upon some of the widespread reports of exploitation reported earlier in this chapter, such suggestions to promote competition seem ill considered. The argument of the pro-market advocates is simply that the number of beds in the nursing home industry will only increase when profitability increases (Dunlop, 1979:89). Moreover, as long as demand continues to rise and shortages deepen because of low reimbursement rates and tight control of bed supply through Certificate-of-Need regulations, the suppliers of nursing home care have little incentive to restrain their costs. The result is that the demand negatively impacts on the lower-paying Medicaid patients who must compete for the scarce beds with higher-paying, private patients. Fairly typical was the announcement of one long-term care chain, Beverly Enterprises, that it would limit the number of Medicaid patients it accepts in order to increase revenues (*Business Week*, 1977:70).

Despite such profit-maximizing behavior, the profit margins for long-term care facilities are lower than average when compared to all U.S. industries (Buchanan, 1981:94). Surprisingly, voluntary facilities, who have more treatment resources, treat even fewer Medicaid patients than the proprietary facilities (Kosberg and Tobin, 1972; Kosberg, 1973). Furthermore, thus far no study has been able to find a significant difference in the types of services offered in a proprietary versus a nonprofit home, and cost differences when they do exist are generally related to case mix rather than quality (Schlender, Shaughnessy, Yslas, 1983:361). Those who promote competition do note that the proprietaries are far more efficient than the nonprofits (Koetting, 1980:95). Nonetheless, most providers in long-term care are not mollified by such reports and still contend that a regulatory model, rather than a competitive approach, is "the lesser of two evils" (Iglehart, 1982a; Relman, 1980).

THE ALTERNATIVES: COMPETITION OR REGULATION?

In a capitalist society, the policymakers must continually strive to balance the interests of efficiency and equity. In long-term care, concern over efficiency has heightened as resources have become more limited, and demand is projected to rise. Historically, the solution to these issues of social justice was for the federal government to provide a program and some added revenue. However, under the present economic conditions, questions of access and quality of care in long-term care are completely overshadowed by the potential bankrupcy of the entire Medicare program. By 1995, the Medicare program faces a $200-$300 million deficit (*The American Nurse,* 1984a:2). Thus, the solutions which are offered are far from entirely painless. Basically, the recommendations include changes from a retrospective to a prospective payment system (like DRG's), an increase in the amount of cost sharing (including children as well as the spouse), tighter regulations, and an emphasis on home care rather than institutional (nursing home) care (Somers, 1982:224).

In Buchanan's analysis of nursing home cost data from 1975 to 1977, prospective reimbursement methods yielded significant savings when compared to retrospective reimbursement methods (Buchanan, 1981:63). Under prospective reimbursement programs, access to services did not appear to be affected. However, there were potential disincentives for maintaining quality care. Specifically, as is the case in hospitals, profits are generated by providing the actual care at less cost than is prospectively allotted. The incentives are opposite those under the retrospective payment systems where the more services/charges nursing homes generated, the more they were reimbursed and the more profit they realized. With a prospective program, less means more and the risk to the quality of care is significantly greater than with retrospective methods. Needless to say, monitoring and regulation to insure that standards of care are maintained is essential with any prospective reimbursement program (Buchanan, 1981:63). There is also the risk under a prospective payment method that the rate will be too low and nursing homes, as is presently the case with some hospitals, will refuse Medicaid patients. In addition, there are disincentives to expand under a prospective reimbursement formula which could easily result in a decrease in the number of total nursing home beds.

Exactly what form the prospective reimbursement program will take in long-term care is open to question, but many experts believe it will be modeled after the DRG's (*The American Nurse,* 1984b:1). However, unlike the hospital sector, where is an elderly person to go after the DRG determines that a patient will no longer be reimbursed for care in a long-term care facility? Or what will happen to an elderly person who has sufficient insurance coverage but, given the scarcity of nursing home beds, cannot be readily placed?

One alternative may be to go home. Estimates vary, but close to 300,000 elderly have been inappropriately placed in nursing homes (Pegals, 1980b:209). Several authors have suggested that the care for such patients would be half as much in the home as in an institution, with a net savings of close to $1 billion (Pegals, 1980b:209; Brickner, 1978:31; Adams, 1980:91). Home care may generate savings for the government, but, under the present system home care is clearly more costly for families (Birnbaum, 1981:13; Kane and Kane, 1982:17). Eighty percent of supportive care received by the elderly living in the community is provided by family members (Institute of Medicine, 1977). In fact, for the greatly impaired (which is about 17% of those over 65), a Congressional Budget Office study found that families and friends provided more than 70 percent of the value of the services received, or about $287 per month for every $120 per month being spent by the government (Congressional Budget Office, 1977). Because of this added expense, the 1981 White House Conference on Aging recommended that tax credits, vouchers, or direct payments be given to families caring for chronically ill family members (White House Conference on Aging, 1981:88).

Even if it is less expensive, is home care a viable alternative for most of the frail elderly? Of those elderly presently in nursing homes, more than 50 percent have no close relatives (Moos, 1977:43). Furthermore, as the size of the average household declines and the numbers of women entering the labor force rises, far fewer family members are available to care for a debilitated, chronically ill family member (Freeland and Schendler, 1983:9). Nor can it be assumed, despite reports to the contrary, that an elderly person would prefer to live in the community cared for by a child, or that even if a child is available he/she is capable of providing round-the-clock supportive care (Hamovitch and Peterson, 1969:3; Lamb et al., 1976:33). Recent studies of elderly abuse victims have found that in 90 percent of the cases the abuser was responsible for the elderly victim, and in greater than 20 percent of the cases, the victims personality, level of dependence, or personal habits evoked the abuse or neglect (Kosberg and Tobin, 1972:126; Hickey and Douglass, 1981). Because of the strain on caretakers, recommendations of the 1981 White House Conference on Aging included state and federal respite programs for families caring for severely or chronically ill family members (White House Conference on Aging, 1981:83).

Home care may not be an available, nor appropriate option for the elderly in all cases. Even in socialist countries or cultures where there are strong familial ties, institutionalization depends upon the availability of relatives to care for the aged person, as well as the degree of mental and physical impairment (Ikegami, 1982; Ovenstone and Bean, 1981; Liberkis, 1981; Trichard, Zabow and Gillis, 1982). In addition, there remains disagreement about the cost-saving potential of home care versus institutionalization. A study by the Department of Health. Education and Welfare found that home care may attract less-impaired clients who had not previously received services or supplement the care presently being provided by family members (Weissert, Wan and Livieratos, 1980). In other words, home care services may be additive, rather than substitutive.

There is little question that home care does cost significantly less than hospitalization which has resulted in aggressive efforts to hasten a patient's discharge. In the past, because the coverage for home health services was minimal, only the local Visiting Nurse Association (VNA) provided such services. The VNA's covered the cost of providing services for indigent clients with donations from philanthropic groups and by charging higher rates to private-paying patients. Recently, proprietary agencies, recognizing that "if the companies can convince all insurers to foot the bill, profits could be spectacular," have eagerly entered the home health care market (Dentzer et al., 1983:73). Between 1975 and 1977, proprietary home health agencies (HHA's) accounted for a 21 percent increase in the number of clients cared for in the home (Callahan, 1977:2). Similar to the tactic used by proprietary nursing homes, the proprietary HHA's are refusing referrals of Medicare/Medicaid clients in order to accept more of the higher-paying private patients. The effect of this practice on VNA's has been disastrous. The proprietaries, by "skimming" the private-paying patients, have severely restricted the capacity of the VNA's to serve indigent clients. Although not anticipated when proprietary HHA's entered the home care market, the plight of the VNA's is now strikingly similar to city hospitals. Both are besieged by growing numbers of indigent patients as more and more "for-profit" agencies and hospitals opt to serve only private-paying patients.

It is difficult to imagine that lucrative profits can be made in long-term care when major programs like Medicare and Medicaid hang in the balance. One naturally begins to wonder, where is the money going to come from? Rising health care costs have been partially attributed to third-party reimbursement mechanisms which shield consumers from realizing actual costs. To improve the "cost-consciousness" of consumers, some economists have suggested increasing co-insurance and deductibles (Newhouse, Manning and Morris, 1981). In long-term care, this philosophy has been translated into proposals which will increase the elderly's out-of-pocket expenses either by: (1) attaching income from private pensions, investments, and savings, (2) restricting the transfer of assets to children, or (3) requiring children to supplement the costs of long-term care (Freeland and Schendler, 1983:30; Dunlop, 1979:97). Whether such mechanisms will deter the alleged "unnecessary utilization" by the elderly and avoid excessive hardship upon the aged or their families is in serious question.

The elderly can hardly be depicted as rampantly overutilizing services when one considers that 30 percent of Medicare's expenditures are paid in the last year of a person's life, and that only one-third of the aged account for slightly greater than three-quarters of the total out-of-pocket expenses (Iglehart, 1982a:71; Rosenblum, 1983:80). Any policy which will increase out-of-pocket expenses for long-term care will adversely impact only those aged who are already well below the poverty line. Presently, 55 percent of the elderly have incomes less than $6,000 and their proportion of out-of-pocket medical expenses equals 5.4 percent. For those with incomes less than $4,000, the proportion is even greater at 8.7 percent (Rosenblum, 1983:86). These figures differ markedly for the elderly with incomes greater than $15,000, whose out-of-pocket expenses are only 1.4 percent of their total income.

The government isn't the only group attempting to generate more capital from the aged. Nursing home administrators have become even more inventive in their efforts to maximize profits. One such scheme has been termed the life care contract. Under the life care contract, residents must pay an entrance fee and transfer to the nursing home all or part of their property in return for the home's promise to provide care for the rest of the person's life (Leonard, 1982). Even if the elderly person should get well, having divested themselves of their property and savings, they are literally trapped in the nursing home. In addition, because the elderly person has now lost the capacity to shop around for other services, there is absolutely no incentive for the owners to provide high quality care.

Hospitals squeezed by prospective reimbursement programs, or suffering from underutilization of beds, are attempting to generate revenues from long-term care by a concept termed a "swing bed unit." Swing bed are hospital beds which, for reimbursement purposes, have been converted to a rate equivalent to the bed rate given in a skilled nursing facility (SNF) or an intermediate care facility (ICF). Typically, a Medicare or Medicaid patient whose immediate crisis has been resolved is moved to the swing bed unit while he/she recuperates and awaits placement. Frequently, there is a lag between the time the DRG terminates payment and a transfer may be made to a long-term care facility. Swing beds insure the hospital that they will be paid if there is such a lag.

Deficiencies in the quality of care, especially the emotional, restorative and social services, have been noted in swing bed units studied in Texas, South Dakota and Iowa (Miller, 1980:98). The morale of nurses on swing bed units is low because, given the limited resources, nurses feel they're giving second-rate care. Families and patients dislike the swing bed units because both expect a higher degree of care than is actually delivered. Even the government loses with swing bed units. Cost calculations indicate that care in a swing bed unit is far more costly than in an existing SNF and that the anticipated economies of scale are not realized to any significant degree (Miller, 1980:100).

For patients with particular types of long-term care needs, day care or hospice services may be the preferred method of treatment, but reimbursement regulations are likely to restrict access. The survival of hospice programs literally hinges on the reimbursement policies of federal and state governments as well as the health insurance industry (Munley, 1983:277). Reimbursement for most health services, either public or private, is dependent upon licensure and certification. To qualify for Medicare and Medicaid reimbursement, long-term care facilities or home health agencies must pass a certification examination and state or local health department inspections. The criteria for certification and licensure include meeting life and safety code requirements (i.e. accessible fire exits) and the maintenance of specific standards of care. Standards of care are measured by the range of services available as well as the types or numbers of personnel available to provide these services. Unfortunately, for some hospices, the criteria for licensure has prevented them from receiving third-party reimbursement (Koff, 1980:141). Predictably, because of mandated licensure, many small, independent, largely volunteer hospices are having major funding problems and are being forced to close (Buckingham and Lups, 1982:461).

Recently, the effects of this bureaucratization were evident at a hearing of the Joint Health Care Committee of the Massachusetts State Legislature. The Health Care Committee was hearing testimony on a bill which would have mandated all Massachusetts hospices be licensed by the State Department of Public Health. The criteria recommended for licensure were extensive, and many small, community-based hospices operated by paraprofessionals and volunteers objected to the bill, claiming that although they provided a smaller range of services, the service they did provide was personalized and met the needs of their particular community. The largest formal organized group of hospices, the Massachusetts Association of Hospice Programs, supported the bill, claiming licensure would protect the public by guaranteeing that certain widely accepted standards of care were maintained. The arguments of the proponents of the bill are not unlike those of other special-interest groups in health care who are covertly protecting their monopolist position under the guise of promoting quality care.

Other innovative delivery models for long-term care have been proposed by the American Nurses Association (ANA), the American Medical Association (AMA) and public health officials (Report of the Joint AMA/ANA Task force, 1983:50). Whether these programs will go from the planning to the delivery stage depends upon future reimbursement policies. The continued hesitancy to fund new home care programs is symptomatic of a long-standing emphasis in America's health care policies on curative rather than restorative or supportive measures. On the surface, the orientation towards research and prevention appears linked to institutional or financial constraints, but it's far more likely that the emphasis is a product of powerful psychological and cultural imperatives (DuBois, 1980:167).

Such imperatives enable monopolists to constrain the entry of alternative, less-costly providers through regulation and licensure. Thus, in the United State there are two parallel systems: one, the private sector driven by the desire to maximize profits, and the other, the public sector with planning, regulation and provision of services divided among a myriad of governmental programs, all attempting to mimic the private sector and at the same time to control costs. Under such conditions, it's no wonder costs are rising, abuses are widespread, and an integrated approach to long-term care needs of the elderly is virtually impossible to achieve.

CONCLUSION

Patchwork reform in long-term care will be completely inadequate given the projected demands that will be placed on the entire health care system. Without major restructuring, the cost of financing the long-term care needs of the elderly may come at the expense of lowering the standard of living for the rest of the population (Grimaldi, 1982:164). Some authors warn that trading off the interests of society and those of the elderly could potentially pit generations of Americans against each other (Estes, 1979:17; Somers, 1980:16).

In the face of such dire scenarios, two alternatives appear plausible: increase regulation or promote competition. Generally, the assumption has been that pursuing one approach precludes pursuing the other. However, especially in the delivery of long-term care, both approaches bear careful consideration. For instance, if one umbrella agency could coordinate, fund, and regulate only the long-term needs of the elderly, including both health care as well as social services, fragmentation and duplication could be minimized. Thus, regulations could be more comprehensive and more readily enforced. Additionally, if less costly non-medical professionals were allowed to develop and provide alternative models of long-term care, competition could be maximized and scant resources used more cost effectively.

The problem with either of these approaches is whether, practically speaking, they can be implemented. The first approach — forming one umbrella long-term care agency — wrests control from innumerable federal, state, and private agencies who have developed their own special niche and are unlikely to willingly relinquish their authority. The second approach — allowing the entrance of alternative providers — is a direct threat to such notoriously powerful special-interest groups as the American Hospital Association and the American Medical Association. Considerations of costs may override these issues of control, but if special interests take precedence over the interests of elderly Americans, then it will be the elderly and their families who will unquestionably shoulder the burden of both costs and the provision of long-term care.

CHAPTER 9

MEDICAL TECHNOLOGY AND THE ELDERLY

MEDICAL technology conjures up visions of gleaming mechanical parts perfectly synchronized to produce an awesome synthesis, a replica if you will, of flawless human functioning. Hardly a day goes by where the mass media does not extol the virtues of one or another of the fruits of biomedical research. These innovations are heralded as "breakthroughs" and "amazing advances" (Panati, 1980).

Stories tell of those who previously could not hear, see, or talk who may eventually have these functions restored through the implantation of electornic devices. The University of Utah's Project and Design Laboratories promises electronic limbs for amputees (Kaercher, 1984). Coronary artery bypass surgery is called "the most important development of the decade in medicine" by a past president of the American College of Cardiology (Cant, 1978). The positron-emission tomography scanner (PET) is hailed as a "boon to body research" (Young, 1981). The CAT scanner is hailed as revolutionary (Bolsen, 1981).

Those with an interests in more than the technical achievements of advances in biomedical science, however, have defined medical technology more broadly. The Office of Technology Assessment (OTA), for example, defines medical technology as "the set of techniques, drugs, equipment, and procedures used by health care pro-

By Kathryn E. Lasch, Department of Sociology, University of Michigan.

fessionals in delivering medical care to individuals and the systems within which care is delivered" (Banta and Behney, 1981).

The OTA definition has generally been used by those engaged in assessments of medical technologies. Several classificatory schemes for these technologies have been suggested for use in determining which technologies are to be assessed. Technologies are classified typically along three dimensions: physical nature, purpose, and stage of development (Wortman et al., 1982). Regardless of classification, the same questions have been asked when these assessments have been conducted. Issues of safety, efficacy and the social, economic, and ethical implications of the use of certain medical technologies are those considered.

To date there has not been a systematic attempt to look at the impact of the use of medical technologies on the aged. In this chapter, the elderly are analyzed in their role as health care consumers, and the suggestion is made that age should be taken more explicitly into account in formulating policies concerning the use of medical technology.

In this chapter, issues are raised related to the safety, ethical, economic, and social implications of the use of medical technologies in the medical care of the elderly. The special needs and problems of applying medical technology to the elderly are explored. The social control aspects of institutional and professional decision making regarding the application of such technology is also examined. Finally, we suggest that those responsible for public policy and the private treatment of the elderly need to examine the relationship between the use, overuse, or underuse of technological medicine and the autonomy of the elderly.

In tracing the historical roots of modern medicine, we present arguments suggesting that the pursuit of the material and ideological interests of the powerful in the health care industry has led to a technical hospital-based medical care system. This system rests on a dependency relationship between those who consume this care and the professionals and institutions which provide services.

THE ELDERLY AS HEALTH CARE CONSUMERS

A disproportionate share of health care resources are consumed by the elderly. Although the elderly comprised only 11 percent of the population in 1978, 29 percent of the health care dollar was spent for their care (Rice and Feldman, 1983). Per capita health expenditures for the elderly exceed those of other age groups by far. Those aged 65 and over spent $2,026 per capita for medical care in 1978. This is over seven times the $286 per capita spent on persons under age 19, and two-and-one-half times the $764 per capita expenditure for those aged 19 to 64 in that year (Fisher, 1980).

The elderly tend to utilize more costly health services than younger populations. Hospital expenditures comprise 43 percent of health care expenditures for the elderly (Fisher, 1980). The aged spent $869 per capita in 1978 on hospital care, which was eight times the per capita expenditure of those 19 and younger, and twice the per capita expenditure for those aged 19 to 64. The elderly, on the average, tend to make more physician visits than the young. The elderly tend to undergo surgery more often than the young and those of less advanced years (Fisher, 1980). Additionally, physicians are more likely to prescribe drugs for the elderly (U.S. Department of Health, Education, and Welfare, 1969).

Higher medical care utilization rates for the elderly and the greater intensity of care represented in that utilization reflects the relatively poorer health of the elderly. The elderly are more likely to have chronic, multiple conditions. In addition, they are more likely to experience some limitation of activity or be unable to carry on major activities (U.S. National Center for Health Statistics, 1971). The number of restricted activity days and bed disability days increase with age for both sexes, although elderly females tend to have more such days (U.S. National Center for Health Statistics, 1973).

Public funding primarily through Medicare and Medicaid pays nearly half of the medical care expenditures for the elderly. Some 5 percent of Medicare enrollees account for 22 percent of program costs (Piro and Lutens, 1973). This disproportionate share of costs is accounted for by the increasingly intense care received by the dying. Approximately 70 percent of all those who died in 1978 were Medicare enrollees (Piro and Lutens, 1973).

USE OF MEDICAL TECHNOLOGY BY THE ELDERLY

Many have noted the aging of the population. Since 1960 the population aged 65 and over has grown more than twice as fast as the younger population (Rice and Feldman, 1983). Declining death rates from diseases such as cerebrovascular disease, heart disease, and others are generally acknowledged as contributers to the swelling of the elderly population. It has been suggested that this growth in the aged population will affect health care utilization and expenditures. By the year 2040 some 27 percent of physician visits will be made by those 65 years and over compared with 15 percent in 1980. Total short-stay hospital days may double, with more than half of the increase due to the aging of the population. One projection estimates that 40 percent of the days of care provided in the year 2040 will be for those aged 75 and over; in 1980 only 20 percent were for those in that age group. Also, nursing home residents may increase three-and-one-half times (Rice and Feldman, 1983).

This increased utilization by the elderly is expected to be reflected in increasing medical care expenditures. Of the total $219 billion spent for personal health care in 1980, $64.5 billion, or 29 percent, was spent on those aged 65 or over. The amount is expected to show a 159 percent increase by the year 2040 (Rice and Feldman, 1983). These are only estimated projections, of course, based on continuation of recent trends in fertility, mortality, and morbidity. It is difficult to tell whether these projections will match actual increases of the aged population, but it is reasonable to suggest that the problems of the costs of medical care for the elderly will only be exacerbated in the future. Health policy decision makers and analysts will increasingly look to the medical care of the elderly as a locus for intervention. Medicare may have solved problems of access for the elderly, but a comprehensive approach to the health needs of the elderly is required.

HISTORICAL ROOTS OF TECHNOLOGICAL MEDICINE

Historians of American medicine have given divergent accounts of the route to the present-day medical care system. This system has been characterized as technologically sophisticated and hospital based; as providing acute, episodic and curative rather than preventive care; as relying on a fee-for-service payment system; and as granting much autonomy to physicians trained in the rubrics of scientific medicine.

Some have looked to a technological imperative as the root of the present medical care system (Mechanic, 1974, 1976; Vogel, 1980). Morris Vogel, for example, argues that hospital medicine grew in part as a result of the specificity and discreteness embodied in the medical style of scientific medicine (Vogel, 1980). He suggests that invention of instruments such as the stethoscope, opthalmoscope, laryngoscope, and x-ray and the discovery of germ theory led to the identification of disease as discrete clinical entities with unique causes, courses, and pathologies which could be determined at the cellular level. As the laboratory translated life processes into quantitative data (the base of scientific medicine), the physician was less concerned with the functioning of the whole person in his environment. The patient, or public, was willing to acquiesce to this kind of medical care because of a generalized "modern" attitude resulting from urbanization and industrialization. According to Vogel's account: "A public increasingly attuned to scientific medicine came to appreciate the curative benefits of this style and to trust the expert authority of the hospital" (Vogel, 1980:134).

Modernization arguments such as this one deny the political, cultural, and economic forces underlying social arrangements. They are tautological in that they essentially argue that modern systems exist because they are modern. In the case of medical care delivery, they cannot explain why other urbanized industrialized countries have nationalized health systems. Nor can they explain why we see dramatic shifts in medical care delivery when countries decide to initiate comprehensive reform as in China after the Cultural Revolution. Others, more convincingly, posit the view that our present-day medical care system is a result of the interaction between technology and economic organization. Theorists from this tradition see today's health care system "deeply rooted in the interwoven history of modern medicine and corporate capitalism" (Brown, E., 1979:1).

Brown, L. (1979), for example, recounts how groups controlling resources and pursuing their material interests forged our hospital-based technical medical care system. Organized medicine by the 1930s, his argument goes, controlled entry into the field through licensure and accreditation of medical schools and teaching hospitals. Through local medical societies the medical profession also controlled the economics and practice of medicine. However, since the 1930s physicians have engaged in a struggle with those who sought to rationalize medical care. The "corporate rationalizers" — hospitals, insurance companies, medical schools, foundations, government health agencies and other groups — supported legislation which would have coordinated medical care and which emphasized capital intensive services. According to this view, hospitals, especially through the American Hosptial Association, were cast as the logical center of any rationalized health system. Hospitals, thus, as the locus of medical technology upon which physicians increasingly relied, became a powerful force in modern health care delivery.

Brown suggests that medical technology and scientific medicine have provided the basis for physicians' claims to a monopoly of authority over the practice of medicine. Analysts sympathetic to this perspective have emphasized social control aspects of the medical profession (Dubos, 1959; Lalond, 1974; Carlson, 1975; Ehrenreich and Ehrenreich, 1978).

Another interpretation comes from analysts such as Paul Starr, who in his book, *The Social Transformation of American Medicine,* points to the development of the cultural sovereignty of the medical profession as the key to the roots of the American health care system (Starr, 1982). Starr recounts how in the nineteenth century the medical profession was relatively weak, divided, economically insecure, unable to control entry into practice or to develop medical standards of medical education. During the twentieth century, however, physicians not only became powerful, prestigious and wealthy as a professional group, they also succeeded in shaping the basic organization and financial structure of American medicine. His analysis traces a sequence of events which he interprets as the conversion of cultural authority of the medical profession into the control of markets, organizations, and public policy.

In the medical care realm, this cultural authority is defined as "the authority to interpret signs and symptoms, to diagnose health or illness, to name diseases, and to offer prognosis" (Starr, 1982:14).

According to Starr, it was this ability to shape the understanding of a patient's experience that guaranteed the control of physicians in the development of the present-day health care system. Scientific and technological change were necessary but not sufficient causes.

Starr argues that this cultural authority on the part of professionals rests on a dependency on the part of patients, Americans became more willing to acquiese, or surrender private judgment, as professional authority grew. The growth in professional authority was a result of in part the growing cohesiveness of the profession. This cohesiveness was a consequence of the growth of hospitals and specialization and the concomitant reliance on peer referral. Cultural sovereignty also depended upon the development of diagnostic technology "which strengthened the powers of the physicians in physical examinations of the patient and reduced reliance on the patient's report of symptoms and superficial appearance" (Starr, 1982:8). Its growth also was accelerated due to the growing cultural belief in science and technological progress. The shift of medical care delivery from home to the hospital further strengthened the dependency of the patient on the physician. Starr also asserts that institutional mechanisms such as insurance reimbursement have contributed to the increased authority of the medical profession.

In all these accounts, the relationship of the individual to the medical care system remains constant. Whether we explain the development of the system as the result of a technological imperative or the pursuit of interests on the part of physicians and corporate rationalizers or as the result of cultural sovereignty, the individual remains in a subordinate role to the medical care system.

What does this dependency mean for the patient? What does this mean for the elderly patient in particular? Loss of autonomy is an overriding issue for the elderly in a society which prizes productivity and the youthful stamina that productivity requires. As medicine becomes increasingly dependent on technology for diagnosis, treatment, and rehabilitation, the dependency of the patient in the patient-physician relationship may also be exacerbated. This loss of autonomy would seem to be intensified for the elderly patient whose autonomy is already threatened by other social institutions and processes.

Medical technology can potentially empower a person. Today's high techology medicine is often restorative of function or has the potential to be so. Dysfunctional hearts and livers can be removed and replaced with functioning transplanted ones. Body parts, like arms, can be synthesized to work and soon look like the original. However, newly emerging technologies such as these are expensive technologies. Each artificial heart, for example, has been estimated to cost $15,000 to $25,000 (U.S. Department of Health, Education and Welfare, 1973). The question of access accompanies the use of such costly care.

The important issue of equitable access has been discussed concerning physician decision making, transplants, and dialysis (Fox and Swazey, 1974; Katz and Capron, 1975). Patients have been less likely to be referred to transplant centers if local physicians felt costs were prohibitive (Simmons, Klein and Simmons, 1977). It has been suggested that unconscious bias on the part of physicians toward the more "socially worthy" middle-class patients has affected acceptance into transplant programs (Sudnow, 1967). The elderly may be considered less socially worthy because criteria such as potential for vocational rehabilitation are applied.

Most new expensive technologies are centralized. For example, 1977, kidney transplants could be performed in less than 200 U.S. hospitals (Simmons, Klein and Simmons, 1977). Centralization poses questions of access for all those who do not reside near the medical centers which serve as repositories for these newly emerging technologies. This problem of access may be especially serious for the elderly, whose mobility may be restricted.

High technology medicine is associated with a high degree of bureaucratization and specialization. It has been estimated that over a five-day period, 141 persons and 21 physicians were involved in one of the early heart transplant efforts (Reinhard, 1970). The impersonal atmosphere of the huge medical center with its shifting personnel may produce stress for the most hearty of those in need of heart or liver transplants. The elderly, whose daily life experiences often involve a relatively simple contained environment and interactions with only a few familiar people, may experience overwhelming stress in the face of this bureaucratization and may thus suffer negative health consequences.

Biomedical technology creates conditions of normative uncertainty, new situations where clear-cut norms have not been established. Resuscitation efforts and other life-sustaining treatment efforts pose such problems of normative uncertainty. There is as yet no agreed-up answers to the questions of who is to decide when a life is to be sustained or what criteria are to be used to make allocation decisions.

The federal government is focusing attention on medical technology through assessment efforts on the part of various agencies. The National Center for Health Services Research lists medical technology as one of its research priorities. The Office of Technology Assessment has a draft of a report which is looking at the issues of medical technology and the costs of the Medicare program. Commissions have been formed to look at specific technologies.

The policy thrust that these efforts will initiate, the effect they may have on the organization and practice of medicine, and the impact they will have on patient populations is unclear at this point. However, endeavors in this area promise to have some impact on the health care of the elderly given their high health expenditure and utilization rates and the significant amount of public resources allocated to the elderly's medical care.

It seems that it is time to stop putting round pegs in square holes. The elderly, by and large, suffer from chronic long-term conditions and with the concomitant problems with every day life activities that those conditions bring. Yet we have a medical care system which treats patients in an acute episodic way. Medicare may have dealt with the problems of access for the elderly, but the hospital-based technologically sophisticated system Medicare helped to underwrite may exacerbate the problems of elderly in their attempts to take care of their health needs.

MEDICAL TECHNOLOGY POLICY

It is our thesis that policies which set the parameters for the use of medical technology in the health care delivery of the elderly exhibit a potential for social control. The formation of public policy regarding medical technology is a recent phenomenon, and mechanisms to develop guidelines or recommendations for the use of medical technology are yet only in the experimental state. Therefore, the long-term and short-term effects of various approaches to the use of medical technology remain uncertain (Banta and Behney, 1981).

Public policy refers to the decision making process at the institutional and professional level. It thus encompasses legislative decisions such as the mandate to establish a National Center for Health Care Technology to formally assess medical technologies. It also includes decisions on the part of third parties to adopt specific reimbursement schedules. It incorporates private sector decisions to produce and develop certain technological innovations. It includes acquisition and utilization decisions on the part of hospitals and medical research centers. It also subsumes the professional decision making at the point of service delivery. It is the confluence of decision making at these levels, and the interactions among them, that results in certain patterns and arrangements of health care provision.

Medical technology has become a focus of attention in health policy debates following the shift from the equity and access issues of the 1960s to the cost-containment issues in the 1970s and 1980s. It has been suggested that it is less contentious to focus on medical technology rather than physician's services or institutional policy as a point of intervention. So, by the late 1970s many began to point the finger of blame at medical technology as the "culprit" responsible for the ever-escalating spiral of health care costs (Altman and Blendon, 1977). Senator Kennedy, chairman of the Senate Labor and Public Welfare Subcommittee on Health, charged during congressional hearings in 1978 that "the American taxpayer in this body has paid an additional $10 billion to $12 billion over the last 10 years because of new technology in health care" and "some studies have estimated that 40 percent of the increase in the cost of a hospital day is due to the use of new technology" (U.S. Senate, 1978).

As the cost of medical care delivery rose, questions were raised as to the effectiveness of that care. While attributing vast improvements in health to advances in medical care, biomedical research and technological innovation, members of Congress and others have expressed concern about the way in which technological innovation has been introduced into medical practice. Concerns have arisen about the timely introduction of new technologies and the phasing out of outmoded ones, the efficient organization and equitable distribution of technologies, and the appropriate and effective use of technologies. A lag between research findings and implementation delays the use of effective technology and results in the continued use of outmoded, harmful or marginally useful technologies. Conversely, many technologies are introduced without sufficient information about their health benefits, clinical risks, cost effectiveness and societal side effects (U.S. House of Representatives, 1978b).

In testimony before the House, for example, computerized axial tomography (CAT or CT scanner) and electronic fetal monitoring were cited as examples of the problem of undue proliferation of certain exotic technologies. Cost appeared to be the central issue with CT scanners, while effectiveness was the major concern with fetal monitors. It was stated that CT scanners cost from $400,000 to $600,000 and "every hospital, or almost every hospital, in the country has wanted one" (U.S. House of Representatives, 1978a). With regard to fetal monitors, a study was cited which indicated that "if we use fetal monitors consistently and often, the number of caesarian sections increases. In fact, the rate more than doubles without convincing concurrent reduction in the likelihood of fetal survival" (U.S. House of Representatives, 1978a).

The Health Care Financing Administration (HCFA), the agency responsible for administering the Medicare program and advising the states on payment decisions under Medicaid, apparently has been beleagured with many questions regarding reimbursement for sophisticated medical procedures (U.S. House of Representatives, 1978b). Third parties have had questions about claims submitted for reimbursement. The professional community has questioned the continued use of procedures presently reimbursed under Medicare when new technologies are not. In fact, it is not unusual for manufacturers to ask about Medicare coverage before making marketing decisions.

By the late 1970s, sentiment was being expressed that the federal government had a responsibility to seek solutions to the problems associated with the transfer of medical technology (i.e. problems of both underutilization and overutilization and uneven distribution of certain technologies throughout the country). The involvement of the federal government was viewed by many as essential because of reimbursement issues. Senator Kennedy, calling for a mechanism to assess medical technologies stated: "The United States has no ability, even though we have virtually an automatic reimbursement for the use of technology, to do any kind of effective evaluation of what the cost of new technology is going to be, or what its impact is going to be on the health of the American people. Nowhere does this capability exist" (U.S. House of Representatives, 1978a).

Others supported a federal role in technology transfer and assessments on the basis of the percent of the gross national product devoted to health care. They pointed out that as a nation we are devoting an ever-increasing percentage of our gross national product to health care. Health care expenditures are the nation's third largest industry (U.S. House of Representatives, 1978b). Iglehart (1976) reported in the *National Journal* that federal officials believe that biomedical research, the bulk of which is federally financed, must move beyond merely probing the mysteries of disease into an assessment of the value of today's medical treatment practices.

There were several legislative and administrative responses to these calls for federal initiatives in the creation and implementation of mechanisms to assess innovations in biomedical research. Included among them was Public Law 95-623, the Health Services Research, Health Statistics and Health Care Technology Act of 1978, which provided for the creation of the National Center for Health Care Technology (NCHCT). Assessments by the NCHCT were to consider the safety, cost effectiveness, social, ethical, and economic implications of health care technologies (Public Law 95-623, 1978). In this law the NCHCT was authorized to provide reimbursement recommendations to the secretary of the Department of Health and Human Services.

One administratively created mechanism was the establishment of the Office of the Medical Applications of Research (OMAR) within the office director of the National Institutes of Health (NIH). The establishment of OMAR was the result of intensive deliberations involving the office of the director, as well as the bureaus, institutes, and divisions constituting NIH (Perry and Kalberer, 1980). OMAR's answer to the query for technology assessment was the Consensus Development Program.

The Consensus Development Program has held over thirty Consensus Development Conferences which have brought together practitioners, researchers, consumers, and representatives from other organizations to seek general agreement on the safety, efficacy, and appropriate conditions for the use of various medical procedures, drugs, and devices. Unfortunately, these attempts to involve the public sector in medical technology assessments have been relatively short lived. Almost two-thirds of the Consensus Development Conferences were held in the years 1978-1979. Only three conferences were sponsored by OMAR in 1981 and 1982, respectively. NCHCT which was disbanded in 1981 was totally eliminated from the 1982 budget. The Health Industry Manufacturers Association and the American Medical Association have been cited as forces in the demise of the NCHCT (Iglehart, 1976).

The only remaining major public sector programs concerned with medical technology assesment are the Office of Health Technology Assessment (OHTA) in the National Center for Health Services Research (NCHSR) and the Office of Technology Assessment (OTA), OHTA, with a staff comprised of two registered nurses and two health service researchers, is hardly equipped to do comprehensive technology assessments. The OHTA has concentrated only on safety and efficacy issues and not on ethical, economic, or social issues. Consensus Development Conferences had become increasingly focused on technical or scientific questions concerning efficacy and safety.

Private sector attempts at assessment have had a relatively narrow focus. The Clinical Efficacy Assessment Program, conducted by the American College of Physicians, emphasizes safety and effectiveness of procedures, tests, and therapeutic interventions within the scope of internal medicine (Seeger, 1983). The American Hospital Association conducts assessments which are primarily concerned with equipment in order to provide hospitals with information on new developments in diagnostic and therapeutic technology. The American Medical Association assesses the benefits and risks of specific technologies for the edification of business, industry, and government through its Diagnostic and Therapeutic Technology Assessment project (DATTA) (Seeger, 1983). The Blue Cross and Blue Shield Association makes determinations about the stage of development of technologies through its Medical Necessity Program.

This program makes recommendations about whether certain diagnostic or therapeutic procedures are outmoded, experimental, or not to be accepted as standard procedure which in turn affects reimbursement decisions.

Every issue on the public policy agenda is surrounded by a political culture, or symbolic environment (Gamson and Lasch, 1983; Lasch, 1984). When the notion of the need for medical technology assessment emerged, the discourse surrounding this issue centered on what role the federal government should play. Two perspectives on this issue dominated the discourse surrounding medical technology assessment in the popular and medical press. Some suggested that due to the complicated questions raised by advances in medical technology, there was a new social imperative for intervention on the part of the federal government. Others fearing broad federal involvement suggested that this involvement could potentially violate the patient-physician relationship, unduly restrict scientific investigation, or inhibit innovation on the part of industry.

At this point the evidence suggests that the "federal intrusionists" have won out. So far, the federal government has played a relatively limited role in medical technology assessment. It has been suggested recently, however, that Medicare's new prospective per-case payment system and its use of diagnostic-related groups (DRG) and 467 disease categories, as a measure on which to base its per-case payment, will affect the use of medical technology and hence create renewed interest in medical technology assessment (Iglehart, 1983).

The congressional staff members responsible for the prospective payment law persuaded Congress to create a new commission for assessment of prospective payment. This commission, which has been created to conduct medical technology assessments in order to provide Medicare with guidelines on appropriate care, will function only in an advisory capacity. The Health Industry Manufacturers Association, fearing repressive effects of cost-control considerations on the part of HCFA, has suggested a congressionally mandated technology-assessment commission and the Institute of Medicine has recommended the creation of a public-private technology-assessment body.

The mechanism, or mechanisms, which will eventually be responsible for medical technology assessment are yet to be developed.

It is reasonable to suggest, in light of the assessment mechanisms that have been developed and employed so far, that who the assessors are and what their purposes for the assessment is, set the parameters within which issues are raised. Recent experience suggests that social and ethical concerns are more likely to be addressed if there is public involvement in assessment.

Regardless of the mechanism employed, standards for the use of medical technologies must take into account the needs of special populations. Given the special health needs of the elderly and the role Medicare has played and continues to play in the organization of medical care, age must be included in assessments of medical technology.

MEDICAL TECHNOLOGY AND SOCIAL CONTROL OF THE ELDERLY

Adding age as a factor in the assessment of medical technologies necessarily complicates the analysis. For example, one can solve the ethical issue of social worthiness and distributional problems in health care delivery by broadening the funding for the treatment of end-stage renal disease to include those of advanced age (Mechanic, 1976; Sudnow, 1967). However, the use of renal dialysis or transplants may be less safe and less efficacious for the elderly. Use of these techniques with the aged may result in more complications and greater need for hospitalization (Rettig, 1979; Fox, 1973). The application of a technology to the aged may decrease quality of life and diminish rehabilitation prospects (Davidson, 1980).

The benefits of a given technology to the aged may also be outweighed by the potential adverse side effects. Digoxin, the most commonly prescribed cardiac medication, can have toxic effects which lead to symptoms such as hallucinations (Stults, 1982). Concerns have been expressed that resuscitation is used too frequently and sometimes it harms rather than benefits patients, particularly elderly patients (Fusgen and Summa, 1978). Over the last fifteen years, cardiopulmonary resuscitation using external compression has become routine in general hospital wards and emergency rooms. Cardiopulmonary resuscitation is now used with everyone with cardiac arrest in most hospitals at a cost of approximately $1,000 per re-suscitation (President's Commission, 1983:234).

The decision not to resuscitate is one of those instances of norma-tive uncertainty described earlier in this chapter. Who makes the de-cision not to resuscitate? What criteria are to be used in making this decision? Will professional, institutional, or public decision making lead to class or age differences in resuscitation attempts? In 1967, BBC-TV reported the following notice in a London hospital: "The following patients are not to be resuscitated: very elderly, over 65, malignant disease, chronic chest disease, chronic renal disease" (President's Commission, 1983:243). Physicians in the U.S. typi-cally serve their gatekeeping function more discreetly. What kind of furor would be aroused if a notice like that were posted in a U.S. hospital?

Intensive care units (ICU), those specialized areas in which med-ical technology and personnel are concentrated for the care of the critically ill, exist in virtually every major hospital. In 1960, some 10 percent of U.S. hospitals with more than 200 beds had ICU's; by 1981, 99 percent did (Knaus et al., 1981). It would appear the aged and chronically ill have become the principal consumers of intensive care. In one study which analyzed 2,693 admissions to an ICU unit, the median age was 62. Most patients in this unit were between 50 and 60 years old, and the greatest number of admissions were males between the ages of 60 and 69 years of age (Thibault et al., 1980).

Questions as to the efficacy of ICU's remain unresolved. One study was conducted to evaluate the impact of intensive care on the results and costs of treatment of patients hospitalized for acute pulmonary edema. Data from patients hospitalized during the year after the unit opened was compared with data from the previous year's experience. No differences in mortality were found. Those in ICU's tended to stay two days longer in the hospital, and the average hospital bill was 50 percent greater for those treated in ICU's (Grin-ner, 1972).

ICU's may be sites for noninvasive monitoring rather than for immediate major interventions. One study, for example, found that 77 percent of 2,693 admissions to an ICU were prompted by the need for noninvasive monitoring, rather than major intervention

(Thibault et al., 1980). Only 10 percent of these admissions had subsequent indications for major intervention. The 23 percent who required immediate intervention accounted for 37 percent of all charges and 58 percent of deaths. Obviously, most of these ICU patients did not require expensive intensive care. The relationship between age and type of intervention was not addressed in this study.

Delirium and acute psychotic behavior have been noted in ICU's (Skillman, 1975). This ICU syndrome, as it has come to be called, seems to more likely with increasing age (Thibault et al., 1980). It seems reasonable to think that the elderly would be more prone to experiencing misperceptions, delusions, and hallucinations, given a dulling of some of the senses with age. The patient in an ICU is highly dependent upon his environment being forced by both his illness and "by the passivity necessitated by treatment, to abdicate the usual decision making process" (Skillman, 1975:45). Induced psychosis seems a high price to pay for noninvasive monitoring which only 10 percent of the time leads to more active interventions.

The ICU itself may induce dependency. A physician related the story of the difficulties of weaning an elderly man from a ventillator: "He frequently said he wished to die, although it was not at all clear to those who were caring for him whether his wish to die was an acceptance of his ultimate fate or whether he was extremely uncomfortable and depressed at the realization of his complete dependency on the ventillator" (Skillman, 1975:32).

When one looks at all the problems associated with the extensive use of intensive care units, one is prompted to ask who's interests are realized by some of our health care expenditures. In 1966, the National Aeronautics and Space Administration (NASA) tried to persuade businesses to invest in monitoring devices like those used in space programs for use in civilian medicine (Jones and Simpson, 1966). Today, intensive care units, based on such monitoring techniques, are flourishing and industry no longer needs encouragement to enter the market. Currently, coronary care units (CCU) account for 5 percent of the beds in community hospitals and more than 15 percent of the costs (Russell, 1979).

Profit incentives may have played a significant role in the proliferations of CCU's (Ehrenreich and Ehrenreich, 1971). Hewlett Packard engineers, together with Stanford cardiologists, developed the first CCU system. This company, and others, have seen steady rises in profit from their medical technology divisions. The ties between academia and the corporate world evidenced by the Stanford-Hewlett Packard development of CCU's is becoming increasingly common.

Physicians also have incentives to utilize technologically sophisticated equipment. First, ever more precise diagnostic tools help them practice medicine defensively. Second, the use of technology too complex for the average person to self-administer or understand supports the cultural authority of the physician. Finally, technological care, the use of which is encouraged by third-party reimbursement structures, may be profitable care. A study conducted at the University of California at SanFrancisco found that physicians could triple their incomes by spending their time ordering tests or performing complicated procedures (Wolf and Berle, 1981).

Some suggest that the consumer sees it as being in his interest to receive sophisticated care. The consumer may demand more sophisticated care because of the influence of mass media and corporate advertising attempts to suggest that technological care is quality care. Theories of social influence would predict that consumers, once exposed to high technology medicine, would rate it positively regardless of differences in health status (Aronson, 1980).

Equity and access issues take on added dimensions in the assessment of the application of ICU's in the care of the elderly. In the past, patients older than seventy years of age were excluded from ICU's. Is age a criterion upon which to base such decisions? To the extent that ICU's help to prolong life and restore people to health, limiting access to certain segments of the population limits options for a longer, healthier life.

Often, institutional policy dictates access to ICU's. At a respiratory surgical ICU of a major hospital, the chief resident on duty was responsible for admissions and discharge decisions. A physician relates the story of a thirty-four-year-old woman who was able to be transferred to a regular hospital ward to make room for an eighty-four-year-old woman who had just undergone hip surgery. He recounts, "Had the young woman been doing poorly the elderly patient might have been kept overnight in the recovery room since her survival potential was far less than that of the young woman"

(Skillman, 1975:9).

Life-sustaining treatment for the elderly poses the host of issues described so far in this chapter. Life-sustaining treatment embraces all those interventions that increase the life span, including respirators, kidney machines, home physical therapy, nursing support for daily life activities, and feeding procedures. In March of 1983 the President's Commission for the Study of Ethical Problems in Medicine and Biomedical and Behavioral Research issued a report on the decision to forego life-sustaining treatment. The ten-member committee, over half of whom were physicians, met over a three-year period and concluded that it is best to sustain life and that life-sustaining treatment decisions should be based on the voluntary choice of a competent and informed patient. However, there are severe constraints on the patient's ability to make a decision, including the violation of physician conscience and professional judgment, the restriction of options due to scarce resources and allocation concerns, and whether a patient is "benefitted or burdened" by treatment (President's Commission, 1983). It appears far more likely that patient decision making regarding life-sustaining treatment depends upon the discretionary power of the physician.

The commission focused on the ethical and legal aspects of competence and informed consent. The issue of access subsumes these issues, but it was never directly addressed. Questions such as the following which tap the social and economic implications of life-sustaining treatment were not entertained: Does one empower a person to maintain his life in a vegetative state? Do we at present sustain all life equally? Are the lives of the middle-class elderly more likely to be sustained than those of the elderly poor? Is a sustained life a healthy life? What are the costs involved in sustaining life and who should bear these costs? Do higher co-insurance and deductible provisions under Medicare and Medicaid prevent some patients from seeking this kind of care?

In 1982, federal legislation enabled hospice services to be reimbursed under Medicare. However, under the provisions attending this legislation, admission to a hospice amounts to a decision to forego many kinds of life-sustaining treatment provided on an inpatient basis in hospitals. Resuscitation, continuous cardiovascular monitoring, and chemotherapy, for example are foregone with hospice admission (Scoy-Mosher, 1982). The elderly person may inadvertently limit his own options through informed consent because these provisions are not made clear.

Hospice care itself poses a set of issues that need to be addressed in the determination of its use for the elderly. Hospice care is a nontraditional method used to deliver care to terminally ill patients. This type of care generally offers services to meet the physical, spiritual, emotional, psychological, social, financial, and legal needs of the dying patient and his family. An interdisciplinary team provides this care and in a variety of setting, both inpatient and at home. It represents a move away from treatment of the dying with highly technological, capital intensive medicine. HCFA's recommendations for hospice care places a 20 percent limit on the utilization of inpatient care (Pryga and Bachofer, 1983). This provision is likely to promote inequitable access to hospice care. The limitation on inpatient care favors the "truly" dying, but it also favors those patients who do not need such care because of adequate family and home support. The result may be a two-class system for the dying.

CONCLUSION

The intent of this chapter has been to shed light on the complicated issues involved in the application of medical technology in the health care of the elderly. The use of sophisticated medicine can potentially empower the elderly if its application takes into account the special circumstances of the aged. Conversely, the use of technological medicine also has the potential to reduce the autonomy of the elderly. Further, medical technology policy, if applied unilaterally without attention to the special needs of the elderly, may unintentionally limit their ability to benefit from the use of certain technologies.

Complex questions about the nature of the relationship between technological intervention and the health of the elderly warrants more attention than they have been given to date. The ways in which the application of various medical technologies affects the health and quality of life of the aged merits the attention of researchers. Specifically, researchers should explore whether the use of specific technologies enhances or limits the autonomy of the elderly. For example, care in a hospice rather than an intensive care unit may be the ideal setting for monitoring a dying elderly patient. The relationship between medical environment, patient characteristics such as age, and resultant health status or quality of life, however, remains an empirical question. Further research into these areas may yield the critiera upon which rational medical technology policy decisions for the health care of the elderly can be made.

These decision, however, often involve difficult choices. The criteria to be used in allocation decisions must be made explicit and examined closely. This examination may reveal that aggressive salesmanship and profit motives lead to the proliferation and use of unnecessary and often harmful technologies. It may indicate that some segments of the population, the poor and the elderly, for example, experience limited access to useful technologies. Policymakers may have to choose between acquiesing to professionals and manufacturers in pursuit of their material and ideological interests and providing rational, humane health care of aged Americans.

CHAPTER 10

MASS MEDIA AS LEGITIMIZERS OF CONTROL

HAVING established by this point that ageism is prevalent in American society and that it facilitates control over the elderly by ensuring their devalued status, we turn to the major cultural agent through which this control is typically expressed: the mass media of communication. Television, radio, newspapers, and magazines, due to their central role in defining and redefining social reality, are the chief disseminators of ageist stereotypes in American culture. Media programming frequently acts to implicitly justify, rationalize, or legitimate the treatment received by the aged in society at large. It thereby contributes to the process of constraining their power, influence, and life options and discourages attempts to alter their status.

As is the case with other socially disadvantaged groups such as women and minorities, the "legitimate role" of the elderly is contained in a set of implicit media messages about what constitutes normative behavior for persons over sixty-five — as workers, consumers, family members, medical patients and so on. Since communication is a dynamic process, these messages not only reflect existing social relations as they are experienced by the elderly but they also reinterpret and refine those relations. For this reason, public policies that dictate whether distorted portrayals of old age

By Lawrence A. Powell, Department of Political Science, Massachusetts Institute of Technology.

are permissible in prime-time programming assume critical importance in determining whether the status of the elderly will be improved or diminished.

A plethora of studies conducted over the past two decades have indicated the presence of substantial ageist biases in media portrayals of old age.[1] Few, if any, however, have related this evidence to the broader social control functions performed by such biases. In our analysis, we attempt to interpret this accumulated evidence in terms of its implications for the issue of social control. In general, we find the evidence from these studies to be consistent with the interpretation that messages contained in mass media tend to legitimize existing patterns of dominance within American society. Negative media stereotyping of socially disadvantaged groups such as the aged, the poor, women, and minorities facilitates control over these groups by rationalizing the subordination, economic exploitation, and devalued status of these groups. In the case of the elderly, stereotyping reflects both intergenerational and interclass conflicts over resource control. Labeling old age as a deviant status via mass media serves to justify the process of denying the elderly access to societal resources like status, power, wealth, and decision making authority.[2] Those who stand to gain the most from this labeling process are the groups who enjoy the most privileged positions in the American social hierarchy and who dominate access to societal resources.

The manner in which society is portrayed by American mass media is influenced by both the market-based economy and the libertarian tradition of an unregulated press. Within this context, mass communications enterprises give higher priority to the imperatives of the market than to the needs of media consumers. An important, albeit perhaps unintentional, by-product of this commercial emphasis is the generation of stereotypes of disadvantaged social groups such as the elderly. Commercial advertisers, who indirectly determine the style of media programming through their bidding for prime-time product exposure, have few incentives to portray the life circumstances of the elderly accurately, since the elderly are not part of their "prime demographic market." Moreover, there are substantial profits to be made in playing upon consumers' fears of loss of youthful vitality, and this reinforces the stigmatization of old age in American society.

Because the elderly are heavy consumers of media, they are particularly vulnerable to negative media depictions of old age. These depictions contribute to self-doubt and feelings of powerlessness among older adults, inhibiting the individual and collective responses to their social environment that might otherwise improve their condition and social status. The end result of this process is that control is exercised over the elderly by reinforcing the behavioral expectations and age constraints that maintain their devalued status.

In our analysis of the process by which media aid in legitimizing the devalued status of the elderly, we shall find it useful in this chapter to address several related questions: (1) What general features of the American societal context are most conducive to mass media stereotyping of old age? (2) Within the communications industry, what predisposes communicators to convey distorted images of the elderly? (3) What is the empirical evidence suggesting the presence of ageist stereotyping in American mass media? (4) Does the extensive use of the media by the elderly render them emotionally susceptible to these biased portrayals of old age? (5) Is the elderly's behavior inhibited as a result of these distorted images? (6) Are there any present or future trends in telecommunications that might hold promise of counterbalancing distorted media portrayals and their inhibitive consequences?

THE SOCIETAL CONTEXT

The process by which control is exercised over elderly behavior via media stereotyping cannot be understood apart from the societal context within which it arises. Historically, two general features of that context have been particularly influential. First, the location of mass media enterprises within a predominantly market-based economy has meant that whenever policy choices must be made between imperatives of the market and the expressed needs of media consumers, the former will usually assume priority. The more consumer-oriented functions of communications media such as education, public service messages, and the provision of accurate information have generally received less emphasis than commercial advertising and light entertainment designed to ensure large audiences. A notable exception to this pattern has been the Public Broadcasting System (PBS), whose greater independence of commercial advertising and profit maximization as economic priorities has made possible an educational and community service orientation.[3]

Secondly, the dominant social ideology of libertarian individualism has resulted in a rather one-sided interpretation of "freedom of the press."[4] The libertarian tradition, best exemplified in the works of John Locke, Adam Smith, and John Stuart Mill, interprets freedom of the popular press to mean freedom from intervention and regulation by government, rather than freedom from programming biases introduced by commercial advertising and sponsorship of entertainment by corporate interests in the private sector.[5] As a consequence of these two aspects of the American social system — market economy and Lockean ideology — the popular press has primarily serviced the private economic interests of American businesses, with minimal intervention by the public sector on behalf of broader social interests.

In colonial days, newspapers reported information about shipping and commerce and carried advertisements by merchants. With the growth of mass production and distribution techniques in the nineteenth century, newspapers, magazines, and trade publications provided a means of stimulating consumer demand through advertising. Twentieth century advances in telecommunications have greatly accelerated these trends. With the advent of syndicated newspapers, motion pictures, radio, and television, the mass media have become huge commercial ventures, marketing packaged images of social reality, and dominated by corporate advertising in the form of "the sponsor."[6] Through their advertising support and concentrated ownership of communications resources, modern corporate interests have come to exert a powerful influence over the policy and content of popular media.

Since they are well served by the existing social order, American corporations are particularly concerned with preserving the status quo and avoiding fundamental changes in the economic conditions within which they operate. The mass media are admirably suited to turn the status quo into social law, and increasingly, organized business has adopted techniques for manipulating mass publics through subtle media persuasion in lieu of more direct and visible means of influence.[7] This use of communications channels to legitimize, maintain, and expand existing patterns of socioeconomic dominance is by no means a novel practice. Throughout human history, in a variety of cultural settings, occupants of dominant positions within a social hierarchy have sought to maintain their hegemony over unequal patterns of resource distribution by successfully inculcating among subordinate groups the belief that existing social arrangements are legitimate, just, and necessary. Disproportionate access to the media by those with economic and social power allows privileged groups to maintain control by imposing their preferred values on subordinate groups.[8]

SOURCES OF STEREOTYPING IN THE MEDIA

Several structural features of contemporary American mass media, as presently organized, predispose them to convey distorted images of the elderly, thereby perpetuating their devalued status. For instance, in order to attract mass audiences and the associated lucrative advertising, producers attempt to maximize potency of media content by constructing recognizable and easily-understandable characters. Time constraints inherent in the medium foster character condensation, which in turn produces stereotyping. Consequently, old-age stereotypes usually perform two functions in entertainment-oriented broadcasts: character condensation and comedy.[9]

When confronted with charges of excessive stereotyping in their dramatic presentations, networks often argue that the ideal of developing characters into intricate personalities is unrealistic, and that the limitations of the medium dictate that characters must be reduced to easily recognizable traits. They argue that this is equally the case for comedy, if not more so, since comedic characters often provoke laughter precisely through the device of stereotypic exaggeration of largely negative characteristics. Defenders of existing network policies are quick to point out that to place restraints and regulations on such portrayals not only takes the humorous edge off comedy itself but is also impinges on First Amendment freedoms.[10]

When all the network rhetoric is cleared away, the bottom line usually turns out to be the salability of the stereotypic protrayals. Networks are supported by television advertising revenues and, hence, have strong incentives to reach the greatest possible audience of potential consumers per dollar invested in advertising. Commercial advertisers, in conjunction with Nielsen ratings which indicate where their market lies, indirectly determine much of the style, and frequently also the content, of media programming through their bidding for prime-time product exposure.

The assumption among advertisers has generally been that the older age group is a weak source of purchasing power relative to younger consumers. The conventional wisdom of Madison Avenue holds that the "prime demographic market" ranges from young un-marrieds through middle-aged adults. Advertisers correctly assume that the income and purchasing power of the average American consumer declines in the later years (Ashmore, 1975:19). To go out of their way to please the elderly population, or to depict their life circumstances accurately, is therefore perceived by both advertisers and networks as a poor investment.[11]

AGEIST BIASES IN THE MEDIA

Research on mass media portrayals of old age has dealt primarily with images of the elderly on television. This research has generally shown that the most obvious form of media misrepresentation of the aged lies in its consistent underestimation of their numbers — implying their lack of importance to American economic and social life. Although the elderly comprise 11 percent of the total population, studies have consistently shown that only 1 or 2 percent of all prime-time characters are cast as elderly (Harris, 1974; Francher, 1973; Gerbner et al., 1977). A comparison of the age distribution of the U.S. population with the symbolic population depicted in prime-time drama reveals television's distortion of the age spectrum. As can be seen in Figure 1, television's portrayal of social reality under-represents both youth and the elderly, with most characters concentrated between the ages of 25 and 50. Moreover, this age distribution of prime-time characters is virtually identical to the age distribution of the "prime demographic market" used by advertisers in targeting consumers — that is, it appears to reflect the distribution of consumer income by age.

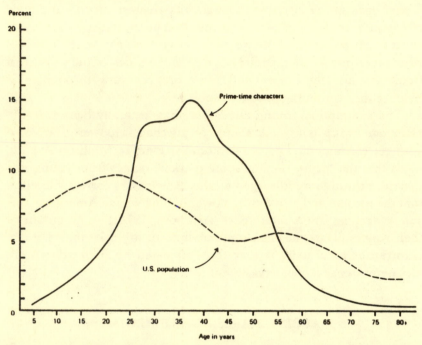

Figure 1. Percentage of United States Population and All Prime-Time Characters by Chronological Age, 1969-1978. From G. Gerbner, L. Gross, N. Signorielli, and M. Morgan (1980:39). Courtesy of Journal of Communications.

Omission of the elderly from media programming becomes even more pronounced in the case of commercial advertisements. A content analysis of 2,200 advertisements appearing in *Time, Ladies' Home Journal, Vogue, Ms.,* and *Playboy* between 1960 and 1979, for example, revealed that advertisements usually portray young adults, substantially underrepresenting the elderly. By far the worst distortions occurred for women. Only 4 percent of adult females featured in the ads were 40 or over, compared with 57 percent in the U.S. population. England, Kuhn, and Gardner (1981:469-471) conclude that "the deprecation of aging is a social process in which advertisers participate."

This consistent pattern of omission apparently reflects the sentiment that since the elderly are "past their prime" as productive employees and as consumers with substantial buying power, they are no longer sufficiently important to American society to merit major dramatic roles or to be used as positive role models in advertisements. Omission implies lack of value. In this sense, media underrepresentation clearly contributes to the devalued status of the elderly in American culture. Omission also implies exclusion from active participation in the mainstream of American social life. It implies that they are not an influential constituency and that their opinions and demands are of no real consequence and can therefore safely be ignored.[12]

When elderly characters do appear in mass media, their roles are usually negative. In television drama, old age is associated with increasing unhappiness, failure, and evil, and older women are disproportionately portrayed as victims (Aronoff, 1974; Gerbner et al., 1977).[13] In addition, media studies have generally shown that when disadvantaged statuses are combined (age + race + gender + class), character distortion is likewise compounded. Conversely, young and middle-aged white males, the most dominant or advantaged group in American society, are most often cast in roles implying access to social and financial opportunities. Content analyses of prime-time network television programming indicate that about three-fourths of all leading characters are male, middle- to upper-class whites, and between the ages of 25 and 55 (Gerbner and Gross, 1976:44; Gerbner et al., 1980:41-42).

American television depicts a world in which physically strong adult white males heroically solve the everyday problems encountered by women, children, the elderly and minorities (Northcott, 1975:184-186; Aronoff, 1974). The latter groups are cast in dependent roles, presumably due to their lesser competence or effort. In short, mature adult white males below the age of 60 are in control of things, and this control is justified by their greater productivity and competence. This depiction is hardly surprising, given that the majority of persons in a position to wield influence over media content — the producers, directors, censors, media executives, and advertisers — are themselves middle- to upper-class white males under 60.

Additional insight into the process of labeling old age as a devalued status can be gained by examining the personality attributes most frequently ascribed to the elderly in media portrayals. Elderly characters are more frequently treated with disrespect than are characters from any other age group. A study of television drama by Gerbner et al. (1980) found that over 80 percent of elderly female characters and 70 percent of elderly male characters were "treated discourteously" or were "not held in high esteem." Older characters were much more likely than younger characters to be portrayed as "eccentric" or "foolish." In addition to the ageist biases in trait ascriptions, considerable male-female discrepancies were also found to exist, and these discrepancies widened with advancing age. Women "age" more rapidly on television than men and are more likely to be cast in roles with reduced romantic possibilities as they grow older. Whereas about half of the older male characters were depicted as "lacking common sense, acting silly, or being eccentric," the proportion rose to two-thirds for older women. Again, note that as socially disadvantaged statuses are compounded (aged + female), prejudicial treatment in mass media increases accordingly (Gerber et al., 1980:42-45).

This general trend toward negative trait ascriptions with advancing age is also illustrated in a 1976 poll which asked readers of a national magazine to describe how persons over 60 are depicted on major television programs (Hemming and Ellis, 1976). The three adjectives most frequently chosen by readers were "ridiculous," "decrepit," and "childish." More positive qualities such as "dignified," "wise," "lively," and "with-it" consistently received lower ratings.[14]

While the distortions of old age in regular programming are considerable, the most blatant and intentionally manipulative cases are to be found in advertisements that exploit fear of aging. Commercial advertising in magazines, newspapers, radio, and television plays upon consumers' fears of loss of youthful vitality and appearance in promoting new products and creating markets. In the fantasy world of Madison Avenue fashion, becoming old is depicted as being a disagreeable experience. Aging is ugly. To be elderly means being constantly plagued with "unsightly age spots," constipation, denture problems, baldness, arthritis, chronic backaches, gray hair, and facial wrinkles.

All of these, of course, require commercially available panaceas in order to revive the look and feel of youth. A further implication usually contained in such ads is that the purchase of the product will restore a lost sense of social acceptability to others by masking overt signs of aging. Sale of the product by advertisers depends heavily on success in persuading consumers to feel uncomfortable with the prospect of being perceived by others as old. The subconscious messages embedded in face cream ads, for example, are not difficult to decipher. Potential female customers are encouraged to feel self-conscious about overt changes that naturally accompany aging since these might become apparent to "friends," who presumably would then love and respect them less as a consequence. They are told to be wary of going outdoors, since this will cause them to look older. Finally, they are urged to purchase a mysterious elixir which will transform them from a deviant status (appearing old) to a socially accepted status (appearing youthful).

USE OF THE MEDIA BY THE ELDERLY

Empirical evidence that has accumulated over the past twenty years has been unequivocal on at least one major point: older adults are heavy consumers of mass media.[15] This is especially true in the case of television. Heavy dependence on the "electronic babysitter" for information, surrogate companionship, entertainment, and emotional gratification renders older adults vulnerable to messages that contain distorted impressions of old age. Repeated exposure to these distortions can have a constraining influence on self-image and perceived life options as aging progresses.

Studies of time use by the elderly have consistently shown that watching television is the single most time-consuming leisure activity among the aged in the United States (De Grazia, 1961:133; Meyersohn, 1961; Schramm, 1969:353; Davis et al., 1976; Comstock et al., 1978). Elderly adults usually have more leisure time available to them than do younger persons, and several recent studies concur that the elderly use television more extensively than at any other point in the life cycle. Schramm (1969) and Comstock (1978), in independent investigations conducted a decade apart, have both found that their is a positive correlation between advancing age and increased viewing of television. A 1976 Nielsen study, for example, estimated that women over 50 view an average of five hours of television daily (Nielsen, 1976).

This heavy use of television takes on added significance if one examines the programming preferences of the elderly. Older adults prefer to watch news and public affairs programming over other types, and elders view these types of programs more often than any other age group (Schramm, 1969; Davis et al., 1976; Danowski, 1975; Comstock et al., 1978; Bower, 1973).[16] Practical information concerning conditions in their social environment is at least as important to them as entertainment, often more so (Hwang, 1974). Similarly, analysis of national election surveys indicates that the elderly have been consistently more attentive to television coverage of political campaigns than have younger age categories (Dimmick, McCain, and Bolton, 1979:25-26).

Unlike the pattern for television, there is a slight decline in newspaper, magazine, book, and radio use with advancing age, especially after 70 (Young, 1979:121, 126-127). This decline is minor, however, and most researchers attribute the decrease to the fact that at least 20 percent of persons over 65 experience some form of sensory loss, rather than to declining interest (Hendricks and Hendricks, 1977; Currier, 1975; Schramm, 1969). Thus, inconvenience and discomfort associated with reading small print may be responsible for reduced print media use, and hearing loss may be associated with reduced use of radio. Television may be preferred to other media because it is a "two-sense medium" that can still be understood by those with either sight or hearing impairments (Chaffee and Wilson, 1975). Despite the slight decline in use, newspapers continue to fill an important informational need for the elderly, and the amount of time devoted by the elderly to reading the newspaper (approximately one hour per day) does not differ significantly from that of the general population (Harris, 1974).

Level of information acquired through the media is closely related to degree of interest in politics and community affairs. Contrary to the popular stereotype which assumes that persons become apathetic about political affairs as they grow old, several key studies have indicated that the highest level of political interest occurs among persons 60 and above (Glenn and Grimes, 1968). One finds that interest in media coverage of campaigns increases consistently with age through the 60-69 category, then tapers off slightly in the 70-79 category.[17]

The question inevitably arises: if the elderly tend to be generally well informed on current affairs and attentive to political issues, then why should they fail as a group to make full constructive use of their potential for political involvement and self-determination? Are they simply too frail? As we have seen, one contributive factor is ageist biases in the presentation of information by media, which often leave the elderly feeling socially insignificant and powerless. Another source of the problem lies in non-informational uses of the media by older adults and their dependence on these uses for emotional gratification and surrogate companionship.

NON-INFORMATIONAL USES OF MEDIA BY THE ELDERLY

A number of recent mass communications studies have identified "extra-informational" or "entertainment-oriented" functions that media use typically performs for the elderly. "Escape from social and personal stress" has been identified as a motivation for television viewing, implying that the high levels of elderly television use may be performing a social disengagement function (Pearlin, 1959:255-259). Conversely, it has been argued that mass media are often used by older adults as a deterrent to social disengagement (Schramm, 1969). According to this interpretation, exposure to communications media is undertaken by the elderly in an attempt to maintain an ongoing sense of participation in society and to combat feelings of alienation and loneliness (Schramm, 1969).

Television viewing acts as a substitute for face-to-face communication that has been lost by an older adult (Hess, 1974). Older adults experience financial, social, and physical losses which lead them to seek compensatory activities. The mass media provide to older persons a socially acceptable substitution that can be used inexpensively, anonymously, and at their own discretion (Graney and Graney, 1974). Media, therefore, play a critical role in maintaining social satisfaction in the wake of reduced contact with friends, relatives, and voluntary organizations in the community (Graney and Graney, 1974).

Graney (1974) has found that there are three major patterns of behavior exchange in late life: (1) losses in reading lead to substitution of television viewing; (2) decreased attendance at religious services and voluntary associations is replaced by television and reading, respectively; and (3) declines in reading are complemented by increased attendance at religious services. Because different activities are substituted for each other, and since each behavior exchange is less effective than the lost activity which preceded it, television viewing is an involuntary "substitute of last resort" at the end of the chain of possible communications substitutions for older adults (Graney, 1974).[18]

In assessing the implications of these research efforts for the issue of social control, it is evident that both informational and noninformational media content play an influential role in the everyday lives of aging adults. Besides obtaining information from media, the elderly use media to counter disengagement, for surrogate companionship, as a substitute for loss of previous activities, and in the process of late-life identity adjustment (Wenner, 1976; Swank, 1979). When one considers that the elderly have the highest media exposure level of any age group, it is apparent that negative media depictions of old age are likely to have an adverse effect. In order to fully understand why the impact of media stereotyping has been so influential in constraining elderly demands for improved economic and social conditions, it is necessary to examine more closely the effects of negative portrayals on self-concept.

INHIBITIVE CONSEQUENCES OF NEGATIVE PORTRAYALS

Negative media portrayals of old age contribute to control over the behavior of elderly adults through two psychological mechanisms. First, they contribute to low self-esteem, and second, they contribute to a sense of helplessness or powerlessness. The combination of these two has the effect of inhibiting the individual and collective response of the elderly to their social environment.

As George Herbert Mead and Charles Cooley demonstrated

years ago, an individual's self-conception develops out of interaction and self-comparison with others. Social validation is necessary in order for elderly persons to maintain their self-esteem as aging progresses.[19] Elderly adults, like persons of all ages, have a strong need for role models. The types of role models available through the media take on a special significance for the elderly because the mass media perform such an important function in providing surrogate companionship and countering disengagement in the later years. If the only role models available for elderly consumption are heavily stereotyped ones, they are likely to become self-fulfilling prophecies to the extent that elderly adults assimilate them and behave accordingly.[20]

A recent investigation by Korzenny and Neuendorf (1980) bears out this relationship between self-concept of the elderly and exposure to mass media. Depictions of the aged on television as "hindrances to society" were found by Korzenny and Neuendorf (1980) to predict a negative self-concept among elderly viewers, while conversely, when the aged were depicted as "assets to society" elderly viewers had a more positive self-concept. Overall, a negative self-concept was predicted by television viewing for any purpose, whether for "information" or "escape." However, watching for "escape" purposes and for "fantasy" content was an even stronger predictor of negative self-concept than watching for "information" or "reality" content.

Another way in which negative media portrayals constrain the behavior of the elderly is by predisposing them to feel powerless. Powerlessness has been variously conceptualized in social science literatures as "learned helplessness" (Seligman, 1975), loss of a sense of "personal control" (Renshon, 1974), and "external control expectancy" (Rotter, 1966; Lefcourt, 1976). Extensive research by Martin Seligman dealing with the phenomenon of "learned helplessness" suggests that the experience of powerlessness is likely to inhibit social and political participation among the aged. As applied to the elderly, this research predicts that if media images give elderly persons the impression that their social circumstances are "uncontrollable" by them, that their responses do not matter, then they will develop a sense of powerlessness. This outcome seems particularly likely given available evidence that the elderly are frequently depicted in mass media as being physically incompetent, mentally slow, sexually impotent, and unproductive to society.[21] Such portrayals have the net effect of suggesting the social and politicial impotence of the elderly. Quiescence among the elderly is thus ensured.

Like other age groups, the elderly tend to embody the role expectations assigned to them by the culture. As American culture's principle symbol-generating apparatus, television actively participates in the process of excercising control over the elderly wherever it portrays them as insignificant, passive, and unproductive. Indiscriminate television use among the elderly can contribute to an attitude of dependence and a passive role in life. The medium's primary orientation toward the younger market produces feelings of helplessness and victimization among elderly viewers (Schalinske, 1968). Because pictorially presented stimuli have strong modeling effects, television commercials, by glorifying youth and devaluing old age, can create tension and anxiety among the aged, contributing to emotional breakdown and even apparent symptoms of senility (Francher, 1973; Oberleader, 1969; Bandura, Ross, and Ross, 1963:601-607; 1969).

On the societal level, media-perpetuated stereotypes reinforce prejudice, discrimination, and age-based segregation, resulting in the isolation of elderly citizens from mainstream economic and social life (Goffman, 1963; Ward, 1977). Widespread belief in negative stereotypes creates gerontophobia among younger cohorts (Meltzer, 1962:831-837). Moreover, stereotypes regarding older adults' physical, cognitive, and emotional characteristics contribute to discrimination in employment practices.[22]

Perhaps most importantly in the long term, biased media portrayals stifle the potential of older adults to meet their needs collectively through the political process. The elderly fail to initiate political action in part because prevailing stereotypes have effectively convinced them that they, and other elderly adults like themselves, are incapable. Reluctant to venture forth to make their grievances heard, the elderly's economic and political demands do not get expressed as vociferously as those of more vocal and aggressive constituencies and, hence, are less likely to receive priority in the making of public policy. This in turn reinforces their devalued social status and limits their share of societal resources. In short, the elderly have been intimidated and effectively neutralized as a social force and come to passively accept their status as legitimate. Intentionally or not, mass media act to maintain the subordinate role of the elderly and reinforce societal patterns of prejudice, discrmination, and resource denial.

THE IMPACT OF EMERGING COMMUNICATIONS TECHNOLOGIES

Up to this point we have discussed the impact on the elderly of mass media technologies which are already in widespread use — television, radio, magazines, and newspapers. A number of qualitative changes in the nature of communications technology are emerging on the mass consumer market which may eventually have dramatic implications for social control. Innovations in the technology of communications can be expected to affect the way in which society is portrayed in mass media, and this in turn is likely to have implications for social control of the elderly (Innis, 1951; McLuhan and Nevitt, 1973; de Sola Pool, 1976).

There are two general qualitative changes in the nature of telecommunications which are expected to gain momentum over the next several decades. First, communications analysts point to a trend toward greater media diversity, allowing for greater personal choice in the programming to which one is exposed. This trend can be seen in the spread of technologies such as cable television, video recorder-playback systems, and subscription "information utilities." Second, media are becoming more interactive. The message carried by communications media is no longer just one way, with the user as the passive recipient of messages over which he/she has little control. This interactive trend is most evident in the advent of the personal computer, teleconferencing via telephone and satellite hookups, and "instant public opinion polling".[23]

These qualitative changes have in common a shift away from packaged "mass" media programming — with its homogenized, mass-produced message geared to the widest possible audience of potential consumers — and toward more differentiated communications in which the viewer is an active participant, selecting among messages according to personal needs and interacting creatively with media. It should be noted that this greater user autonomy is merely a possibility inherent in the technology of the new telecommunications advances. Whether these advances will facilitate autonomy or exercise additional control over viewers' attitudes and buying habits, however, will depend on the extent to which these advances are applied to satisfy popular versus commercial interests. The new telecommunications technologies are a two-edged sword that could conceivably either expand or constrain the control the elderly exercise as consumers of media.

Elderly adults have a need for age-specific information about available services, organizations, resources, and events in their surrounding environment. Access to such information through communications media is necessary if they are to effectively control important aspects of their life situation, both individually and collectively. Particularly promising in its possibilities for this sort of specilized programming is cable television. This technological advance, which has already been introduced in most major cities in the United States, has the capacity to open up virtually limitless numbers of additional channels.[24] By opening up multiple channels, cable TV creates opportunities for diversity in programming which could cater to previously underrepresented societal interests such as those of the elderly, women, blacks, hispanics, intellectuals, and groups with non-mainstream political and religious beliefs. Since cable TV has much greater potential than network TV for making communications systems available for use by nonprofessionals, it could provide a valuable resource to such groups (Gillespie, 1975; Real, Anderson, and Harrington, 1980).

These potentials in cable television have thus far remained largely unrealized due to the social context within which the innovation has taken place. The cable companies, like almost every other agency in the communications industry, are primarily oriented to the imperatives of the market and only secondarily to the expressed needs of media consumers. Thus, instead of trying to expand the possibilities for public access and programming diversity, there has been a tendency for cable companies to rely on broadcasting what is already available through established media (Ashmore, 1975). So far, cable operators have resorted to a combination of inexpensively produced light entertainment, movies, and frequent repeats of the same material in different time slots. Columnist Russell Baker has aptly described this current cable programming strategy as "dividing among 180 channels material already inadequate for twelve" (Waters et al., 1981:46).

On the positive side, there have been several pioneering applications of cable technology in recent years that point to the potential of the medium for expanding elderly autonomy. The most successful cable experiment to date was the Berks Cable project conducted in Reading, Pennsylvania, which was designed to allow the elderly to produce television programs. By using the two-way capability of the closed-circuit television station, the elderly were able to take classes and hold discussions on elderly concerns. Independent follow-up research evaluating the effects of the project indicated that elderly participants had improved their personal communication skills, successfully mastered a complex telecommunications system, and became enthusiastically involved in program production. For elderly viewers, exposure to the programs was found to have increased awareness of available public services in the community (Carey, 1978; Moss, 1978; Felton, Moss, and Sepulveda, 1978).

Another exemplary attempt to actively involve the elderly in the television production process was the PACE (Public Access to Cabletelevision by and for Elders) project in San Diego. Funded through Title I provisions of the Higher Education Act of 1965, PACE taught video production courses to 95 elderly persons. Participants were instructed in camera operation, directing, editing, and on-camera skills. Elderly adults and undergraduate students worked together in producing approximately 50 senior-oriented programs dealing with exercise, nutrition, educational opportunities, political advocacy, and other topics of interest to the elderly. The Senior Planning Council, composed of elderly volunteers from the project and from the surrounding community, was established to set programming policy and supervise operations. The resultant PACE programs were then cablecast to 110,000 homes via the public access channel and to 250,000 homes thoughout the United States on the local origination channel (Real, Anderson, and Harrington, 1980). What is noteworthy about these successful applications of cable technology is that they were funded through government grants, such as the National Science Foundation, and viewer contributions.

Another recent technological breakthrough that could be used to disseminate more age-specific programming is the videorecorder. The potential benefits that videorecorder self-education could hold for the elderly is perhaps best illustrated in a project conducted at Consummess River Community College in Northern California. Under a Title III grant, the college produced a series of 24 tapes for closed-circuit use. The tapes contained age-specific information directly addressing salient life problems experienced by the aged. They were packaged for easy access at video reception stations provided in community libraries. Topics covered by the tapes included retirement, Social Security, Medicare and Medicaid, housing, legal and consumer rights of the elderly, how to avoid being victimized by health fraud schemes, forced retirement, and opportunities for volunteer service in the community.[25] Particularly noteworthy is a three-part program entitled "What is Old? Myths and Realities of Growing Older." Part I counters prevalent stereotypes of old age with factual research and presents numerous examples of elderly adults who do not fit the conventional images. In Part II, eminent gerontologists take on myths regarding the physical and mental aspects of aging, and in Part III a group of elderly adults discuss their reactions and emotions while watching images of the elderly on film (Davis, 1975:315-321).

Besides offering wider programming choice, the interactive nature of some of the new communications technologies opens up the possibility for elderly adults to tap vast stores of information for personal use and for political organizing — via information utilities, telephone and satellite linkups, and home computers. The electronics revolution in communications has reduced the importance of physical distance and with it the importance of physical mobility. This trend could prove to be liberating for the elderly, for whom lack of mobility sometimes imposes a formidable handicap. Because "disengagement" among the aged is often a result not of physical infirmity per se but of the reduced mobility that accompanies it, technologies such as teleconferencing, remote photocopying, electronic mail, and text editing could create new opportunities for the formation of interest groups and voluntary associations around age-specific issues. As a consequence, reduced mobility may cease to be the inhibitor to social and political activism that is has been in the past.

If "push-button voting" is adopted in the near future as an economical alternative to ballot boxes and voting machines, getting physically to the polls will be eliminated as an impediment to elderly electoral turnout. Similarly, if the "instant public opinion polling" techniques that have already proven successful in cities like Columbus and Cincinnati are put into more widespread use, the rate of elderly responses to public opinion polls can be expected to increase. Since interactive TV is a "two-sense medium" (Chaffee and Wilson, 1975), sight and hearing problems would no longer constitute the deterrent to participation that has been the case with mail and telephone surveys. Voting and "instant polling" on local and national issues of concern to the elderly would be reduced to a mere choice of which button to push on an interactive television console located in the home, nursing home, or hospital. Given the adoption of this electoral technology, it is not inconceivable that even the most chronically bedridden of the elderly would be able to take part in the electoral process on a regular basis.

In summarizing the implications of these various communications advances, it is clear that substantial possibilities exist for using these innovations to expand the autonomy and influence of older Americans. But, unfortunately, substantial possibilities also exist for further stigmatizing old age and exercising even greater control over their lives through subtle media manipulation. The decisive factor will be whether the present pattern of commercial dominance over media technologies continues unchecked or whether some of the democratizing possibilities inherent in many of these technologies are allowed to develop.

One can anticipate that corporate interests will put up considerable resistance to the democratizing possibilities of some of these telecommunications technologies. Resistance to democratizing access to communications resources can already be observed, for instance, in corporate efforts to tighten copyright laws so that consumers would be prevented from photocopying printed materials or videotaping televised materials for distribution to others at no cost.[26] The underlying intent of these legal efforts is to maintain a legitimate monopoly over the production and distribution of information and images, thereby ensuring a captive consumer market, high demand for products, and a disproportionate influence over the way social reality is portrayed. The greater consumer choice in media use made possible by the emerging technologies presents a direct challenge to this pattern of dominance by threatening to decentralize control over the use of society's communications resources and by making them available as a public resource.

CONCLUSION

At the outset of this discussion we noted that although there is substantial evidence indicating the presence of ageist biases in American mass media, this evidence has not been linked to social control processes in American society. In our analysis we have suggested that studies of the mass media have clearly demonstrated that existing societal patterns of dominance and subordination are reinforced. Media stereotyping aids in the process of keeping socially disadvantaged groups, such as the elderly, "in their place" by legitimizing their devalued status. By labeling the aged as unworthy, mass media serve to justify segregation of the elderly from direct access to wealth, power, and status.

The process by which control is exercised over elderly behavior via media stereotyping cannot be understood apart from the societal context within which it arises. Mass communications enterprises are an extension of the corporate-industrial order, which affords primacy to the imperatives of market mechanisms over the expressed needs of consumers. A by-product of this commercial dominance is the disinterest networks and commercial sponsors exhibit relative to the elderly audience because they are not part of the "prime demographic market." The stigmatization of old age in American culture is also accentuated by advertisers' efforts to derive profits by capitalizing on consumers' fears of loss of youthful vitality and appearance.

The elderly are heavy consumers of mass media and are dependent on media for information, surrogate companionship, entertainment, and as a substitute for loss of previous activities. Repeated exposure to messages that contain distorted impressions of old age contributes to self-doubt and feelings of powerlessness. This in turn inhibits expression of elderly needs and demands, effectively neutralizing them as a social force. The result is that social control is exercised over the elderly by reinforcing existing age constraints and behavioral expectations that maintain their devalued status and limit their share of societal resources.

The question remains as to how future communications advances will be used — as mechanisms of control or to facilitate greater personal choice and need-satisfaction among the elderly. On the basis of the foregoing analysis, we can predict that the answer will depend on the extent to which telecommunications advances are applied to meet commercial versus popular ends. If funding for communications projects continues to stem primarily from private enterprise and corporate advertising revenues, one can expect that mass communications technologies will continue to be used in ways that reinforce stereotyping and manipulative control of the elderly, as they have in the past. To the extent that funding can be accomplished through public sector grants and viewer contributions, bypassing corporate dominance over programming priorities, one can expect to see at least some relaxation of ageist biases in media and, hence, a more realistic view of old age in American culture.

NOTES

1. Among the most frequently cited studies documenting ageist biases in media content are Francher (1973), Petersen (1973), Aronoff (1974), Northcott (1975), Harris and Feinberg (1977), Signorielli and Gerbner (1977), Smith (1979), Gerbner et al. (1980), and England, Kuhn, and Gardner (1981). Kubey (1980), and U.S. House of Representatives Select Committee on Aging (1977), provide useful overviews of these literatures.
2. "Deviant" is used here to mean non-normative.
3. Even PBS has not been entirely devoid of commercial influences. Corporate grants to public television are often undertaken as a public relations ploy to boost a company's image in the eyes of consumers. Programming contributions from multinational corporations are given selectively to support projects that do not directly challenge their preferred interpretation of economic reality. Mobil Oil, for example, would be unlikely to fund a documentary that contained criticism of excessive oil profiteering at the expense of consumers.
4. See Hartz (1955), MacPherson (1962), Lodge (1975), and Devine

(1972) for accounts of the historical pervasiveness of the Lockean individualist ideology as the dominant American belief system. Hartz (1955:11) argues that "the American way of life" can best be understood as "a nationalist articulation of Locke," including the notions of rugged individualism, competition, limited government, sacrosanct property, and regulation of economic life through market mechanisms. Devine (1972) provides empirical evidence, based on an exhaustive study of nationwide polls, that these ideas do in fact comprise the underlying belief system of the majority of Americans.

5. See Siebert, Peterson, and Schramm (1956) on the evolution of the libertarian theory of the press in the American context. This is in contrast to the "social responsibility" theory of the press, which holds that freedom of the press cannot be defined apart from the responsibility for the social consequences of its actions. Social responsibility theorists place greater emphasis on the functions of promoting democratic processes and fostering public enlightenment and less emphasis on the functions of servicing the economic market and providing entertainment. See Commission on Freedom of the Press (1947), Gerald (1963), and Rivers and Schramm (1969).

6. George Gerbner (1961) has described contemporary mass media as "the cultural arm of American industry."

7. On the issue of social control and status quo maintenance via mass communications media, see Klapper (1960), Lazarsfeld and Merton (1971), and Garnham (1979).

8. In traditional societies, dramatic stories and folk-tales contain warnings that, should the rules that uphold the present order of things be upset, retribution will inevitably follow for the violators. With the development of advanced communications technologies, these authority-maintenance functions are increasingly assumed by mass media. Innis (1951) argues that in any era or cultural setting, the available media influence the social order. Control of communications implies control of both social organization and consciousness. Ball-Rokeach (1980:50) argues, from a conflict theory perspective, that a hierarchical social structure is legitimized by convincing the public at large that inequalities are "necessary and proper."

9. A stereotype is defined here as a simplified, largely inaccurate conception or image which has become standardized through popular usage. For discussions of the most prevalent old-age stereotypes in American culture, see Tuckman Lorge (1953), McTavish (1971), Wood (1971), Bennett and Eckman (1973), Weinberger and Millham (1975), and Green (1981).

10. See, for example, U.S. House of Representatives Select Committee on Aging (1977:32-33, 50, 96-97).

11. Note that we are not suggesting that there is a conscious conspiracy by broadcasters and advertisers to frustrate the needs of elderly media consumers but rather that neglect of their needs is an unintentional by-product of the predominance of profit maximization over other priorities. One of the reasons that negative media stereotypes are so difficult to eradicate is that the process of perpetuating them is inadvertent and largely unconscious for the persons who participate in it. Advertising boards for the major corporations are merely attempting to market their products according to the rules of the game as they understand them and are thus not consciously planning to tighten the noose of social control on the elderly.

12. There is an interesting parallel here between prime-time television which substantially underrepresents youth and the elderly and theories of age stratification suggested by Martin, Bengtson, and Acock (1974) and Agnello (1973). Martin's research on alienation and age has shown that the highest levels of alienation consistently occur among youth and the elderly. Martin's explanation for this phenomenon is that in modern industrialized societies the middle-aged generation effectively controls most of the resources of the social system, tending to dominate or "command" its activities. This makes integration into mainstream social life difficult for both youth and the elderly, who find themselves alienated and relegated to a subordinate status by the dominant, middle-aged "command generation." Consistent with Martin's work, research by Agnello indicates that youth and the elderly experience the highest levels of "political powerlessness." Like Martin, Agnello argues that this pattern reflects dominance over societal resources by the middle-aged generation, which leaves youth and the elderly feeling powerless and excluded.

13. Gerbner et al. (1977) observed that elderly black women "are only cast to be killed. They rarely have any other role."

14. Results of this Hemming and Ellis (1976) poll should be treated as illustrative rather than confirmatory, since the survey was based on an unscientific sample of readers.

15. See Opinion Research Corporation (1957), Meyersohn (1961), Schramm (1969), Israel and Robinson (1972), Bogart (1972), Harris (1974), Chaffee and Wilson (1975), Davis et al. (1976), Nielsen (1974), Doolittle (1977), Comstock et al. (1978), Young (1979), and Kubey (1980:17-18).

16. For corroboration of these trends, see also Chaffee and Wilson (1975)

and Davis et al. (1976).

17. Calculations were made by the author based on University of Michigan Institute for Social Research archive data (originally analyzed by Dimmick, McCain, and Bolton, 1979). The percentage of respondents who indicate that they watched "a good many" programs about political campaigns during national election years increases from 29.2 percent in the early adult phase (21-29 years) to 51.5 percent among elderly adults in the 60-69 age category, then levels off to 47.6 percent in the 70-79 category.

18. Additional support for Graney's (1974:88-86) explanation can be found in studies by Petersen (1973), Danowski, (1975), Davis (1971:156), Wenner (1976), and Swank, (1979). Petersen (1973) suggests that television personalities such as soap opera characters compensate for lost personal relationships and thereby reduce the sense of social isolation. Danowski (1975) points out that personal and mediated forms of communication tend to be inversely related over the life span, and that therefore the relationship between mass media use and more direct interpersonal communication is probably substitutive. Davis (1971) finds that television serves a companionship function, and that is aids in dividing the day into time segments for the elderly. Wenner (1976) has isolated the major uses of the media by the elderly, namely, social disengagement, combating disengagement, and as a source of conversational material. Swank's (1979) findings demonstrate the tendency of elderly media consumers to match needs with gratification sources.

19. See Mead (1934:142-255) and Cooley (1902:151-153). In making their point that reality is socially constructed, Berger and Luckman (1966:150) argue that feedback from significant others is particularly important for the ongoing confirmation of one's identity.

20. Estes (1979:3) observes that "an examination of the social definitions of aging is important because these definitions are likely to become social reality. . . ."

21. See Signorielli and Gerbner (1977), U.S. House of Representatives Select Committee on Aging (1978b:88-95), Aronoff (1974), Francher (1973), and Hesse (1974).

22. Supervisors have been found to view older employees as being more resistant to change, less promotable to a position requiring innovative thinking, less interested in learning about new technological developments, less capable of handling jobs requiring physical exertion, and less trainable in new skills than younger employees of equal ability (Rosen and Jerdee, 1976). These preconceptions are often in-

volved in managerial decisions to avoid investments in continued development of older workers. See also Palmore and Manton (1973) for evidence that older employees are more frequently subjected to discrimination and unjust treatment on the job than other categories of workers.

23. See de Sola Pool (1968), Baer (1978), and Reid (1977) for discussions of anticipated trends in telecommunications technologies over the next several decades and their social implications.

24. The QUBE cabletelevision system in Cincinnati, for instance, provides up to 60 channels, in addition to a two-way interactive connection which permits viewers to talk back to the tube by punching viewer-input buttons. For a description of the Cincinnati CATV project, see Steiner (1972). Other major cities that already have cable television systems (or are in the process of installing them) include New York, Los Angeles, Boston, Miami, Dallas, Houston, Chicago, Pittsburg, Detroit, Cleveland, Columbus, Philadelphia, Indianapolis, and Milwaukee.

25. In a 1977 survey of elderly viewer preferences, 70 percent of the respondents felt there were too few educational offerings, 61 percent felt there was too little information about available social services and 61 percent felt existing televison programs did not provide enough programming on problem solving (Real, Anderson, and Harrington, 1980).

26. Two landmark cases in recent years were *Williams and Wilkins* v. *the United States* (copyright infringement by photocopying) and *Universal City Studios and Walt Disney Production* v. *Sony Corporation* (copyright infringement by consumer videotaping). In the latter case, Universal and Walt Disney launched a heavily financed legal battle against Sony Corporation, makers of Betamax® videorecorders. Entertainment industry spokesmen argued that the sale of Betamax recorders to consumers should be curtailed because owners were routinely using the devices to tape copyrighted materials, and that taping diminishes the potential marked for sale of those materials. A San Francisco U.S. Court of Appeals ruled in 1981 that consumer use of the machines violated federal copyright law, but this ruling was overturned by a 5-4 U.S. Supreme Court decision in 1984. While Sony Corporation was absolved, the decision did not rule out the possibility that producers may sue individual Betamax owners for "illegitimate use" of the machines. See Rubin (1984:1,7) and Press, Huck, and Clausen (1981:119).

CHAPTER 11

THE EVOLUTION OF AGEISM IN AMERICA

AGEISM, like racism and sexism, implies segregation, prejudice, discrimination, and an inferior social status for those affected.[1] Ageism is an ideology, or an action-related system of ideas
(Friedrich, 1963:89), whose purpose is to explain and justify society's customs regarding old persons[2], ranging from the distribution
of rewards to old people to norms about what constitutes proper age-
related behavior.

The concept of ageism can be analyzed both in terms of cultural
and institutional ageism. Cultural ageism refers to basic "values, tra-
ditions, and assumptions" about the nature of old persons.[3] On an
individual level these assumptions take the form of prejudice or pri-
vately held beliefs about what old people are like,[4] and these beliefs
are frequently supported by stereotypes (systematic prejudices) promoted at a societal level. Persons come to be judged or categorized
on the basis of group membership. Our mental images of "the old"
are learned.

Institutional ageism is the conceptualization at the institutional
level of these beliefs. It frequently involves discriminatory behavior
in the form of policies and procedures of institutions — such as corporations, unions, or schools — which systematically exclude old
persons from options available to others.[5] Merton has pointed out
that discrimination can occur in the absence of individual prejudice
(Merton, 1970). When discrimination is legitimized as part of bureaucratic policy, it can be justified as "unintentional," "beyond individual control," or "normatively based." Individuals carrying out

discriminatory policies may or may not themselves be prejudiced. Mandatory retirement rules represent an example of institutional ageism.

Gerontologists as a group tend to hold cultural and institutional ageism equally responsible for the devalued status of the elderly in America, although cultural ageism is sometimes considered more salient. Some of the most-quoted commentators — e.g. Fischer, Achenbaum, and Linden — emphasize cultural values which have contributed to increased segregation of the old over the years. Linden points to a decline in respect for old persons due to a loss of authority, the exaggerated premium on the physical and psychological attributes of youth, and the shift away from family responsibilities towards the elderly (Linden, 1956). Fischer speaks of increased secularism, industrialization, an egalitarianism of age promoted by the French and American Revolutions, and transcendentalism as probable catalysts for the development of ageism (Fischer, 1978). And Achenbaum, focusing on the period between 1865 and 1914, mentions a growing population of old persons, negative descriptions of senescence in medical literature, and a new valuation of youth as the symbol of progress (Achenbaum, 1974).

While agreeing with these analyses, we do not feel that they sufficiently capture the relationship between the causes and effects of ageism. It is our contention that cultural ideas in the form of values and prejudices cannot be separated from their material context. To distinguish between cultural and institutional ageism is to artificially sever the production of ideas from their systemization at the institutional level. For example, what changes in resource control and/or labor policies may have underpinned a decline in respect for the elderly or a premium on the physical and psychological attributes of youth? We know from our discussion of social control in Chapter 2 that an increased division of labor in the nineteenth century, as evidenced in Taylorism, reflected managements' desire to simultaneously make laborers interchangeable while eliminating any need for skilled older workers.

In this chapter we shall argue that ageism is an outgrowth of the more encompassing ideology of liberalism which itself was used by early capitalists in England to explain and justify capitalist expansion. American colonists embraced an unusually narrow version of liberalism, one advanced by Locke. We shall further argue that this more narrow and harsh ideology of liberalism was reinterpreted in the nineteenth century and used to rationalize ageism in the interests of an emergent corporate class. We are thus arguing that the ideology of both liberalism and ageism arose in response to transitions and disruptions within the economic realm and in support of the interests of certain economic groups. And finally — and with no small sense of irony — we shall suggest that because of the specific roots of ageism in America, it may only seriously recede when older Americans are denied systematic retirement and are subject to the same job market controls as other adult age groups.

A case has been made elsewhere that an ideology of sexism was necessary to rationalize the economic basis of discrimination against women.[6] According to this reasoning, the development of private property, based on accumulated surplus of agricultural products as a significant power source, caused men to be concerned with inheritance rights and family lineages. The quest for clear paternity rights led women to be bridled with a double standard of sexual conduct and increasingly segregated from direct access to economic resources. Concurrently, an image of their innate inferiority and economic marginality was perpetuated to justify their oppression and segregation.

Similarly, others have argued that an ideology of racism evolved to rationalize the expansion of and exploitation by mercantilist European powers overseas.[7] It is our contention that an ideology of ageism developed within late-1800 American society to reinforce the economic disengagement of older workers deemed necessary by the owners and managers of the new private corporations.

We are not arguing that ageism, as a mask for economic interests, is a new phenomenon nor that capitalism is a prerequisite for its existence. But we shall make the case that early America's dominant ideology reflected economic interests and was modified to the detriment of old persons when economic changes so required.

We begin with a discussion of the ideology of liberalism, its close affinity with capitalism, and ways in which Locke's, and therefore, America's, liberalism differed from earlier versions.

LIBERALISM, LOCKE, AND THE ROOTS OF LAISSEZ-FAIRE

Liberalism is a set of ideas that evolved over a long period of English history and eventually justified a separation of political power and institutions from economic institutions. Enlightenment thinkers advanced liberalism as a cohesive ideology to justify this separation only after the state had assisted the establishment of capitalism. The emergence of liberalism was closely associated with the implementation of mercantilism in England, an economic philosophy that attempted to reconcile vestiges of feudalism, certain religious beliefs, and an increasingly secular outlook.[8] England's mercantilist period is generally defined as extending from 1550-1763, and it was no accident that it followed in the wake of Henry VIII's reign.

Henry VIII, in breaking with Rome, confiscating Church properties and distributing them to his supporters, opened the door to numerous ideological questions, not the least of which was who or what was to replace the Church at the center of collective and individual life. Henry's answer was that the state in the form of God's monarchy now assumed the functions of the old universal church. In doing so, he made the Church and state one, sanctified worldly processes, and set up a situation where church and state could only be separated in the future by denying God's direct will in secular activities (Williams, 1966:36-37). His actions also underpinned questions about what the relationship between private property and religion was to be, as well as eventual tensions between the Crown and Parliament and between the individual and the state. These tensions did not fully erupt for one hundred years, and in the meantime mercantilism reconciled these philosophical loose ends with a religiously informed economic theory.

Merchantilist policies were pursued by virtually all of the Elizabethan and Stuart monarchs who reigned after Henry VIII and until the Cromwellian revolution in the 1640s. These policies were informed by feudalism in depicting England as a "manor" whose members had reciprocal responsibilities, protections, and obligations and by the biblical injunction to promote the welfare and common good of God's corporate world and inhabitants (Williams, 1966:40).[9] The beliefs of both St. Thomas Aquinas and Jean Calvin underscored the idea that monarchs and subjects had to control economic changes to promote the common good as well as anticipate and offset social consequences of these changes. St. Aquinas, for example, had argued earlier that the state had to regulate property for the common good, and Calvin said that while any calling was a satisfactory way for showing discipline to God, if an individual had two callings, it was his responsibility to choose the one that contributed most to the common good. There were arguments about who should control the central government in England but not about the need for a national state (Williams, 1966:37).

Materially, the mercantilist economic theory was grounded in beliefs that foreign policy was the key to domestic welfare and that the common good was best served by monarchs encouraging internal protections (tariffs) and external markets. This economic theory provided the rationale for empire-building, a part of which America would someday be. While monarchs subsidized explorations abroad and dispensed corporate charters to establish commerce on the monarchy's behalf, legislation was passed to encourage food production and provide for relief. Poverty was viewed as a corporate or system problem — not an individual frailty — and expansionist and protectionist economic policies were assumed to benefit England and therefore its poor (Williams, 1966:40-43).[10] Through these policies England's economy was slowly transformed from a land-based one to a capitalist one.

Many of the values associated with the ideology of liberalism, such as the sanctity of property, individualism, competition, political representation, and the harnessing of nature for humankind's use, were all present, if subdued, during this early mercantilist period. It is important to note that England's emergent liberal tradition carried with it the concept of community responsibility and thus had a generosity of spirit that was to come under attack with Cromwell and that would be essentially absent from Locke's brand of liberalism. In the wake of Cromwell's Puritanist Revolution and the Glorious Revolution of 1688, Locke formalized a version of liberalism that would eventually justify an unrestrained interpretation of individualism in American society. But Locke's liberalism was also premised on an assumption of economic expansionism (Williams, 1966:65; Gough, 1979).

Questions spurred by Henry VIII's actions, such as who was to run the state and what was the relationship to be between the Crown and Parliament, between the individual and the state, and between property and religion, became paramount during the seventeenth century. Answers took twists that combined capitalists' concerns with religious and political changes. Locke's particular ideology reflected all of these twists.

To the extent that religion and the monarch were one, the Glorious Revolution of 1688 servered religion from the state in consolidating political power within the Parliament. This formal separation of church and state was augmented by the arguments of many Protestant capitalists that God resided in individuals, not the state, and could best be served thorugh the free exercise of individual industry (Williams, 1966:47-48). This last reference was a criticism of the state's delegation of corporate charters to some persons and not to others and thus a case for unbridled competition and serverance of economic activity from state oversight (Laslett, 1967; Webb and Webb, 1927). Also, during the post-Cromwell period (1650-1688), Puritan and Calvinist beliefs were recast to mean that individual worldy success was a sign of religious virtue, and poverty, a function of sin — particularly of lust and laziness (Weber, 1958:155-161, 177-180, 263-268; Tawney, 1954:98-106).

All of these shifts in beliefs helped sanctify private property and sever religion from the polity and the polity from the economic arena. Religion would again be used as a rationale for unbridled economic competition and accumulation of wealth in nineteenth century America, but, as we shall see, morality would be associated with the fruits of economic activity, not with the activity itself.

Locke articulated an ideology that reinforced the property interests of a rising bourgeoise upper class (Kellner, 1978:46). Now that capitalists had benefitted from state development of foreign markets, the upper echelons of this capitalist class saw the major purpose of government as the protection of property. This belief served as the linchpin of the Lockean paradigm which also emphasized individualism, competition, a limited state, and scientific specialization or fragmentaiton.[11] All reinforce one another. Individualism states that no community is greater than the sum of its parts. Scientific specialization, to the contrary, declares that the whole of nature can be comprehended through study, mastery, and dominance of its parts. This atomized perspective on community and nature was extended to the market, and the emphasis on competition (as eventually articulated by Adam Smith) states that the use of private property can best be controlled by each individual proprietor vying in the marketplace to satisfy consumer wants.

When all of these values are considered together, a somewhat anarchistic or laissez-faire picture emerges,[12] a picture underscored by Locke's ambivalence toward the state. The state was to be essentially severed from economic activity while responsible for protecting property and its unequal distribution. At a later point this would mean the government should "clean up" social problems created by capitalist expansion without trying to prevent social problems through economic planning. The state was thus invested with the difficult task of appearing neutral in order to maintain its legitimacy while simultaneously facilitating capitalist expansion and aligning with the needs of that group in which Locke always intended power to rest: upper-class capitalists.[13] Locke's liberalism was void of any community ethos or notion of the collective social good; it emphasized limited government activities and suggested that human beings could be politically free through exercising the franchise while economically unfree.[14] Locke's laissez-faire liberalism served as the basis for a conservative revolution in late-1800 America when laissez-faire became emergent corporations' bailiwick; in his own country, England, Locke's views lost out to a more generous version of liberalism, one that retained its communal core.

The suggestion that certain religious values anticipated Locke's ideology may help explain why the values he promoted were so aggressively and unquestionably embraced by American colonists.[15] Many colonists were Puritans and Calvinists who accepted the harsh interpretations of their religions that were unleashed in the wake of Cromwell. Success in one's "calling" was viewed as God's approval and poverty as an emblem of lust and sloth. The huge tracts of territory available (unlike in England) no doubt implied that hard work could pay off in property ownership, at least if one was not a slave, black, an Indian, or a woman (Rossiter, 1953:70-71). Thus, there was no religious or material reason for invoking the state to protect the common good, since it would presumably evolve through individual and congregational efforts to master nature and to prosper.

The protection of property was ensconced within the *Federalist Papers* and the Constitution as the purpose of government, and people were deemed to be free "in proportion to their property".[16] Nature was to be taken apart to be used and controlled, and individuals competing in the pursuit of economic gain could only contribute to the good of the community. What this particular brand of liberalism added up to was a definition of success as the individualistic production of wealth and income, and fulfillment as a lonely struggle where the fit will survive and the nonsurvivors will cope with the onus of being unfit.[17]

The seeds of communal ostracism of any nonproductive persons were always present, but the agrarian nature of the society prevented economic and familial segregation of the elderly for a long time.[18] Religion, since it was invested with an age hierarchy, also helped protect older Americans from the impact of this materialism for a while. Perhaps of most importance was a tendency among early American political leaders to impose the mercantilist policies with which they were familiar and as a consequence delay the full-fledged blooming of laissez-faire liberalism. Laissez-faire was the specific version of liberal ideology that explained and justified the ostracism of America's old, but, as we shall now see, it had to be recast in order to do so.

REINTERPRETATION OF THE IDEOLOGY AND THE RISE OF AGEISM

Interestingly, the concept of laissez-faire which was always implicit within the Lockean paradigm originally took the form of Jefferson's independent farmer — at the same time that the federal government was openly and directly overseeing economic development. It was not until the period between 1850 and 1900 that the emerging corporate community seized upon the concept to try and repel state intervention within the economic sphere. Up until then, Hamilton's mercantilist vision of a government assisting growth prevailed (Lerner, 1963).

The federal government had built roads, bought stock in canal companies, conducted surveys, improved waterways, constructed telegraph lines, issued protective tariffs, and made interest-free loans, to mention just a few "interventionist" activities. All of these activities helped provide a subsidized infrastructure for economic expansion. By 1850, the government also initiated one of its first "cleanup" projects on behalf of the business community as industrialization came to require an unskilled but basically disciplined labor force. By building old-age homes, almshouses, and mental institutions, the government segregated the "less eligible" competitors of society thereby freeing up relatives to work, putting the fear of God in those who might feign poverty, and making it clear that social and political participation are predicated upon economic participation (Scull, 1977:15-40).

Up until about 1830, government facilitation of economic growth took the form of charters granted to public corporations for building roads, bridges, canals, etc. By the 1830s a distinction was increasingly made between these public corporations chartered for community purposes and the emerging private corporation formed for profit. It was also at this time that the Lockean ideology was being recast and business preparing to wave the banner of laissez-faire. And, as has been noted, the government had begun to move toward cleaning up the social fallout of capitalist growth by tending to those who did not fit into the new economic order and away from direct oversight of growth. It was not until the Civil War, however, that the individualistic and materialistic core of the Lockean liberal ideology had its most profound fruitions.[19]

By 1865 the corporate status was no longer a special privilege chartered to a few on behalf of community needs. Rather, it was now presented as a useful form for any economic activity, and its new functions were to concentrate and accumulate capital through profit maximization and stimulated consumer demands. Eventually these goals were to become so legitimized that the purpose of law was interpreted to be enlarging the private corporations' maneuverability; indeed, in 1919 the Michigan Supreme Court declared that the competitive pursuit of profits, not pricing in the interests of workers or the community as a whole, was management's primary obligation (Hurst, 1970:82-83). This definition of a corporation's purpose represented a total break with the concepts of just price based in feudalism and the common good which rationalized much of mercantilist capitalism.

Business managed to effect this legitimization of unbridled competition by shifting the right to pursue property from the individual to the private corporation. Jefferson's idealized farmer working a plot of land no longer epitomized individualistic pursuit of property rights. Rather, the corporation was now promoted as the embodiment of property and business as the protectors of the American ideology. Ironically, as individualism was interpreted more and more in terms of survival of the fittest within the new private corporate sector[20], the workplace itself suppressed individualism with its increasingly rationalized organization. Indeed, this was one of the corporation's objectives.

The new corporate goal of increasing profits at the least cost called for extracting surplus value from workers by deskilling work, making laborers interchangeable, and thereby suppressing wages. Hierarchical control within factories, speedups, long hours, and fines were some of the tools used to assure desired output levels (Edwards, 1979). Efficiency and growth became the watchwords for a drive for accumulation unprecedented in history. Between 1850 and 1900 industrial development radically altered both the workplace and society and management was continuously trying to break the traditional work and social habits of natives and arriving immigrants.[21]

Older workers were specifically portrayed as impediments to these changes. An argument sometimes offered against their employment was that the socialization of laborers, particularly immigrants, to the new regime required time and money, and thus older workers should be removed to allow newcomers' advancement — or at least the belief that they would advance (Achenbaum, 1974:56). As was suggested in Chapter 2, the evidence indicates other reasons for increasing discrimination against older workers. Many were highly skilled and accustomed to working autonomously, and both skill levels and worker autonomy were prime targets for elimination as corporations sought surplus labor value (Braverman, 1974). Older workers were also undesirable because, having experienced a more humanely paced work life, they tended to resist the drive toward ever-rising output. And they were, of course, more costly in the short run due to seniority and sometimes more stressed by workplace changes than their younger peers.

Corporations' reinterpretation and promotion of laissez-faire were not only directed toward increased profits and control over the stock and flow of labor (Graebner, 1980) but also toward state governments whose labor protection laws were viewed as obstacles to economic "progress." A major goal of laissez-faire policies was to regularize the marketplace through acquisitions and rationalization while simultaneously defining the marketplace as a national rather than a state problem. By doing so, corporate leaders hoped the Supreme Court would invoke the due process clause of the Fourteenth Amendment and nullify all state restrictions on private property, that is, on corporations as now defined.[22]

It is important to note that just as revised Protestant beliefs had reinforced Locke's conceptualization of laissez-faire liberalism, so were they used to justify laissez-faire capitalism in America. These beliefs, however, were applied to the rich and the poor with a double standard. The Calvinist idea that godliness was expressed through individual industry was transformed to mean that godliness was connoted through individual prosperity — at the same time that an individual capitalist's economic actions were void of morality (Gutman, 1976:80-84). Thus, any economic activity among capitalists was morally fair, but to interfere with an entrepreneur's freedom by regulating his corporation was to violate "divine" or market law (Fine, 1956:3-166). At the upper levels, the marketplace knew no morality. At the lower levels, twelve-hour days were justified to keep workmen and children from "vicious amusements" and to assure their moral reform (Gutman, 1976:19). Poverty and a failure to prosper were equated with sin. These beliefs conveniently liberated the consciences of the upwardly mobile while demoralizing the poor, many of whom had accepted the axioms of Christianity about brotherhood on earth.[23] Individualism was now truly unrestrained and incarnate in the "acquisitive" corporate men.

In addition to this ruthless definition of individualism, late nineteenth century America experienced a number of other cultural changes that boded poorly for old people. Older Americans had indeed increased as a proportion of the population, youth was now glorified as the means to "progress," and families were less willing to care for their members. Unquestionably, these cultural changes facilitated ageism. But it is our contention that the increasingly respectable profit motive of emergent private corporations underpinned the chain of events. Certainly Darwin's theory of evolution, its application by Spencer to the social and business worlds, and James' pragmatism, with its implicit experimental opportunism, all contributed (Hofstadter, 1944; Spencer, 1868; Dewey, 1939). And the industrialization process, so frequently cited by gerontologists as a cause of ageism in America, played a part.

But all of this occurred within a context where laissez-faire liberalism was used to justify and reinforce the economic interests of the private corporation. The industrialization process may be speeded up through increased worker efficiency and output, but it does not require this efficiency in itself — profit goals do. It is also interesting to note that some of the earliest studies of senescence conducted during this late 1800 period were sponsored by or directed toward the new insurance industry.[24] So again, while negative descriptions of the aging process put out by medical personnel no doubt contributed to ageism, neither the purposes for the research nor the distribution of its findings occurred in a material vacuum. Increased profits were the goal, and elimination of older male workers was one desired means.

Just as the idealization of youth helped reinforce the corporation's need for a certain kind of laborer, so did it underscore its need for a certain kind of consumer. Youth is a metaphor for energy, restless mobility, appetite, and a state of wanting (Sontag, 1972:31); what combination of features could reflect a more malleable worker or a more ravenous consumer? Youth was a commodity whose exploitable and marketable apex had come. Young and middle-aged men came to epitomize the "norm," the "good," and "adulthood," while old men joined women on the sidelines of resource control.[25]

Even if the elderly's authority had begun to wane by 1800, as some claim,[26] there is no question that their increased segregation from the labor force contributed to a stereotype of their being helpless, dependent, incompetent, and nice — a stereotype similar to those that were already in place for women and blacks.[27]

Studies suggest that Americans associate "deviants" with being "out of control" (Lemert, 1972). Within this society there is probably no more serious impetus to being out of control than losing access to critical resources such as jobs and incomes. Thus, it is not surprising that the newly found economic marginality of older American males led to a revision of their image. For many years old men were vested with the virtues ascribed to "masculinity" (Fischer, 1978:226) — competence and autonomy — but with their fall from economic participation, they joined women, blacks, and other dependent categories outside the mainstream. If ageism at core involves a "dread of powerlessness," as some have argued[28], the material and class bases for this dread were laid in the late 1800s.

Prior to the Civil War, old persons were characterized by qualities of stability, self-control, and piety, and in the early aftermath of Darwinism, *they* were portrayed as the fittest.[29] But by 1880, white male professionals were emphasizing physical and mental disabilities that accompany old age and arguing that longevity in the absence of health and a capacity to work is undesirable. It had in fact become so. Writers went so far as to describe the old as alienated, anxious, resentful, morose, and welcoming death.

A complex and pervasive theory of ageism thus appeared to help rationalize the privileged position of white middle-aged workers and corporate owners. As the proportion of gainfully employed males over 65 dropped precipitously, academic commentators also did their part in rationalizing this exclusion. Older workers were described as slow, worn out, and demoralizing for other workers (Hoffman, 1906:3). Since women had long been economic dependents, their employment rate after age 65 did not change much. Elderly unemployment was perceived as a male problem, a drop from grace or a privileged status, as it were.

Two aspects of this transition need to be emphasized. One is the fact that some of the descriptions used to justify discrimination against the old had been around for centuries and remain with us today. And second, while these prejudicial tools had always been available, their application in the late 1800s epitomized the victim-blaming strategy which was implicit within Locke's brand of liberalism and its economic and social anarchism.

Stereotypes of old persons were nothing new and usually reflected intergenerational tensions over resource control. From the time of Horace (20 B.C.) onward, the elderly have been depicted in literature as having a desire for gain, being miserly, praising the good old days, and condemning younger generations.[30] Cicero (44-43 B.C.) further argued that old age is adjudged unhappy because it takes away from life activities, diminishes physical vigor, lessens sensory pleasures, and is only a short distance from death (Cicero, 1967:10).

The physical descriptions of old age advanced by Cicero have remained basically unchanged for 2,000 years, and old age has routinely been invested with a presumed loss in hearing, taste, sight, sexual appetite, and vigor.[31] And, in fact, research indicates that *some* loss tends to occur with extreme old age along these dimensions, though findings are not conclusive and in some cases contradictory.[32]

What has been of much greater importance than the stereotype or its basis in reality are its content and purposes. Who promotes it, toward what ends, and how well defended are the targets? Prior to the growth of industrialization and a wage-dependent labor force, old persons were capable of using property or agricultural independence as protective weapons against any greed or resentment among offspring. They might be ridiculed or hated, but they could not as a group be excommunicated from the productive force.

As large numbers of people became dependent upon employers for economic survival, the extant values of the Lockean liberalism were reinterpreted and latent prejudice against old people took increasingly restrictive forms. The concept of "natural rights," as originally advanced by Locke, referred to a presumed equality among men in nature and was interpreted by American colonists as a celebration of each white male's ability to cope for himself and to create a new society. With the introduction of Darwinism and the notion of individual atavism (or nonequality in nature), the concept of natural rights was altered to mean that society could be improved through the transformation of individuals (Davis, 1975:1-35; Schrag, 1978:236-241). As the needs of capital became more specific and the population more pluralistic, the belief in controlling nature by concentrating on its parts (scientism) was focused upon individual behavior modification; those who did not conform to the white middle-aged male ideal were viewed as atavistic, nonproductive, deviant, and in need of rehabilitation, or at the very least in need of social management.[33]

The ideology of ageism which solidified during the late 1800s was thus the product of a perceived need by employers to discriminate against the old and a culmination of ideological forces begun years earlier. Specifically, we are arguing that institutional discrimination triggered a process whereby the elderly became segregated from the mainstream and increasingly controlled, a process that occurred rapidly and formidably because corporations successfully reinterpreted uniquely American values in the interests of maximizing profits. Concurrently, the rise of wage dependency underscored the idealized value of competition. A scarcity ethos was fostered, and labor groups also discriminated against those labeled "less eligible" or different.[34]

One of the paradoxes of American life is that while industrialization led to what has been called a "modern" economy, individuals have been motivated through fear of survival, a characteristic usually associated with "primitive" societies.[35] The only way to be "safe" in America is to be a success, and Americans have functioned under an assumption that others' gains are their losses and vice versa.[36] This in itself undermines a sense of community.

The emphasis upon individualism, as noted, contributed to a situation where those deemed "less eligible" producers could be ascribed with negative characteristics. Their differences — in this case, senescence — were used to explain their exclusion from the labor force, and the precipitous decline in resource control which followed further contributed to their reputations for being nonproductive, inferior, and eventually in need of special attention. The unemployed elderly thus became an official social problem at the turn of this century.

The sanctity of private property and the value of a limited state, promoted by Locke, always implied difficulties for the government in solving social problems. The government, while being expected to clean up the fallout of private enterprise, has always been limited by the kinds of solutions that are acceptable to the business community. And so it was that Social Security eventually passed in a form that emphasized work-related criteria for eligibility, avoided redistribution of wealth, and actually exacerbated economic inequalities (Lubove, 1968; Pechman and Okner, 1974).

The most important aspects of Social Security legislation for the purpose of this discussion were the ways in which it officially legitimized existing employment discrimination against the old and created a recognized population of economically deviant and socially devalued persons — old people. Both of these changes helped to further solidify stereotypes of older Americans.

STEREOTYPES

Earlier in this discussion we pointed out certain images of the elderly which have appeared in literature over the past 2,000 years. These have included the ideas that age brings miserliness, praise of the good old days, condemnation of younger generations, and loss in sensory and activity levels. Some of these imply generational struggles, but as was noted, the systematic loss of economic leverage among the elderly, as a group, only took place with rationalization of the workplace. And because of the vigorous primacy accorded market mechanisms in America, this fall from grace was particularly harsh.

Up until the 1880s religious beliefs and the familial age hierarchy were still strong enough for writers to invest old men with such attributes as benevolence and stability of character (Achenbaum, 1974; Fischer, 1978). After 1880 the presumed fitness of the elderly which had been associated with their longevity was played down, and longevity was not valued in the absence of employment. As older workers became more frequently disengaged from the work force, they were characterized as sickly, alienated, anxious, resentful, unpleasant, and suicidal. Interestingly, while Social Security legislation assisted people in "succeeding" by being able to pay their own ways, it did not resolve the stress experienced by old people or lead to a cessation of negative images.

Studies of attitudes toward old persons as well as content analyses of media portrayals suggest that putting money in their pockets and transferring their dependence from employers to the community probably augmented the status decline they were experiencing.[37] Dependence upon contributions, even when disguised as an "insurance program," not only implies an inferior socioeconomic position but can reinforce it.

The contention of ancients that old people praise the good old days finds expression today in commonly held beliefs that they are "not very open-minded and adaptable," "rigid and dogmatic," and "conservative" (Harris, 1975; Rosen and Jerdee, 1976; Tuckman and Lorge, 1953). The idea that they condemn younger generations is manifest in the belief of younger persons that old people "tend to resent younger people" and "are sometimes inconsiderate of the views of younger persons" (Kogan and Shelton, 1962a; McTavish, 1971). The physical losses with which they have been associated over the years now take the form of such descriptions as not very physically active, not too bright and alert, dependent upon children, and always hurting themselves; the prevalent belief that old persons are not active sexually speaks to a presumed loss of sensate capacities (Harris, 1975; Cobb, 1982b:38).

Just as our forebearers in the late nineteenth century began to focus upon old people's physical appearance, so do many Americans today link age with undesirable physical characteristics (Weinberger and Millham, 1975:343-348). Older Americans are still variously depicted as fearing death, clinging to life, and seeking death, and the same mixture of fear, pity, and sympathy seems to cloak these images.[38] Old people's abilities to participate within the productive sectors of the country are strongly downplayed with beliefs that they are "not very good at getting things done," "not very useful members of their community," and not preferable to younger workers on any dimensions except reliability and honesty (Harris, 1975:53; Rosen and Jerdee, 1976).

An argument can be made that these accusations and the attributes themselves, to the extent that they exist, are situationally based for the most part. For example, there is some evidence that exposure to old persons in everyday life helps mitigate against negative images (Bell and Stanfield, 1973), and the elderly's legitimized exclusion from the mainstream has only facilitated the acceptance of such ideas. Second, studies suggest that an enhanced class position can overcome the stigma of age, but in our society aging has become automatically associated with a decline in income. Our institutional arrangements thus help set up old people for problems related to age and to class position.[39] By pushing the old out of productive roles, Americans created a self-fulfilling prophecy whereby the elderly could be and have been seen as something less than human — as not functioning in an effective adult manner.

WHITE NONAGED MALES AS THE NORMATIVE STANDARD

It must be remembered that the standard for the effective adult is the white young to middle-aged workers who became the idealized and economically protected species with the rise of factories and private corporations. This is the model against which old people, women, blacks, and children are presumed to compare inadequately. The inclusion of children is important because women, blacks, and the elderly have all been invested with child-like (read not quite human/inferior) qualities over the years. There is more than a hint of atavism implied in popular portrayals of these groups.

Women have been acceptable when girlish, blacks when "primitive," and the elderly pitied when in a "second childhood." The first two groups have been denied full entrance into adult statuses, while the elderly male was presumed to have experienced but then lost the ideal status. This may help explain why older men show a high degree of sensitivity to occupying the position of "old person" (Flaste, 1979; Kogan and Shelton, 1962b). The suicide rate of older white males, for example, is higher than that for white older women and elderly blacks. One explanation of this discrepancy is that white males experience a status decline with age that blacks and women, due to previous discrimination, do not encounter.[40] The most positive images of old people detected to date among the public revolve around the notion that they are "nice," "warm," "friendly," and "wise from experience" (Harris, 1975:53). Clearly, the first three comprise part of the traditional female sex role stereotype, and to suddenly be associated with such "feminine" qualities must underscore the elderly male's sensitivity.

Women's relegation to a less than adult social position helps explain why their aging processes are so severely judged and feared. Because they have been reared to be never fully adult, they are declared obsolete earlier than men. In deviating from America's standard for female beauty (the girl), an aging women with wrinkles, flabby breasts, or veined legs is regarded with revulsion.[41]

As was noted earlier, the ideology of sexism has relied upon a pre-sumed inferiority to justify and reinforce male privileges and has in fact meant that adult roles have been most unequally distributed be-tween the sexes. The prejudices that accumulate against women as they grow older are an important manifestation of male privilege. Their many adult roles give men the freedom to age. For example, to the extent that class helps offset the stigma of age, economically solvent males are deemed "successful" at sixty-five while their poorer and more dependent female counterparts are viewed with pity and horror (Bell, 1976). Further, while the defined female role has in-volved "being" rather than "doing,"[42] one of the things males do is choose women. Their selection of younger women has been a bottom-line contributor to the double standard of aging.

Although this double standard of aging is reinforced with stereo-types of old persons presented on television and in jokes, qualities identified with masculinity (e.g. competence, autonomy, and self-control) are denied elderly males to some extent as well.

Probably no medium epitomizes America's gerontophobia as much as advertisements. One study, for example, found that 57 per-cent of monitored television ads promised "youth, youthful appear-ance, or the energy to act youthful" (Francher, 1973). Commercials suggest that the elderly are preoccupied with bodily discomforts, such as constipation, backaches, and loose dentures, and both men and women are encouraged to wash the grey away. There is evi-dence that this preoccupation with looking old was intensified if not launched in response to the systematic disengagement of older workers from the labor force in the late 1800s.

Along with articles on how hard it was for a man to get or keep a job after a certain age, magazines of that period began to run recipes for men's hair dyes and mentioned facial age as a deterrent to em-ployment. The excluded older worker was openly referred to as "the product of an industrial and economic system that thrives only on young blood," but it was inferred that he brought on his plight by not successfully masking evidence of age.[43] Thus, the correctness or morality of discrimination was not addressed, only the individual's culpability in his dilemma.

Television ads today put a particular onus on the aging woman by suggesting that she needs to soften her wrinkles, eliminate "tell-ing" age spots on her hands, and by all means not look older than her husband. Since the average woman is chronologically younger than her spouse, for reasons mentioned earlier, this playing upon a fear of appearing older underscores the more rigorous criteria of obsolescence being applied to women (Cobb, 1982a).

At the same time that women face heavy sanctions for not complying with a girlish ideal, they are also ridiculed for trying to mask the aging process. In analyzing ten popular joke books for attitudes on aging, Palmore found evidence of negative stereotypes toward men and women, but the most negative ones were reserved for women (Palmore, 1971:181-186). About 50 percent of the jokes reinforced images of the elderly in general as infirm, mentally deteriorated, sexually inactive, unhappy, or useless — images found to exist at the individual level also. The majority of jokes which dealt with retirement or sexual inactivity involved males and were mixed in terms of positive, ambivalent, or negative references. But those dealing with women as subjects — all old maid jokes and almost all age-concealment jokes — were consistently negative in viewpoint.

Even as women are relentlessly encouraged by advertisements to protect themselves from aging and its social consequences, they are simultaneously viewed sarcastically for trying to extend their sexual eligibility. It appears women are blamed for being vulnerable and for trying to lessen their vulnerability and thereby undermine their proper "place." Just as class helps offset the stigma of age for men, so does it help women offset the aging process. Those few who slip by the rigorous cultural standard and are admired for being exceptions to the "no-win bind" tend to have both money and leisure disproportionately (Sontag, 1972).

Older women's social vulnerability is further reflected in televison characterizations. The implied nonadult or nonperson status, which we have argued accompanies all but white young to middle-aged males, is reflected in the invisibility of old people, children, women, and blacks on television in comparison with their percentages of the population. Additionally, those women presented are disproportionately youthful and attractive. When older characters (1.5%) are portrayed, the women are likely to be hurt, killed, or to fail, whereas the men of similar ages more often play settled adult roles with romantic possibilities (Brown, L. 1979:18).

In keeping with the invisibility or scarcity of some groups and the vast overrepresentation of adults 30 to 54 years of age, televison depicts a world where the young and the old invariably suffer problems that are solved by adult males.[44] In both frequency and competence, the dominant figure on television is the young to middle-aged man. This has been called the "cult of competency" by one observer (Northcott, 1975:184-186). Those who "produce" also "solve," and the idealized and economically protected worker spawned in the late 1800s has penetrated all aspects of cultural life as the unstigmatized hero. White middle-aged males monopolize prime time as well as primary sector jobs.[45]

Within a context where the economic producer is viewed as the "norm," the "good," and the "healthy," this depiction of old persons, children, blacks, and women as lacking competence, autonomy, and self-control is understandable. They are, in fact, "out of control" of the means to attain society's approval and rewards. Judged by an ideology which glorifies acquisition, views individual material success as an end in itself, and portrays lone persons in a never-ending competition for limited rewards, those in less lofty or dependent positions can be ascribed with generalized incompetence. Those who are deemed unsuccessful or devalued are thus in a position to experience further discrimination, victimization, and social control.[46]

IDEOLOGY AND GROUP CONTAINMENT

It cannot be accidental that members of groups adjudged socially weak are victims of abuse within our society. It has become common knowledge that old people, women, and children serve as punching bags within some American homes. Physical characteristics, which were a primary weapon used by corporations to eliminate older workers in the late 1800s, now underpin the rationale for targeting and beating on certain individuals.[47]

The terrible irony is that those who do not measure up to the idealized successful producer are often the perpetrators of abuse. For example, many of the criminal attacks on old persons in cities are made by unemployed nonwhite adolescents who view them as easy marks for quick revenue (Antuns et al., 1977). Elderly abuse within the family has been labeled by some as a "woman's issue," not only because 80 percent of the victims are women, but also because in many instances the abuser is a woman (Kirchheimer, 1981:12). Usually these abusers are primary caretakers without access to other adult (and more highly esteemed) roles. By virtue of their gender, women *are* assumed to be nurturing, but both elderly and child abuses attest to the difficulties of "being" in a culture that values and rewards "doing."

While the assumption about women's "nature" is itself suspect, our social context mitigates against either men or women aspiring to a cult of nurturance. Since some authors see a link between being nurtured in childhood and being able to nurture in adulthood[48], the relatively low value placed on giving, as opposed to acquiring and achieving, in America may have some direct bearing on the elderly's position.

Evidence exists, for example, that the capacity to nurture is related to tolerance of and positive attitudes toward old persons.[49] On the other hand, individuals who are negatively disposed toward the elderly also tend to be somewhat high in anomie and/or authoritarian.[50] Both anomie and authoritarianism can be viewed as predictable outcomes of America's rigorous value system.

Those persons who do not measure up to expectations in the long quest for success and rewards may become pessimistic about the future, feel helpless against powerful forces, or be unable to find meaning or purposefulness in life — all of which are presumed indicators of anomie. The anticommunitarianism which is implicit in the American ideology only exacerbates the likelihood of anomic individuals as by-products. And, not surprisingly, a characteristic of an authoritarian-type person is strong contempt for weakness, being exposed, or appearing vulnerable — features associated with old persons, children, women, and the disabled in particular, and which clearly connote incompetency, nonproduction and a lack of authority within our culture.

By putting so much pressure upon societal members to succeed at any cost and holding them responsible for any shortcomings, even in the face of structured failure rates, an environment of fear and intolerance is guaranteed. The existence of anomic, authoritarian, or nonnurturing persons bodes poorly for the elderly's interpersonal welfare and represents an indirect method by which institutional arrangements contribute to the perpetuation of stereotypes and social constraints that they helped create in the first place.

The liberal ideology that emphasizes private property, individualism, competition, a limited state, and scientific fragmentaiton has resulted in a neat paradigm where victims of discrimination feel less eligible, and the economic monopoly of white young and middle-aged males remains essentially unchallenged.[51] Individuals must change, cope, or adjust to devalued positions; the structure must not be seriously altered. Behavioral scientists devise theories for and earn incomes from assisting individuals in adjusting to the status quo.

When an ideology is broadly accepted as depicting "the way things are," with consensus inferred, the ideology is hegemonic and can be maintained through "indirect rule" rather than coercion (Kellner, 1978:49-50).[52] Locke's liberalism has long been hegemonic in American society, and recognition of the importance of competition, money, and compliance with work rules serves as a blueprint for survival while masking inequities and their causes (Kellner, 19788:50). Acceptance of this particular ideology also involves blaming one's self for not measuring up, and to some degree old persons have responded to the ideologies of liberalism and ageism by being hard on one another and themselves. For example, much evidence exists that old people have internalized age norms of what is and is not appropriate behavior[53] and have been sufficiently impressed with the consequences of perceived or real vulnerability within America to be horrified of aging.

Many old persons hate the idea of aging and grow depressed with the passage of years (Clark and Anderson, 1967). Others avoid association with peers who have health problems. For some the removal of work threatens the very core of their personal and social identity which was fostered by the American way of life. And for many a cultivated dislike for old persons can only end in self-hate. Perhaps nothing helps keep devalued people in their "place" so quietly and effectively as self-hate and the debility it generates.[54] There is one school of thought that argues that even senility is a social artifact, a role grasped to end the tension and anxieties of aging, most of which are institutionally and culturally induced (Oberleder, 1969).

Earlier in this discussion we argued that a reinterpreted Lockean liberalism in conjunction with profit-oriented discrimination against older workers launched intense stereotyping of old persons. This stereotyping in turn rationalized even greater social distance of old persons from the mainstream. We further argued that this social distance contributed to older Americans' invisibility over the years, as well as to permission to victimize and abuse them. Throughout our discussion we have attempted to show the parallelism between old people's relegation to a less eligible category and that of other groups rendered inferior and deviant so as to rationalize privileges of the dominant group.

As the workplace became more and more rationalized in the late 1800s and white nonaged males solidified their privileged position, other groups became economically superfluous. Those who did not fit the competent producer model were increasingly labeled as problem categories, and attempts were made to handle these persons without altering resource or power distributions. Social Security and other employment-related insurance programs passed in the 1930s represented one response. Another one was the evolution of the treatment or medical model as a vehicle for managing parasitic or economically excommunicated population categories.

As corporations demanded higher profits and productivity, tolerance of differences lessened, and difficult relatives — be they old people, the poor, or women who did not know their place — were increasingly subject to the care of doctors and social workers. While unemployment became an accepted fact of life, political and economic dilemmas were converted into "problems" of mental illness, age, and individual maladjustment. Probably no American policies better epitomize the distilled consequences of profit making, scientism, and a limited state than nursing homes and drug management programs today.[55] When these are combined with ageism among professionals themselves,[56] legitimized victimization is the outcome.

GOVERNMENT SUPPORT OF AGEISM AND THE POTENTIAL FOR REVERSAL

The American belief in science took on new dimensions as nonorganically based behaviors came to be labeled as psychiatric disorders, and happy adjustment to the status quo, no matter how unattractive for the individual, became the treatment goal. Over the past seventy years this medical model has expanded with government support, and its cadre of personnel has become the arbitrator of what constitutes "sick," "dysfunctional," and "inappropriate" behaviors. Certainly the fact that the poor, the old, blacks, and women have been disproportionately labeled and processed through this system attests to its "cleanup" and control functions for economically superfluous groups. Widespread use of drugs has permitted the mellowing out of these dependent, uncooperative, and ugly people in greater numbers and at lower costs as institutionalization is increasingly reserved for the elderly.

The federal government has thus been busy trying to manage the casualties of private enterprise without daring to make full employment a goal or to shift resources from medical and social intervention to major improvements in the elderly's autonomy and social integration. The first strategy employs many middle-class persons; the second would render them obsolete.

Essentially one type of ageism — one of economic discrimination and exclusion — has led to a second type whereby the image of old persons as a special category must be perpetuated in order to justify tax resources now subsidizing the "aging enterprise."[57] This failure or incompetency model of old persons is easy to sustain as long as the elderly are denied access to the idealized producer positions.[58] The fact that Americans tend to stereotype old pesons as pathetic rather than arrogant, for example, is a reflection of their relatively low social power.

With few exceptions, programs and policies implemented "on behalf" of old persons over the past ten years have carried no reference to or indication of eventual termination (Estes, 1979; Schrag, 1978). Nor has responsibility for the implementation of these policies ever been seriously delegated to the elderly themselves. Both of these facts presuppose a continued defintion of old persons as failures and dependents. It is not too strong of a statement to say that advocates for the elderly have a vested interest in the existence of ageism — in both of its forms: economic exclusion and their resultant definition as a "problem" group. These advocates probably will not be the agents through which ageism is eliminated in America.

It is our contention that ageism will only be dissipated by a reversal of the process which was its impetus. As has been shown, the ideology of ageism intensified to accommodate the needs of capital. With the emergence of the private corporation and increased control of the labor force and process, many older workers were forced out of the labor market by 1900. This action was accompanied by very negative stereotypes of old persons to rationalize the solidifying of privileges among young to middle-aged males.

We foresee the likelihood that market demand for old persons is going to increase in the long run and that this change will release them as a group from ageism and the vast social controls it subsumes. We predict two major stages in the future course of ageism: (1) ageism will probably intensify during the next twenty years; (2) ageism will decline after that time for the elderly in general. The majority of old persons will be maintained in the labor force and subject to market controls, while a smaller group will be controlled by the government-financed treatment apparatus already in place. Let us briefly comment on these possible short-and long-run scenarios.

A SHORT-RUN SCENARIO

In spite of the founding colonists' intent for and the American people's myth of a limited state, all evidence suggests that Americans increasingly look to the state to resolve struggles over resource distribution, be it jobs, subsidies, or profits which are involved. Class conflict has become more politicized as numerous groups seek state support.[39] And the state which has been facilitating capital accumulation over the years through government-financed subsidies of the private sector (e.g., tax loopholes, social insurance) has become more and more fiscally hard pressed. Even as Americans speak of "too much government," they simultaneously look to the government to reduce inflation and offset its casualties. Specifically, two trends in process right now bode poorly for the elderly in the short run.

One is reluctant acknowledgment among Americans that econimc growth and improved economic circumstances are not "givens" in their lives. Many factors have contributed to this aware-

ness, including energy shortages, demands from less-developed nations for more of the world's resources and rewards, reduced foreign
markets, continued unemployment, and rising costs of living.

Whatever the sources, this recognition has resulted in a mood of
scarcity, and the old standby values of individualism and competition are being relied upon as a means for determining who is going
to "survive" the scourge of perceived scarcity. Since America has
never had a communally oriented theory of distributive justice, the
me-first and survival-of-the-fittest ethos is being openly presented as
an appropriate sorting-out device. It appears that Americans'
largesse to less well-off peers is most noticeable when perceptions of
economic growth abound.

Evidence of this niggardly approach ranges from a documented
"meism" among Americans today to the latent and overt issues of political campaigns during the early 1980s. A case can be made, for example, that much of Ronald Reagan's support came from
economically privileged groups — corporate leaders and white male
workers — who perceived an encroachment of their privileges in the
form of antidiscrimination efforts on behalf of women, blacks, and
old persons, and an unwillingness among women to keep their subordinate "place."[60] This concern with maintaining economic and social privileges was unquestionably exacerbated by the usual
assumptions and presumed losses for self if others experience gains.

One likely offshoot of this scarcity mentality will be more fighting
among single-issue lobbying groups for government resources along
with disgruntlement about revenues targeted for others. And as we
have already seen with various "tax revolts," this reluctance to share
resources with others is going to intensify the government's fiscal
bind.

The government's fiscal problems are related to a second trend
that bodes poorly for old people over the next twenty years, namely,
retrenchment in commitments to social programs. An early version
of this trend was the decarceration movement launched in the 1960s
whereby inmates of total (and costly) institutions, such as prisons
and mental hospitals, were released into communities where follow-
up care was supposedly, though infrequently, provided (Scull,
1977:134-160).

When this dumping of mental patients led to increased demands for nursing homes, the government likewise responded with maximum regard for budget restraints. Entrepreneurs were free to make money off the elderly and the government, while costs were kept down through inadequate and poorly enforced guidelines.

Today this retrenchment process and the increased jockeying of special interests for government resources are combining to underpin efforts to get the Social Security eligibility age extended (Hayes, 1980:20). Essentially, the federal government is trying to find a way to contract its commitment to America's old people. As concern mounts about a projected shrinkage in the number of producers available per retiree, presidential commissions have been charged with making recommendations for change (Cash, 1980). Whereas five persons are of working age for every person over 65 today, this figure could drop to three by the year 2030 (Greenhouse, 1980:20).

Some politicians have begun to respond to budgetary and lobbyists pressures by trying to frighten future workers about the burdens posed by old persons, and in some instances they appear to be pitting one group against another so that demand will mount for them to perform unpopular monetary surgery (Coltin, 1981:12).[61]

In the short run we believe this atmosphere of scarcity could result in some political defeats for old persons. But of most importance is the likelihood that ageism is going to continue if not intensify at the same time that the Social Security eligibility age is extended. What this means is that many older Americans could be trapped between limited employment prospects on the one hand and no Social Security payments on the other.[62]

Since wages and salaries represent less than 25 percent of the elderly's incomes, and 65 percent of aged families would be poor or near-poor without Social Security (Girschick, 1980), many persons would be in dire economic circumstances if the government alters its commitment to Social Security in the near future without guarantees for employment. And indeed, given Americans' traditionally harsh views of the poor, an increase in the number of poor old persons would intensify ageism.

Factors which might offset these events include political mobilization among old persons to unparalleled heights[63] and an unforeseen counter-hegemonic capacity on their part. Older Americans could, for example, keep whittling away at ageism by providing in-

novative solutions to their material and ideological hardships. Job
sharing and house sharing are two such strategies with considerable
potential. We are, however, somewhat reserved about the possibility
of a decline in prejudice leading to a reduction in discrimination,
rather than the reverse.

A LONG-RUN SCENARIO

A favorable aspect of this generally pessimistic assessment is that
the same demographic changes which are used to justify government
retrenchment on Social Security are also likely to alter the needs of
capital in the longer run. Just as youth became the idealized producer and consumer categories among business at the turn of the
century, so might the elderly be actively sought as workers when the
supply side of the labor force falls off. As we noted in Chapter 2,
American corporations have lost their international competitive
edge, and many have come to view routinized retirement as inefficient and non-cost effective. Some managers have even begun to
publicly extol the virtues of older workers.[64] If industries become less
energy intensive or more service oriented in the future, pursuit of
older workers will be still more likely.

Certainly there are questions about the fairness involved in encouraging the elderly to work after years of propagandizing the virtues of retirement. In fact, if the market does come to need the
presence of older workers, "encouragement" will become coercion.
The same Social Security system which has been used to legitimize
the elderly's economic discrimination could once again be used to
reinforce the needs of capital.

If for some reason the eligibility age for Social Security has not
been extended (as we suspect it will be) by the time market demand
seriously alters, it unquestionably will be at that time. Thus, the majority of older Americans may find themselves subject to workplace
discipline well into old age. The only foreseeable source of labor that
might rival the elderly under these circumstances would be immigrants deliberately drawn to America for employment purposes.[65]

CONCLUSION

Regardless of the amount of coercion or fairness involved in reintegrating old people within the economy, it is our belief that such integration is the most salient means by which ageism can be drastically undercut in America. Just as economic discrimination against old people gave rise to stereotypes of inferiority, increased social distance and thousands of caretakers benefiting from their reduced circumstances, so will economic inclusion provide their only full-proof means of being deemed productive and competent and thus for shaking off the failure model and its perpetrators.

Unlike some observers, we are not suggesting that a reduction in cultural ageism will pave the way for decreased institutional ageism or indeed even precede it, although it might. Based on our analysis of the roots of ageism in America, we contend that market needs will probably prevail. Now that employers can count on the government subsidizing certain costs of older workers, some are already finding profit-based arguments for preferring them.

According to this reasoning, it is often more economical to keep a high-paid veteran than to hire a younger one who will work for less because the older worker takes less compensatory time and requires cheaper insurance due to Medicare coverage.[66] The impetus for ageism in America swelled from ignoble motives and so will the impetus for its demise, in all likelihood.

The one dark spot on this long-term prediction centers on those segments of the elderly population who will end up in nursing homes. If discrimination against women prevails in terms of employment and Social Security benefits, then nursing homes will continue to be filled disproportionately with very old and very poor white women who outlive their spouses or peers.[67] This segment of the population will continue to be controlled by state-funded facilities and caretakers and will represent an acutely disenfranchised group or what one gerontologist refers to as the "drop-out aged."[68] They will be dropped out of the very same competency model that we predict will become more accessible — perhaps coercively so — to other old persons and will continue to provide clients for the treatment model.[69]

As older Americans come to represent a larger proportion of the population and to have more money available though participation in production, they will be more aggressively pursued by business and education facilities as consumers. Perhaps it is a fitting end for this discussion to note that a commodity such as the aged, which used to be valued for its rarity and presumed quality, is gaining value today as both a political threat and an economic resource on the basis of its relative quantity.

NOTES

1. Butler (1969) is often credited with the first conceptualization of ageism as a system of ideas.
2. This is an adaptation from Huber and Form (1973:2) where the purpose of an ideology is defined as the explanation and justification of social institutions. Because of our specific use of the term "institution" in the discussion that follows, its broader sociological meaning has been replaced here with the word customs, referring to particular social elements.
3. This definition is an adaptation of a definition of cultural racism in Jones (1972:116).
4. For a discussion of prejudice, see Allport (1958).
5. Feagin and Feagin (1978) present an overview of various ways in which institutional racism and sexism can be analyzed. These same dynamics are applicable to ageism.
6. See Engles (1902), Sacks (1974), and Amundsen (1971) for examples of this type of emphasis.
7. See Blauner (1972) and Heckter (1975) for discussions of this cause-effect sequence.
8. This discussion of mercantilist England is heavily based on the excellent analysis of the 1550-1763 period in Williams (1966:27-74).
9. See Huntington (1968:98-121) for a somewhat different interpretation of Elizabethan England's legacy in America.
10. See Owen (1965) for a history of how the meaning of poverty in England altered over the years.
11. Lodge (1975) makes reference to Locke's ideology as paradigm, and much of the discussion of Locke's legacy in America is informed by this synthesis. Scientism or scientific specialization refers to the idea that all things can become known by studying each of the parts. Prior to the works of Copernicus and Newton, those who studied nature

tended to take an organic or holistic view. But since Newton, scientific thought has been dominated by a concern with specialization, reductionism, objectivity, rationalism, and materialism. That which is tangible counts for more than that which is not. Lodge (1975:317) points out that concentration on the parts does not mean the whole takes care of itself. Interdisciplinary linkages and latent functions and dysfunctions go missed as scientists are rewarded for knowing more and more about less and less. Focusing on a mental disorder's course at the exclusion of its context is but one example of the short sightedness of this approach.

12. Laissez-faire or laissez-nous-faire, as it is presented by some, refers to a "let us" or "let us be free to do" philosophy.

13. See Laslett (1967) for a discussion of the material interests justified by Locke's works. Locke was essentially justifying the previous one hundred years of struggle in England whereby the values of individual liberty and religious toleration had successfully been used to dissipate the concept of absolute monarchy. Lodge (1975) and Randall (1970) discuss Locke as ideologue. See O'Connor (1973:6) and Wolfe (1977) "Introduction" for discussions of the capital facilitation and legitimacy functions of the state. Wolfe (1974:152) also notes that capital accumulation requires a government to maintain enough social order to allow this accumulation, in spite of capitalists' vocal criticism of "regulating" state activity. See Locke (1937).

14. Polanyi (1944:34-38) discusses the wrenching aspects of this period for nonpropertied groups and refers to the transition out of feudalism as essentially a "revolution of the rich against the poor. . ." Bridges (1974:174) notes that by conceptually separating the economic from the political, Lockean values unleashed individuals from their moorings of feudal dependence and left them to struggle for survival in an unregulated economic arena. Thus, individuals who were vastly unequal in resources were presumably "equal" under the law imposed by a limited state. A reading of Aristotle (1885) and Plato (1930:1935) provides evidence of how the ancient world functioned on a more communal approach to the uses of property. See also Barker (1959).

15. For discussions of Locke's application by American colonists, see Bailyn (1967), Haraszti (1952), Laslett (1967), Macpherson (1962), Lodge (1975); and Northrop (1946). For a discussion of the link between Christianity and individualism, see Gierke (1927). Rosenstock-Hussy (1949) notes the Christian assumption of "progress" toward a kingdom of heaven and its implications for technolog-

ical innovations.

16. Handlin and Handlin (1969:29) refer to this statement.

17. Macpherson (1962:3) refers to this ethos as possessive individualism. Gouldner (1970:65-78) suggests that in a context where utility is a thinly disguised excuse for the uninhibited pursuit of self-interest, unemployment means failure, and wealth, no matter how derived, is a badge of distinction. He goes on to argue that not only does utilitarianism render disvalued those goods or activities which do not "sell," such as some artistic creations, but useless people are disposed of and controlled as well. More and more the state has taken over the control of these groups through subsidies, institutionalization, and medicalization so as to protect the environment for the individualistic acquisition of the propertied.

18. Gerontological literature is full of works suggesting that agricultural-type economies are more hospitable for old persons than modern ones — partly because old people can hold onto their means of survival, such as land or work, right into old age. See Achenbaum and Stearns (1978), Palmore and Manton (1974), and Sheehan (1976).

19. See Hurst (1970) for the development and documentation of this transition of the corporation. His scholarship informs much of this discussion.

20. See Hofstadter (1944) for one of the most penetrating discussions of the social Darwinism promoted during this period.

21. See Gutman (1976) for an excellent analysis of this process as well as Thompson (1967).

22. Williams (1966:327-328) ascribes these goals as the primary concern of laissez-faire proponents during this 1850-1900 period.

23. See Hobshawm (1959) for a discussion of laborers' interpretation and use of scriptures and religious beliefs.

24. For an early example of this link between medical descriptions of old age and concerns of the emerging insurance industry, see Allen (1874:108).

25. See Clark and Anderson (1967:3-30) for a discussion of how the "normal" is everywhere a function of how the "good" is defined — that which society values and rewards. Dowd (1980) provides one of the more developed analyses within gerontological literature on the relationship between resource control and the existence of ageism. To some degree this thesis was anticipated by Simmons' (1945).

26. This is a thesis of Fischer (1978).

27. Achenbaum (1974) traces in detail the transformation of old people's image in America. See Hacker (1975) for a discussion of the stereo-

types of women and blacks which had been in place for many years. Williamson, Evans, and Munley (1980:126-135) provide comparisons among all three groups with respect to stereotyping and relegation to a minority group status.

28. Butler (1969) mentions a "dread of powerlessness" as a core component of ageism.

29. Information provided about this transition is heavily based on Achenbaum (1974).

30. Coffman (1934) presents a content analysis of literature's depiction of old people.

31. For a brief overview of presumed losses, see Levin and Levin (1980:1-34). Assumptions among professionals about such losses are discussed in Holtzman and Beck (1979).

32. A good summary of numerous studies on physical and mental changes with aging is Botwinick (1978). One example of those studies that challenge the assumption of loss with ageism is Nesselroade, Schaie, and Baltes (1972).

33. The concept of social control as a subject for study by social scientists surfaced during this period — as did social scientists.

34. See Graebner (1980) for an excellent account of labor unions' involvement in discrimination against older workers.

35. Obviously, the way in which Americans are motivated by a fear for survival differs from inhabitants of primitive societies in its form and extent. But the idea that people must be forced to work through anxiety about survival was a major argument against passage of work-related insurance programs enacted in the early 1920s and 1930s. This attitude still underpins certain arguments against public assistance today and development of a "welfare" mentality. See Lubove (1968) for a discussion of the political and ideological contexts surrounding passage of Social Security. Also, Crowley (1980) notes certain primitive aspects of American society in his observations of what it is like to be an octogenarian in America.

36. For a discussion of the idea that social safety in America demands economic success, see Clark and Anderson (1967:16). Wellman (1977), as quoted from personal correspondence with Feagin and Feagin (1978:9), suggests that the concept of "privilege" implies a dynamic relationship whereby one group is "fat" because another is "skinny." A more recent term for this phenomenon is "zero-sum society" in Thurow (1980).

37. One of the most obvious symptoms of this status decline was older Americans' resistance to retirement. Graebner (1980:224-241) gives

an excellent account of how strenuously mandatory retirement had to be marketed in order to get a modicum of willing compliance from older workers. Palmore and Manton (19773:363-369) also comment on the relationship that appears to exist between occupying a recipient or dependent status and an inferred inferiority or lack of prestige. Chapter 2 develops this thesis further. Also, see Evans and Williamson (1981:18-20).

38. Some of these conflicts are evident in Kogan and Shelton (1962a; 1962b), where young people depict the elderly as being preoccupied with death and fearing it. The elderly themselves do not register similar responses, and the authors suggest that believing old people are preoccupied with death, through fear or desire, is a convenient way to justify low contact levels.

39. Levin and Levin (1977). Further evidence of this overlap between class position and ageism comes from Silverman and Townsend (1977), who found that outmoded clothes trigger stereotypes of old people as conservative among college students rather than specific physical characteristics, such as wrinkles. See Levin and Levin (1980) for an excellent overall discussion of ageism and the various prejudices against the old that help sustain it.

40. For a summary of this argument, see Williams (1982).

41. Much of this discussion on the double standard of aging is based on Sontag (1972:29-38). This article is one of the most insightful and well-written available on the subject.

42. There is much to indicate a detrimental impact of the traditional image of women as "being." It not only stresses physical appearance and passivity, which can be destructive to the ego and sometimes survival, but also has required living through others. As Lopata (1974) notes, probably no group of old persons is as invisible as widows, and again class is involved since the less-educated woman has tended to view her role as servicing a spouse and has no separate identity to rely upon in widowhood. While more than one out of two women over 65 will be widowed (Klemesrud, 1980), many are grossly underprepared in terms of necessary assertiveness. That the institution of marriage benefits men is evidenced in their strong motivation to take a new wife, particularly if she will assume housekeeping and caretaking duties. See Foreman (1980). Thus, men are usually taken care of til death while many surviving women, due to a number of economic and social patterns, end up in institutions. Not surprisingly, survival rates in nursing homes are positively related to attributes women are socialized to avoid, e.g. being demanding and aggressive. See

George (1980).

43. Both of these emphases of the earlier period are reported in Achenbaum (1974:57).

44. This depiction of middle-aged males as problem solvers to others is found also in television ad voice-overs, where 92 percent are done by males in the afternoon and 90 percent in the evening. See *Boston Herald American* (January 3, 1981).

45. With all the recent talk about what a large number of women have entered the labor force over the past twenty years, it is important to note that most of their jobs have been in the low-paying service (labor intensive) sector. See U.S. Department of Labor (1980). This sector is very vulnerable to economic downturns and belt-tightening. See Rothschild (1981) for elaboration. Older women are particularly exploited and earn less upon re-entering the labor force than they did fresh out of college twenty or twenty-five years earlier. See *Boston Globe* (August 31, 1980).

46. One of the more grotesque manifestations of the American emphasis on success, lone individualism, and distaste for less eligible members was the unwillingness of a crowd in Chicago to save a man from being struck by a subway. According to the *Associated Press* (1980) account, the 32-year-old man had an arm in a sling, could not hoist himself out of the track pit, and was "laughed and jeered" at by the crowd. No doubt the fact that he appeared down on his luck and intoxicated only reinforced justifications for inaction. As one observer put it, "When he heard the train, he tried to get up, but he couldn't. His arm was in a sling. Everybody, 60 to 70 people, saw him. They didn't help. He didn't ask for any." The man was crushed.

47. For typical popular treatments of abuse, see Wald (1980) and Koch and Koch (1980). For a more thorough comparison of elderly, child, and wife abuse, see Block and Sinnott (1979).

48. See de Beauvoir (1972) and Linden (1956) for linkages between childhood nurturance and ability to nurture.

49. Kogan (1961) was one of the first to report on factors influencing attitudes toward old persons.

50. Here anomie refers to pessimism about the future, helplessness in the face of powerful social forces, and an inability to find

meaning or purpose in life. See Kogan (1961). Roberts and Ro-keach (1956) and Srole (1956) found authoritarianism to be directly related to prejudice toward minorities, whereas Kogan (1961) found that it was not directly related to negative attitudes toward old people. But to the extent that old people lack author-ity (are seen as weak), those with authoritarian tendencies, in-cluding contempt for weakness, would tend to be harshly disposed. Those with positive sentiments about nurturance tend to view dependency positively, while those who view weakness with hostility tend to be negatively disposed toward nurturance.

51. Over and over in the gerontological literature, including theories of aging, an emphasis is placed on individual adjust-ment to aging. And criticisms of the structure tend to go only as far as suggesting "reforms" that will permit greater intervention by middle-class professionals. See Levin and Levin (1980) for a strong analysis of exceptualism and individual orientations and George (1980) for an example of the "social adjustment" model. Goldenberg (1978) makes some interesting observations about social intervention and its built-in social control mechanisms. Also, see Estes (1974).

52. This article provides an excellent discussion of how and why ideologies can become hegemonic.

53. For examples, see Kogan and Shelton (1962b) and Ward (1977:227-232).

54. Both Agnello (1973) and Martin, Bengtson, and Acock (1974) discuss the self-containment that results from self-censorship.

55. See the following for some of the most penetrating discussions of nursing home/drug care operations: Vladeck (1980), Men-delson (1974), Schrag (1978), Townsend, (1971), Fontana (1978), and Ingram and Barry (1977). Everyone is implicated with profiteering — corporations, legislators, professionals — and the impotence (at best) of the state or its out-and-out collu-sion (at worst) deserves full treatment as a topic all in itself.

56. See the following sources for evidence of ageism among profes-sionals working with the elderly: Coe (1980), Holtzman and Beck (1979), Levin and Levin (1980), and Stannard (1980).

57. This term was first used by Estes (1979).

58. Kalish (1969) was one of the first to note the dangers for old

people in professionals emphasizing the elderly's problems.

59. O'Connor (1973) provides evidence for this argument.

60. Possible reasons for why many older Americans supported Reagan include Reagan's age and a presumed sympathy with old-age issues, and Reagan's promotion of a balanaced budget may have been interpreted by the elderly to mean fiscal stability and therefore solvency for a commitment to Social Security. As it turned out, Reagan was fairly unsympathetic to senior causes, huge military outlays precluded a balanced budget, and an absence of Social Security refinancing has left the system's long-term solvency undecided.

61. An example of an article by an economist that could rouse intergenerational tension is Feldstein (1977).

62. If the number of age discrimination suits filed with the Equal Opportunity Commission is any indication of the actual level of discrimination, then employment discrimination against older persons is on the rise. Between 1979 and 1981, for example, the number of suits filed rose by 75 percent. See Weaver (1982:12).

63. See Williamson, Evans, and Powell (1982) for an analysis of the potential political clout of older Americans.

64. See Trausch (1981:33, 36). Some industries, such as computer software, are already reporting labor shortages.

65. See Bernstein (1980) for elaboration of this idea.

66. *U.S. News and World Report* (1980) ran a major piece, "Life Begins at 55," in which the economic benefits of employing older Americans were discussed.

67. One of the ironic consequences of discrimination against blacks is that the individualistic upward mobility goal has not been prevalent enough to undermine a sense of familial and community responsibility. Single black women do not end up in nursing homes at rates anywhere near those of unattached white women.

68. See Birrens (1978) for a discussion of a possible schism between the vast majority of older Americans and the few who will not benefit from future opportunities.

69. Some observers predict a scenario that would turn nursing homes into congregate living spaces with mobile teaching units, talking books, and a lot of prior preparation for residents in re-

tirement living. See McClusky (1978). Presumably all of these pastimes would require employment of service providers and educators — thus absorbing persons who may no longer be needed in other areas of elderly care.

CHAPTER 12

FUTURE PROSPECTS: PARTICULARISTIC VERSUS UNIVERSALISTIC REFORMS

THROUGHOUT this book we have attempted to highlight the contradictions, structural inadequacies, and reform limitations of major policies that affect the elderly. We view policies such as Social Security, Medicare, and Medicaid as having improved the quality of life for the elderly but also as having some problematic social control consequences which to date have not been adequately examined. Similarily, we identify those aspects of the media and medical technology which unwittingly serve as agents of control. In the case of medical technology, the control and expense are considerable, yet attempts to regulate application and innovation have only been marginally effective (Banta, Burns, Behney, 1983:180). With the media, the control is more subtle, reinforcing our expectations of the elderly as dependent, incompetent and "hindrances to society."[1] Our goal has not been to suggest that existing programs should be limited or cut back, for despite their limitations the net impact of these programs has generally been quite positive. Rather, our goal has been to emphasize that the social control aspects of public policies affecting the aged must be openly acknowledged if we are to reduce the number of similar shortcomings in the future.

In the present chapter, we want to analyze the prospects (or lack thereof) of future public policy gains for the elderly. Given the policy shift to the right in recent years, it might seem more appropriate to discuss where cuts in programs for the aged are to be made. However, as we do not anticipate further major cuts at this point, it is reasonable to at least consider the prospects for future gains. The political realities of the current era are reflected in our attention to such issues as cost containment. We discuss how this can be done in such a way as to minimize the negative impact on the elderly. Before we turn to an analysis of a number of public policy reforms that are currently being debated, it will be useful to review those factors which contributed to the public policy gains the elderly made during the 1960s and 1970s.

THE ELDERLY'S "DESERVING" STATUS

When Medicare and Medicaid were enacted in the 1960s, and mandatory cost-of-living adjustments (COLA) were added to the 1972 Social Security Amendments, policymakers and politicians alike were narrowly addressing issues of equity and access. The policy preference was for programs that were universalistic to the extent that the goal was to provide benefits to as many of the aged as possible, but particularistic to the extent that the focus was on programs for the elderly to the exclusion of other age groups. This focus was influenced by political as well as philosophical considerations. At that time, because the plight of the elderly was beyond question, and the perceived strength of the elderly electorate was considerable, opponents dared not risk engaging in open conflict with America's senior citizens (Marmor, 1981:114; Hudson, 1981a:263).[2] Means tests were also avoided because it was generally assumed that stereotyping and stigmatization would occur if eligibility criteria singled out a particular group for assistance (Hudson, 1981b:181). And finally, with America's economy at its height of productivity, relatively little attention was given to the long-run costs of these programs.

In recent years the economy has deteriorated and the worthiness of the elderly, as well as their political strength, has come into question. By the mid-1970s, reports began to emerge which refuted the perception that large numbers of the elderly were impoverished (U.S. Bureau of the Census, 1977; 1979). Although the median income of the elderly relative to other age groups had increased only modestly, when cash and in-kind benefits to the elderly were considered, the standard of living for the aged had improved substantially over the decade of the 1970s (Schulz, 1985:18; Johnson and Williamson, 1980). Fairly typical was a study by Brotman (1978:1625) which reported that in the mid-1970s 14 percent of those over 65 were in poverty. A Congressional Budget Office (1977b) study reduced this estimate to 6 percent after considering in-kind government transfers. However, after twenty years of virtually uninterrupted declines in poverty for those over 65, between 1979 and 1980 the number of aged poor increased by 300,000 (U.S. House of Representatives Select Committee on Aging, 1982b:VII). In 1981 the number in poverty totaled 3.9 million or 15.3 percent of the aged (Schulz, 1985:35). This trend suggests that the economic advances the elderly enjoyed during the decades of the 1960s and 1970s were starting to recede in the 1980s.

THE STRENGTH OF THE ELDERLY ELECTORATE

Increasingly, the elderly's ability to maintain visibility for their economic concerns has been separated from their ability to actually wield political power. Groups like the National Council of Senior Citizens (NCSC) continue to be quite successful at persuading legislators to support income-maintenance programs, mobilizing their membership, and targeting key legislators for direct contact (Pratt, 1981:149). But, in general, elderly organizations including the National Council of Senior Citizens, the American Association of Retired Persons (AARP), and the National Association of Retired Federal Employees (NARFE) tend to focus their efforts solely on Social Security and Medicare, rather than Medicaid or other programs of benefit to the indigent aged (Binstock, 1981:59, 67).

A closer look at voter polls and studies of the elderly's attitudes towards public policies suggests that on issues other than those involving direct economic benefit, the elderly could hardly be described as a cohesive constituency. Particularly on issues such as abortion and racial integration, the elderly's voting behavior follows traditional party and demographic voting patterns.[3] The inability of aging organizations to redress the problems of the disadvantaged or frail elderly, and the clear absence of bloc voting behavior by aged

Americans, has led some authors to conclude that there is little possibility the elderly will ever fully develop into a strong, viable political constituency (Weaver, 1981:39; Binstock, 1983:139).

The increasing skepticism over the intensity of the elderly's needs, the growing absolute and real costs of aged programs, and mounting competition over dwindling social-welfare dollars will present a tremendous challange for the elderly's public policy advocates in the years ahead (Hudson, 1981a:266).[4] Demographic projections have been enumerated thoughout this book and consistently conclude that in future years the percentage of elderly Americans to the general population will markedly rise as will the aged's demand for supportive services (Vladeck and Firman, 1983:146). Nonetheless, it is also important to note that this significant growth in the number of elderly citizens only explains a small portion of the anticipated increases in future program costs (Clark and Menefee, 1981; Judge, 1982).

PROPOSED PROGRAM REFORMS

Medicare, Medicaid and Social Security have all been plagued by high rates of inflation. Low productivity and high unemployment have also added to the problems with the Social Security trust funds (Congressional Budget Office, 1981:14). In the case of Medicare and Medicaid, both the volume of services per beneficiary and the rise in the costs of those services have intensified (U.S. House of Representatives, 1984:7). Given that these are the primary reasons costs for programs benefiting the elderly have dramatically risen, it seems illogical that the proposed reforms focus upon the beneficiaries rather than the broader structural flaws.

Basically, health care costs can be brought into line by paying hospitals and physicians less or expecting the elderly and other taxpayers to pay more (U.S. House of Representatives, 1984:9). At the 1984 Conference on the Future of Medicare, the three possible options for maintaining solvency in the Medicare/Medicaid program included: paying for fewer services, paying less for each service, or shifting a greater financial burden to the beneficiaries or taxpayers (U.S. House of Representatives, 1984:7). Only one of these possible solutions — paying less for each service — targets those who bear the primary responsibility for these cost increases: providers.[5]

One physician has characterized this struggle as "a classic pocket-book issue pitting the economic standing of physicians against the out-of-pocket liability of the elderly beneficiary" (U.S. House of Representatives, 1984:350). If because of political pressure from the AMA or the American Hospital Association (AHA) the choice is to increase cost sharing among the elderly beneficiaries, then the elderly will be forced to shoulder the burden of medical costs. If, on the other hand, there is a clear understanding that the providers are a primary force behind skyrocketing health care costs, then the choice will be to aggressively regulate the industry and institute prospective payment mechanisms for both hospital and outpatient treatment.

There are indications that despite the political influence of the AMA and the AHA, efforts will be made by Congress and the Executive Office to freeze hospital and physician reimbursement. However, the president has also called for increases in the Medicare premium from 25 percent of program costs to 35 percent of program costs by January 1988 (Message from the President of the United States, 1983:6). Further, although by definition Medicaid is for the medically indigent, President Reagan has proposed Medicaid co-payments for hospital and physician services.

Voucher programs are a relatively new payment scheme endorsed by policymakers and a variety of medical economists. Vouchers would allow Medicare beneficiaries to shop for less expensive health insurance coverage and keep the monetary difference between that plan and Medicare. In theory, by opening up the health insurance marketplace, the elderly should find more cost-effective health care coverage (U.S. House of Representatives, 1984:77-79). In practice, given that the elderly are a high-risk group, it is unclear that in the open market they will be able to secure any health insurance at all (Cohodes, 1982:77). In fact, due to adverse selection (that is, the refusal of many commercial insurers to even accept the high-cost aging population), it is a distinct possibility that within a few years Blue Cross/Blue Shield, which does not refuse coverage on account of age or disability will be forced out of the health insurance market entirely (Luft, 1982:47).

Other reforms, such as the Kennedy-Gephardt Medicare Rescue and Health Care Reform Act of 1984, would place the responsibility for holding down costs squarely on hospitals and physicians. Through a comprehensive prospective payment program for hospitalization and physician services, as well as incentives to decrease hospitalization, the net savings projected under Kennedy-Gephardt would be $1,184 billions (U.S. Senate, 1984a). By comparison, the net savings under Reagan's proposals equal approximately $4.3 billion (Message from the President of the United States, 1983:7).[6] Clearly, the more cost-effective approach tightens the belt on those who have benefited the most from escalating health care costs (i.e. the providers) and spares those least capable of shouldering any more of the burden (i.e. the elderly).

A key question in this debate over controlling health care costs is whether the elderly should be held more personally responsible for their medical and hospital bills. Some medical economists argue that increased cost sharing will hold down excess utilization and enhance competition (U.S. House of Representatives, 1984:32-33). Others note that 28 percent of all Medicare expenditures are expended in the last year of a person's life, hardly implying an abuse of services (Lave and Silverman, 1984:155). Furthermore, if cost sharing was to be increased, those who could most afford supplemental health insurance would purchase additional protection, placing added financial pressure only on those who can least afford any increased out-of-pocket expense (U.S. House of Representatives, 1984:203-209).

In similar fashion, solutions to maintain the solvency of Social Security call for either bureaucratic maneuvering or for the elderly to assume more of the direct costs.[7] In it's purest form, reliance on income maintenance programs could be severely curtailed by limiting accessibility and promoting reliance on the private pension system through more favorable tax laws (Myles, 1984:116-117). More moderate reforms, recommended in 1982 by the National Commission on Social Security Reform, include: delaying the cost-of-living adjustment (COLA), accelerating payroll tax increases, taxing the benefits for high income persons, and requiring Social Security coverage of new federal employees and all non-profit organizations

(U.S. House of Representatives Select Committee on Aging, 1983:4).[8]

Attempts to improve the economic security of the elderly that rely upon individual responsibility, not government intervention, stress the importance of individual retirement accounts (IRA's) Keogh plans, and employee stock ownership plans (ESOP's) (Olson, 1982:221). Inherent in this emphasis on individual responsibility is the supposition that economic hardship is a product of one's unwillingness, not inability to save. Therefore, there is a risk that greater divisiveness will be created among the elderly by pitting those who are perceived to be "frugal" against those who are unwilling or unable to save.

Even in the private sector, over the last four years American workers' retirement security has been seriously threatened by the termination of 114 private pension plans and the subsequent reversion to employers of over $1 million (U.S. House of Representatives Select Committee on Aging, 1984:9).[9] In some cases, the pension plan has been transformed into an employee/stock ownership plan (ESOP) — a concept heralded by both labor and management. However, by not diversifying the investment, there is the potential danger that the employee could completely lose his or her retirement income (U.S. House of Representatives Select Committee on Aging, 1984:14).

Other legislative initiatives, such as lowering the minimum age for pension participation, granting pension credit during maternity or paternity leave, and safeguarding survivor benefits are all sincere efforts to make the private pension system more equitable (U.S. House of Representatives, 1983b; U.S. Senate, 1983b). Despite the virtues of such reforms, making the private pension system more equitable through the Employee Retirement Income Security Act (ERISA) or any other legislated means is not going to be of any great value to a little less than half (45.4%) of all Americans who are not even participating in a private pension program (Schieber and George, 1981:25).

PARTICULARISTIC OR UNIVERSALISTIC REFORMS?

Perhaps the basic problem with current public policies benefiting the aged is that they fail to account for the prominent differences that presently exist in the aged population. For example, in the age group over 85, 57 percent are limited in their ability to carry on major activities compared to 34 percent in the 65 to 74 age group (Callahan, 1981:185). Only a very small percent (4.8%) of all the elderly account for over half (53%) of all Medicare expenditures (Hirsch, Silverman and Dobson, 1982). By the year 2000, the over-85 population will increase by 84 percent compared to a 56 percent increase in the 65 and older age group (Callahan, 1981:185). In the future, we can anticipate it will be the over-85 age group who, due to their projected numbers and sheer intensity of debilitation, will require far more services than those aged 65 to 75.[10]

There are also significant differences between older men and older women. Seventy-two percent of all those over 65 who live in poverty are women (U.S. Senate, 1983b:14). In 1981, only 10.5 percent of women over 65 received pensions averaging $2,427 a year compared to 27.7 percent of men who received pensions averaging $4,152 a year (U.S. Senate, 1983b:14). Living arrangements between men and women also differ greatly, with far more men over 65 than women (82.9% to 57%) living with a spouse or relative (U.S. House of Representatives Select Committee on Aging, 1982a).

Economic differences among the aged have been widely recognized for some time. Overall, older women have substantially lower incomes than older men, and more older blacks and Hispanics live in poverty than older whites (Allen and Brotman, 1981:57). Less widely known is the extent to which out-of-pocket expense, particularly for health care, impacts to a far greater degree on the poor, whom Medicare and Medicaid are supposed to protect, rather than the fairly well-to-do. For instance, the proportion of out-of-pocket health expenses for those with incomes less than $6,000 is 5.4 percent, and 8.7 percent for those with incomes less than $4,000. However, for those with incomes greater than $15,000, the proportion of out-of-pocket health expense is only 1.4 percent (Rosenblum, 1983:86). Under these conditions, it's not surprising that the fairly well-to-do elderly seldom identify with aging issues (Riley and

Foner, 1968).

In the face of such disparities and given the scarcity of economic as well as human resources, would targeting benefits to the elderly in the greatest need be a feasible policy alternative? In other words, despite Americans' historical dislike of means or eligibility tests, has their time now come? Given that only 15 percent to 20 percent of those over 65 actually require some special form of health or social services, are we overserving the vast majority of aged Americans and underserving those truly in need (Neugarten, 1982:26)? Should, as Governor Bruce Babbitt of Arizona advocates, those who have "fortunate economic circumstances" forego government subsidies in order to target a tight federal budget where the need is greatest (Babbitt, 1984:A7)?

There are certain political advantages for the elderly in pursuing particularistic policy reforms. Narrow particularistic programs offer a recognizable rallying point for advocates and proponents (Hudson, 1981b:181). A clearly defined program serving a very circumspect group can also facilitate monitoring to ensure program goals are met. In keeping with this view, although it did not differentiate among the aged themselves, the 1981 White House Conference on Aging did propose strong resolutions to continue separate aging programs.

Differentiating need according to an economic yardstick certainly has presented a plethora of problems to other social-welfare programs such as AFCDC, Medicaid and WIC (Women, Infants and Children Program). Fragmenting programs to serve particular populations can make it easier for policymakers to gradually erode funding support. By definition, particularistic programs serve narrow populations which many times are not large enough to sustain significant opposition should continuance of a program be threatened.

One group whose "deserving" status has rarely been questioned are the disabled; yet, between March 1981 and September 1983, nearly one-half million beneficiaries of the Social Security disability program were terminated (U.S. Senate, 1984b:3). More disturbing was that upon review by administrative law judges, approximately 70 percent of those removed from the liability rolls were reinstated (U.S. Senate, 1984b:3). The hardship this callous and precipitous action by the Social Security administration incurred on scores of disabled persons is amply documented in testimony before the U.S. Senate Committee on the Budget (U.S. Senate, 1984b).

The other potential danger of particularistic reforms is that they heighten competition between groups who must vie for scarce resources. There is also the possibility that as the elderly make gains in their political influence, others in society, in particular the taxpayers who will be called upon to fund additional aging programs, will rise up in opposition. The potential for such a backlash is not unprecedented. One only has to witness the firment between pro and anti-abortion activists to see how mounting strength in one constituency mobilizes an adversarial response in another. It is also possible that as younger taxpayers perceive the aged population to be less debilitated and dependent, the more likely they are to characterize the aged as "undeserving," and the less willing they will be to subsidize aging programs (Samuelson, 1978).

If one assumes, as does Etzioni (1976), that particularistic programs heighten tension between the aged and the rest of society, then perhaps the elderly will ultimately loose more than they could gain by pursuing particularistic reforms (Schram, 1981:233). Given these political considerations, it may be far more fruitful to avoid singling out the aged as special, different and dependent and instead focus the energies of the elderly upon policies that will be of benefit to all Americans. For example, cost-effective national health insurance is not only advantageous to the elderly, it is advantageous for all Americans.[11] With of some social problems, such as abuse, alcoholism, and housing, the actual service may differ according to the age of the individual, but the need for the service is not specifically age related (Austin and Loeb, 1982:274-275).[12] However, not all programs now targeted for the elderly may be easily expanded to include other age groups.

Currently, the work cycle is fairly fixed with leisure and retirement set arbitrarily at age 70 and uninterrupted participation in the work force occurring through the middle years of an individual's life. In such a system, the displacement of older workers to make room for the younger aspirants is encouraged and facilitated by Social Security and private pension programs. Yet, one study found that four out of five workers would prefer to reduce their years of retirement and redistribute more leisure time during the middle portion of their working years (Best and Stern, 1977).

Redefining and redesigning the work cycle to accommodate both the needs of working adults and the elderly could ease the strain on the Social Security trust funds. But, pragmatically, the immediate demands of the marketplace are not likely to yield to the long-term interests of labor. It is far more likely that inflexible work schedules will be maintained, and, in addition to substained participation in the work force throughout adulthood, the elderly will be enticed or expected to extend the length of their work life.[13]

Policy analysts who support universalistic reforms claim that comprehensiveness will facilitate administration, minimize fragmentation and duplication, and ultimately be more cost effective. Other advantages include spreading the risk among a larger pool of beneficiaries and expanding the funding base.[14] But, again realistically, given the impact of economic scarcity and Americans' values of individualism and limited government, any effort to expand existing programs is unlikely to gain widespread support.

Moreover, for programs covering a wide range of ages to be implemented, the elderly and their advocates would have to form political alliances with other disadvantaged Americans and their advocates or with the population at large. On a variety of public policy initiatives, competition among special-interest groups has made coalition building extremely difficult. Whether those who are similarly repressed identify together and join forces to mandate universal reforms, or view each other as adversaries in a struggle to capture limited resouces, remains to be seen. In either of these scenarios, the definition of "beneficiary" is the critical component of the reform. In neither instance is attention given to economic restraints or sanctions on those who provide or indirectly benefit from programs for the elderly.

FORCES MITIGATING AGAINST REFORM

Although by the end of the 1960s, the NCSC, AARP, and NCOA (National Council on Aging) received $10 million for aging programs, their activities did little to address the economic and social problems confronting the disadvantaged aged (Binstock, 1981:66-68). The public posture of the major aging organizations has been to insist that "all programs benefiting the aged, and those who make their living off them, are sacred . . . without much attention to those who are not saved by Social Security or any other programs" (Binstock, 1983:142). Unfortunately, it would appear that this pattern of pursuing self-interest to the detriment of the disadvantaged elderly is not confined to aging organizations. Nowhere does this self-serving behavior appear more apparent than in health care where seventy times more dollars are spent annually than on social services (Newcomer et al., 1982).

The American Medical Association (AMA), the American Hospital Association (AHA), and two groups representing the insurance industry, the Life Insurance Association of America, and the National Association of Blue Shield plans, have all consistently opposed any government-sponsored national health program.[15] It has been this insistence by the insurance and medical industry to maintain regressive financing mechanisms that has assured no serious debate on national health insurance has ever taken place, and that efforts to hold down costs have placed excessive burdens on the consumers of health care services (Harrington, 1980:74). In fact, even though liberal reimbursement policies (on a fee-for-service basis for physicians and a cost basis for hospitals and nursing homes) amply rewarded providers, by 1970 gross gaps in coverage were apparent in Medicare and Medicaid, as well as private insurance.

Today, not only are the elderly paying more out-of-pocket expenses, but medical costs in general are consuming larger and larger portions of a family's total budget (Health Insurance Association of America, 1982:64). Clearly, neither employer-based health insurance nor Medicaid on Medicare are any guarantee that Americans will be adequately protected under the existing health insurance programs.[16] Remarkably, on an issue that impacts all ages, no coalition has yet to be formed among the elderly, business, and labor to limit health care providers' "overwhelming sense of self-interest and self-preservation" (Tomayko, 1978:87).

In the area of medical technology, especially as it relates to the aged, where every type of technology is applied more often than to the general population, the question of cost has far-reaching social and ethical implications (Banta, Burns, and Behney, 1983:178). The cost of medical technology can be controlled either by: decreasing demand by increasing costs to the consumer, limiting distribution by assessing the cost/benefit of individual technologies, or changing the reimbursement procedures to reverse the monetary incentive for physicians and hospitals (Banta, Burns and Behney, 1983:178).[17]

How one weighs psychological aspects and measures the potential for improvement in the quality of an individual's life have polarized the medical community (Najam and Levine, 1981:114). The use of cost-benefit analysis which completely avoids addressing larger questions of social justice has dire connotations for the elderly who are presumed to have a higher cost-benefit ratio (Fox, 1979). Undaunted by issues of distribution, fairness, and equity, some have argued that with demand exceeding supply, the only option is to evaluate explicitly, systematically, and openly using an approach like cost-benefit analysis or continue to evaluate implicitly, haphazardly, and secretly as has been the pattern in the past (Fuchs, 1980:937).

Any regulatory approach that relies upon subjective guidelines for the distribution of capital-intensive technology is obviously subject to bias (Banta, Burns, and Behney, 1983:178). A number of analysts agree that even with such regulations, unnecessary utilization will continue as long as doctors and hospitals can reap enormous profits from extensive reimbursement policies (Wolfe and Berle, 1981:95; Relman, 1980:966; Russell, 1979:4; National Research Council Committee on Technology and Health Care, 1979:12). Ultimately, a choice will have to be made whether the rights of the individual, the state, or providers will be infringed upon in an effort to reasonably control the application of medical innovation (Bloom, 1979:1271; Callahan, 1973:14; Fishel, 1967:515).

The conflict between the interests of capital and those of labor is also evident in the Social Security system. Back in 1972, when amendments to the Social Security Act were enacted, aging organizations had gained a strong political foothold, the economic need of the elderly was beyond reproach, and the solvency of the program appeared certain. Barely a decade later, the Social Security trust fund seemed doomed to bankruptcy, assertions were made that Social Security was a bad investment for younger generations, and critics characterized the program as an instrument of social control whose redistributive effect was minimal (Feldstein, M.S., 1977; Davis and van der Oever, 1981). Although only a few business lobbyists and administration officials dared question the effect Social Security might have on the federal budget and inflation in the early 1970s, the funding crisis of the late 70s irrevocably changed the image of Social Security as a "sacred" entitlement program.

The compromise negotiated in 1983 to maintain the solvency of Social Security is an example of how in a crisis it is the beneficiaries and the American taxpayers who are called upon to make sacrifices. We should anticipate that heightened antitax sentiments on the part of business and the American public will significantly limit those options which call for added revenues through substantial tax increases in the future. State governments, in particular, are very vulnerable to threats by businesses to relocate their industries if local taxes become too costly (Estes and Newcomer, 1983:259-260). In light of these considerations, when the President's Commission on Pension Policy (1980) recommended a sweeping reform, termed MUPS (Manditory Universal Pension System), concern was expressed that even with a generous tax credit of 46 percent on a 3 percent employer contribution, the slight increase in cost to business could potentially result in higher unemployment, lower wages, lower benefits, or both to employees.

CONCLUSION

In America, our pluralist public policies attempt to maintain individualism and liberty while simultaneously sanctioning limited government intervention should the free market be incapable of providing certain necessary social goods. Not surprisingly, contradictions erupt between the state — charged with redressing social and economic inequities — and the capitalist economy — driven by profit. Some economists refer to this struggle as the balance between equity and efficiency. We have attempted to document throughout this book that, due to a variety of constraints, the redistributional effect of American old age policies has been limited.

In this chapter, we have raised questions regarding the "worthiness" or "deservedness" of the elderly. Although originally it appeared that during the 1970s the economic status of the elderly had improved, more recent income tabulations suggest that the proportion who are poor has been increasing. Assuming that the economic need of the elderly is once again intensifying, we have examined whether the aged have sufficient political power to push forward either particularistic or universalistic reforms. Public opinion polls and other studies of the elderly's voting behavior suggest they do not form a strong voting block. Therefore, it appears unlikely that the elderly will markedly improve their political influence in the near future. Further, even if the elderly could be mobilized around a particular policy initiative, growing skepticism that the elderly are not as dependent and incapacitated as once perceived has put them in a vulnerable position when their interests are pitted against the interests of other groups.

As for the type of program reform the elderly might most effectively promote, we have analyzed the advantages and disadvantages of particularistic versus universalistic reforms. Pragmatically speaking, particularistic reforms are probably easier to enact, but by targeting one narrow group for assistance, by implication, the remainder of the population is more directly accountable for their own well-being. Universalistic reforms which recognize the heterogeneity of the aged would expand government's role (a prospect most American's oppose) and diminish or curtail the activities of various special interests in the private sector (i.e. the AMA, the AHA, and American business). Even with these limitations, there are certain elderly programs which may well benefit from each of these approaches.

The long-term care needs of the elderly seem well suited to a reform measure that would comprehensively administrate and fund a program addressing both the social and health care needs of the frail elderly regardless of economic status. Currently, five pilot projects are underway in the United States to create Social-Health Maintenance Organizations (SHMO's). SHMO's coordinate the health and the chronic care needs of the frail elderly through a prospective, pre-paid plan using a variety of alternative less expensive providers (Daly, 1984:35). The SHMO's represent a reform that is particularistic in its focus on the needs of the frail elderly but universalistic in availability to the frail elderly in all income groups.

A particularistic reform measure of significance to elderly women is the Private Pension Reform bill enacted in August of 1984. The Private Pension Reform Act provides additional protection of women's pensions rights by improving both joint and survivor benefits, reducing the minimum age for pension plan participation, and granting credit for maternity or paternity leave. Representative Ferraro describes this reform as "a practical cost-effective approach to many of the problems women face in the private pension system," which will hopefully go far in "making a difference between poverty and comfort for retired women" (U.S. House of Representatives, 1983b:145).[19] This measure is universalistic to the extent that it is available to women in all income groups, but it is particularistic in its focus on women to the exclusion of men.

Whether a particularistic or universalistic reform measure is appropriate and implementable will largely be determined by the degree to which the elderly are perceived to be in need and the extent to which all the interested parties can agree upon the cost-effective solution. The difficulty with the first step is that the elderly are not a homogeneous population. Nor does it appear likely that even if pockets of "deserving" elderly could be identified, they would be capable of strengthening their position by forming coalitions with other similarly disenfranchised groups.

As for the second step, virtually all of the recent reforms have held down costs by placing added financial burdens on the elderly beneficiary. Those who tend to promote this approach are administration officials, representatives of American industry, professional organizations, and the American taxpayer. We anticipate that if this trend continues, the inadequacies of public policies will become more apparent, discord from those in need who are adversely affected will intensify, and ultimately pressure will once again be brought to bear on the government to more evenly balance the interests of government, the private sector, and the public at large.

To date, advocates for the elderly have done well emphasizing programs and policies that are particularistic in providing benefits targeted for the elderly to the exclusion of other age groups, but universalistic in the sense of providing benefits to as many of the aged as possible. In the years ahead, it would seem that two alternative strategies might be viewed as being more just and at the same time prove to be more cost effective. One would be to emphasize programs for the aged that are particularistic in the sense that they are aimed at the aged who are clearly disadvantaged. The second strategy would be to emphasize programs and policies that are universalistic in the sense of providing benefits to the non-aged as well as the aged and to middle- as well as low-income groups.

The first or particularistic strategy is designed to deal with the criticism that many of the aged have adequate means to provide for themselves. By restricting program benefits to persons who can demonstrate need, the resources which we know will be limited would go to those who are most in need. In addition, this emphasis will undercut the opposition of those who tend to view the elderly as a homogeneous and relatively affluent segment of the population.

The second or universalistic strategy is designed to deal with the criticism that the elderly are already getting more than their fair share of government resources. To the extent that the elderly are viewed as a homogeneous and relatively well-off group, there will be continued opposition to new programs and policy changes that tend to benefit the elderly to the exclusion of other age groups. But if a way can be found to design more universalistic programs that benefit the non-elderly as well, it might be possible to obtain the political support needed.

Today, neither the particularistic nor the universalistic strategies we have described would be likely to result in support for bold new social program initiatives that will directly or indirectly benefit the elderly. However, these strategies will become increasingly appropriate if and when the nation returns to a period of sustained economic growth similar to that of the 1960s. Until then, it would seem that there is no plausible strategy for increasing the share to our national product that goes to the elderly. The one major exception to this generalization will be the increases due to purely demographic changes. As the proportion of the population eligible for Social Security and Medicare increases, we can expect at least some increase in the share of the national product spent on programs for the aged.

In any case, meaningful political change will only be effected as a response to the sustained collective action of the elderly and other groups acting on their behalf. Success also requires attention to cost-effective solutions and not merely reliance on social justice rhetoric, which, of late, has lost much of its persuasive appeal.[20] And, finally, trade-offs will have to be made between particularistic and universa-listic reforms — choices which should be governed by the needs of the aged and not political expediancy or private gain.

NOTES

1. Korzenny and Neuendorf (1980) found that depictions of the aged on television as "hindrances to society" predicted a negative self-concept among the elderly. Numerous authors have claimed that the elderly are frequently depicted in the mass media as physically incompetent, mentally slow, sexually impotent and unproductive to society (Signo-rielli and Gerbner, 1977; U.S. House of Representatives Select Committee on Aging, 1978b:88-95; Arnoff, 1974; Francher, 1973; Hesse, 1974).

2. In fact, in 1972 when a federal income guarantee was enacted for the aged, it was rejected for children (Burke and Burke, 1981:173).

3. Weaver (1981) analyzed date from the 1970 Survey Research Center of the University of Michigan and concluded that bloc-like behavior is not found in areas removed from direct economic interest. Additionally, exit polls during the 1982 congressional elections showed differences within age groups but not between age groups (New York Times/CBS Poll, 1982).

4. Social Security actuaries anticipate the Social Security funds under normal economic conditions will have an average surplus of $9 billion from the year 1990 to 2015 (U.S. House of Representatives Select Committee on Aging 1983a:6). However, unless some policy changes are implemented in Medicare, the hospital insurance trust fund is projected to be depleted by 1990 (U.S. House of Representatives, 1983a:6).

5. In addressing the issue of inflated physician fees and volume of services, one physician, Ben Lawton, M.D., noted that "Physician fees are not related to the style of practice, but rather to the style of life" (U.S. House of Representatives, 1984:356).

6. The cumulative Medicare deficit is $1,018 billion. Thus, under Kennedy-Gephardt there would be a net surplus of $166 billion (U.S. Senate, 1984a).

7. To temporarily remedy the financial difficulties in the Old Age and Survivors Insurance (OASI) fund in the first part of fiscal year 1982, the Congressional Budget Office recommended borrowing from the Disability Insurance fund and the Hospital Insurance fund (Congres-

sional Budget Office, 1981:xi). In keeping with this recommendation, $12.4 billion was transferred from the hospital insurance trust fund to the OASI trust in 1982 and is slated to be repaid by 1987.

8. COLA has been a frequent target of budget cutters who claim that the income of Social Security beneficiaries rises faster than that of working Americans (Binstock, 1983:137). Others, however, note that any lowering or delaying of COLA would, at a minimum, move 500,000 elderly people into poverty between 1982 and 1985 and an additional 1.2 million by 1990 (U.S. House of Representatives Select Committee on Aging, 1982b:VI).

9. It would appear that the threat of bankruptcy or financial distress were not the primary factors leading to the termination of the 114 pension plans. Rather, after the accrued plan liabilities were satisfied, the so-called "surplus assets" were used to fund new acquisitions, retire long-term debts, fight off takeovers, or boost corporate profits (U.S. House of Representatives Select Committee on Aging, 1984:1).

10. The over-85 age group is now popularly refered to in the literature as the "frail elderly."

11. A Department of Labor study found that in 1979 about three-quarters of American workers had group health coverage — a figure 13.3 percent lower than in 1977 and 13.9 percent lower than in 1976 (U.S. Senate, 1983a:2). It is this uninsured population and Medicaid recipients who are much less likely than those with Medicare or private insurance to have a usual source of medical care (U.S. Department of Health and Human Services, 1982:3).

12. See Jacobs (1982) on financial arrangements enabling the elderly to remain in their homes while converting home equity into cash.

13. Former Secretary of Health Education and Welfare Joseph Califano dismisses the idea that longer participation in the work force will result in unemployment for younger workers. Califano is a strong supporter of incentives such as the amendments to the Social Security Act in 1977, which increased a worker's retirement benefits by 3 percent for each year of work past sixty-five (Califano, 1981:286).

14. See the President's Commission on Pension Policy (1980) on the Mandatory Universal Pension System (MUPS) and Altman (1981) on the design of a National Health Insurance Program for the United States.

15. See Marmor (1981) and Sundquist (1968) for an analysis of the political maneuvering by various interest groups leading to and culminating in the enactment of Medicare.

16. Specifically, over the next three years the budget for Medicare and Medicaid is slated to be reduced by $14.3 billion forcing 615,000 people off the Medicaid roles and even greater out-of-pocket expenses for the elderly (Iglehart, 1982:839).

17. A structure was in place at the National Center for Health Care Technology (NCHCT) to access the net gains and costs of various technologies. Budget cuts under the Reagan administration in 1981 dismantled the center, and now a smaller staff in the Office of Health Technology Assessment (OHTA) is attempting to undertake such evaluations.

18. Incremental attempts to reform the private pension system have also been resisted by American businesses who are not receptive to any effort that threatens their control over pension funds projected to total $1 trillion by 1985 (Stephens, 1979:181; U.S. Senate Special Committee on Aging, 1980:13).

19. One of the more recent studies examining the economic status of women conducted by the non-partisan Urban Institute and entitled, "The Reagan Record," once again confirmed that the incomes of families headed by women declined from 1980 to 1984 (McGinley, 1984:48).

20. Galbraith questions the common perception that the present erosion of support for those in poverty is rooted in economic scarcity. Instead, he argues, it is as America becomes more affluent that the plight of the poor is increasingly ignored or rationalized (Galbraith, 1984).

BIBLIOGRAPHY

Abrahamson, M.
  1978   Functionalism. Englewood Cliffs, New Jersey: Prentice-Hall.
Achenbaum, W.A.
  1974   "The obsolescence of old age in America, 1865-1914." Journal
          of Social History 8:48-62.
  1978   Old Age in the New Land. Baltimore: Johns Hopkins Univer-
          sity Press.
  1980   "Did Social Security attempt to regulate the poor? Historical
          reflections on Piven and Cloward's Social welfare model." Re-
          search on Aging 2:470-488.
Achenbaum, W.A., and P.N. Stearns
  1978   "Essay: old age and modernization." Gerontologist 18:307-
          312.
Adams, J.
  1980   "Alternative forms of care benefit young and old." Hospitals
          54(May 16):91-94.
Agnello, T.J.
  1973   "Aging and the sense of political powerlessness." Public Opin-
          ion Quarterly 37:251-259.
Aiken, L.H., and R. Blendon
  1981   "Nursing priorities for the 1980s: hospitals and nursing
          homes." American Journal of Nursing 2:324-330.
Alford. R.
  1980   "The political economy of health care." Pp. 449-481 in D. Me-
          chanic (ed.), Readings in Medical Sociology. New York: Free
          Press.
Allen, C., and H. Brotman (eds.)
  1981   Chartbook on Aging in America. Washington, D.C.: U.S.
          Government Printing Office.

265

Allen, N.
　1874　"The law of longevity with special reference to life insurance."
　　　　Medical Record 9:108.

Allport, G.
　1958　The Nature of Prejudice. Garden City, New York: Anchor/
　　　　Doubleday.

Altman, S.H.
　1981　"The design of a national health insurance system for the
　　　　United States." Pp. 205-223 in S.H. Altman and H.M. Sa-
　　　　polsky (eds.), Federal Health Programs. Lexington, Massa-
　　　　chusetts: Lexington Books.

Altman, S., and R. Blendon (eds.)
　1977　Medical Technology: The Culprit Behind Health Care Costs?
　　　　Washington, D.C.: U.S. Government Printing Office.

American Nurse
　1984a　"Advisory panel approves Medicare Rescue Plan." 16(Janu-
　　　　ary):2.
　1984b　"Sophisticated clinical nursing key under DRG plan says
　　　　Joel." 16(January):1, 18.

Amundsen, K.
　1971　The Silenced Majority. Englewood Cliffs, New Jersey:
　　　　Prentice-Hall.

Antunes, G.E., F.L. Cook, T.D. Cook, and W.G. Skogan
　1977　"Patterns of personal crime against the elderly: findings from a
　　　　national survey." Gerontologist 17:321-327.

Archibald, W.P.
　1976　"Face-to-face: the alienating effects of class, status, and power
　　　　divisions." American Sociological Review 41:819-837.

Aristotle
　1885　The Politics of Aristotle. Translated by B. Jowett. Oxford,
　　　　England: Clarendon Press.

Aronoff, C.
　1974　"Old age in prime time." Journal of Communication 24:86-87.

Aronson, E.
　1980　The Social Animal. Third edition. San Francisco: W.H.
　　　　Freeman and Company.

Arrow, K.J.
　1963　"Uncertainty and the welfare economics of medical care."
　　　　American Economic Review 53:941-973.

Ashley, Sir W.J.
　1893　An Introduction to English Economic History and Theory.

Volume II. Second edition. London: Longmans, Green.

Ashmore, J.S.

1975 "Commercial television's calculated indifference to the old." Center Magazine 8:18-20.

Associated Press

1980 "Man is crushed by subway train as crowd laughs." Hartford Courant, October 9.

Austin, C.D., and M.B. Loeb

1982 "Why is age relevant?" Pp. 263-288 in B.L. Neugarten (ed.), Age or Need?: Public Policies for Older People. Beverly Hills: Sage Publications.

Babbit, B.

1984 "It's time for a universal means test." Boston Globe, August 12.

Baer, W.S.

1978 "Telecommunications technology in the 1980s." Pp. 61-123 in G.O. Robinson (ed.), Communications for Tomorrow. New York: Praeger.

Bailey, M.

1980 "Older women abused." Boston Globe, August 31.

Bailyn, B.

1967 The Ideological Origins of the America Revolution. Cambridge, Massachusetts: Harvard University Press.

Ball-Rokeach, S.J.

1980 "Normative and deviant violence from a conflict perspective." Social Problems 28:45-55.

Bandura, A.

1969 "Social learning theory of identificatory processes." Pp. 213-262 in D.A. Goslin (ed.), Handbook of Socialization Theory and Research. Chicago: Rand McNally.

Bandura, A., D. Ross, and S.A. Ross

1963 "Vicarious reinforcement imitative learning." Journal of Abnormal and Social Psychology 67:601-607.

Bankers Trust Company

1980 1980 Study of Corporate Pension Plans. New York: Bankers Trust Company.

Banta, D., and C. Behney

1981 "Policy formulation and technology assessment." Milbank Memorial Fund Quarterly/Health and Society 59:3445-479.

Banta, H.D., A.K. Burns and C.J. Behney

1983 "Policy implications of the diffusion and control of medical technology." Annals of the American Academy of Political and

Social Science 468:165-181.

Barber, R.
1982 "Pension funds in the United States: issues of investment and control." Economic and Industrial Democracy Journal 3(February):31-73.

Barker, E.
1959 The Political Thought of Plato and Aristotle. New York: Dover Publications.

Bassuk, E.L., and S. Gerson
1978 "Deinstitutionalization and mental health services." Scientific American 238(Februrary):45-53.

Battistella, R.M., and T.G. Rundall (eds.)
1978 Health Care Policy in a Changing Environment. Berkeley, California: McCutchan.

Bauknecht, V.
1983 "More budget cuts slated for health agencies." The American Nurse 15(January):2.

de Beauvoir, S.
1972 The Coming of Age. Translated by P. O'Brian. New York: G.P. Putnam's Sons.

Becker, H.
1963 Outsiders, New York: Free Press.

Bell, B.D., and G.G. Stanfield
1973 "The aging stereotype in experimental perspective." Gerontologist 13:341-344.

Bell, I.P.
1976 "The double standard." Pp. 353-363 in J. Blakenship (ed.), Scenes from Life. Boston: Little, Brown and Company.

Bennett, H.S.
1937 Life on the English Manor. New York Macmillan.

Bennett, R., and J. Eckman
1973 "Attitudes toward aging: a critical examination of recent literature and implications for future research." Pp. 575-597 in C. Eisdorfer and P. Lawton (eds.), The Psychology of Adult Development and Aging. Washington, D.C.: American Psychological Association.

Berger, P.L.
1963 Invitation to Sociology: A Humanistic Perspective. Garden City, New York: Anchor/Doubleday.

Berger, P.L., and T. Luckman
1966 The Social Construction of Reality. Garden City, New York:

Anchor/Doubleday.

Bernard, L.L., and J. Bernard
1965   Origins of American Sociology. New York: Russell and Russell.

Bernstein, M.C.
1980   "Shifting age patterns won't do Social Security in." New York Times, September 21.

Best, F., and B. Stern
1977   "Education, work, and leisure: must they come in that order?" Monthly Labor Review 100:3-10.

Betten, N.
1973   "American attitudes toward the poor: a historical overview." Current History 65:2-5.

Binstock, R.H.
1981   "The politics of aging interest groups." Pp. 47-73 in R. Hudson (ed.), The Aging in Politics: Process and Policy. Springfield, Illinois: Charles C. Thomas.
1983   "The aged as scapegoat." Gerontologist 23:136-143.

Birnbaum, H., et al.
1981   Public Pricing of Nursing Home Care. Cambridge, Massachusetts: Abt Books.

Birren, J.
1978   "A gerontologist's overview." Pp. 197-208 in L.F. Jarvik (ed.), Aging in the 21st Century: Middle-Agers Today. New York: Gardner Press.

Blau, P.M.
1964   Exchange and Power in Social Life. New York: Wiley.

Blaug, M.
1963   "The myth of the old poor law and the making of the new." Journal of Economic History 23:151-184.
1964   "The poor law report reexamined." Journal of Economic History 24:229-245.

Blauner, R.
1972   Racial Oppression in America. New York: Harper and Row.

Bloch, M.
1961   Feudal Society. 2 Volumes. Translated by L.A. Manyon. Chicago: University of Chicago Press.

Block, M.R., and J.D. Sinnott (eds.)
1979   The Battered Elder Syndrome: An Exploratory Study. College Park, Maryland: University of Maryland Center on Aging.

Bloom, B.S.
1979   "Stretching ideology to the utmost: Marxism and medical

technology." American Journal of Public Health 69:1269-1271.

Bluestone, B., B. Harrison, and L. Baker
    1981   Corporate Flight: The Causes and Consequences of Economic Dislocation. Washington, D.C.: The Progressive Alliance.

Bogart, L.
    1972   "Negro and white media exposure: new evidence." Journalism Quarterly 49:15-21.

Bolsen, B.
    1981   "CT scanning of the brain: a revolution in only eight years." Journal of the American Medical Association 246:2667-2668, 2675.

Borgatta, E.F., and H.J. Meyer
    1959   Social Control and the Foundations of Sociology: Pioneer Contributions of Edward Alsworth Ross to the Study of Society. Boston: Beacon Press.

Boston Herald American
    1981   "TV ads denying women an equal voice." January 3.

Botwinick, J.
    1978   Aging and Behavior. New York: Springer.

Bower, R.T.
    1973   Television and the Public. New York: Holt, Rinehart and Winston.

Bowker, L.H.
    1982   Humaninzing Institutions for the Aged. Lexington, Massachusetts: Lexington.

Bradford, W.
    1962   Of Plymouth Plantation. New York: Capricorn Books.

Branco, K.J., and J.B. Williamson
    1982   "Stereotyping and the life cycle: a focus on views of the aged." Pp. 364-410 in A.G. Miller (ed.), In the Eye of the Beholder: Contemporary Issues in Stereotyping. New York: Praeger.

Braudel, F.
    1967   Capitalism and Material Life: 1400-1800. Translated by M. Kochan. London: Weidenfeld and Nicolson.

Braverman, H.
    1974   Labor and Monopoly Capital: The Degradation of Work in the Twentieth Century. New York: Monthly Review Press.

Braverman, J.
    1982   The Consumer's Book of Health. Philadelphia: W.B. Saunders.

Bremner, R.H.
1956   From the Depths. New York: New York University Press.
Brickner, P.
1978   Home Health Care for the Aged. New York: Appleton-
        Century-Crofts.
Bridges, A.
1974   "Nicos Poulanzas and the Theory of the Capitalist State." Poli-
        tics and Society 4:161-195.
Brotman, H.B.
1978   "The aging of America: a demographic profile." National
        Journal 10:1962.
Brown, E.
1979   Rockefeller Medicine Men: Medicine and Capitalism in
        America. Berkeley: University of California Press.
Brown, L.
1979   "Study finds stereotyping in TV casts." New York Times, Oc-
        tober 30.
Buchanan, R.
1981   Health-Care Financing. Lexington, Massachusetts: Lex-
        ington.
Buckingham, R., and D. Lups
1982   "A comparative study of hospice services." American Journal
        of Public Health 72:455-463.
Buraway, M.
1978   "Toward a Marxist theory of the labor process: Braverman and
        beyond." Politics and Society 8:247-312.
1979   Manufacturing Consent. Chicago: University of Chicago
        Press.
Burke V., and V. Burke
1981   "Supplemental Security Income." Pp. 162-175 in R. Hudson
        (ed.), The Aging in Politics: Process and Policy. Springfield,
        Illinois: Charles C. Thomas.
Business Week
1977   "Nursing the nursing homes back to health." December 5.
Butler, R.N.
1969   "Age-ism: another form of bigotry." Gerontologist 9:243-246.
Caldwell, J.M., and M.B. Kapp
1981   "The rights of nursing home patients: possibilities and limita-
        tions of federal regulation." Journal of Health Politics, Policy
        and Law 6:40-48.

Califano, J.
   1981   "The aging of America and the four generation society." Pp.
           282-294 in R. Hudson (ed.), The Aging in Politics: Process
           and Policy. Springfield, Illinois: Charles C. Thomas.
Callahan, D.
   1973   The Tyranny of Survival. New York: Macmillan.
Callahan, J.J.
   1981   "The impact of federal programs on long-term care." Pp. 177-
           192 in S. H. Altman and H.M. Sapolsky (eds.), Federal
           Health Programs. Lexington, Massachusetts: Lexington.
Callahan, J., and S. Wallack
   1981   Reforming the Long-Term Care System. Lexington, Massa-
           chusetts: Lexington.
Callahan, W.
   1977   Medicare Use of Home Health Services. Washington, D.C.:
           Department of Health and Human Services.
Cant, G.
   1978   "Is the heart bypass necessary?" Time, April 3.
Carels, E., D. Neuhauser, and W. Statson
   1980   The Physician and Cost-Control. Cambridge, Massachusetts:
           Oelgeschlager, Gunn and Hain.
Carey, J.
   1978   "Interactive television: a frame analysis." Pp. 245-308 in M.L.
           Moss (ed.), Two-Way Cable Television: An Evaluation of
           Community Uses in Reading, Pennsylvania. Final Report to
           the National Science Foundation. Volume I. New York: New
           York University, Graduate School of Public Administration.
Carlson, R.
   1975   The End of Medicine. New York: Wiley.
Cash, W.R.
   1980   "Changes in Social Security benefits next year." Boston Globe,
           December 3.
Chaffee, S., and D. Wilson
   1975   "Adult life cycle changes in mass media use." Paper presented
           at the Annual Meeting of the Association for Education in
           Journalism, Ottowa, Canada.
Cicero
   1967   On Old Age. Translated by F.O. Copley, Ann Arbor, Michi-
           gan: University of Michigan Press.
Cipolla, C.M.
   1976   Before the Industrial Revolution. New York: W.W. Norton.

Clark, M., and B.G. Anderson
  1967   Culture and Aging: An Anthropological Study of Older
          Americans. Springfield, Illinois: Charles C. Thomas.
Clark, R.L., and Menefee, J.A.
  1981   "Federal expenditure for the elderly: past and future." Geron-
          tologist 21:132-137.
Clawson, D.
  1980   Bureaucracy and the Labor Process. New York: Monthly Re-
          view Press.
Clinard, M.B.
  1974   Sociology of Deviant Behavior. New York: Holt, Rinehart and
          Winston.
Cobb, N.
  1982a   "What's ahead after the 20s: not-so-sweet 16." Boston Globe,
          January 24.
  1982b   "Disspelling misconceptions about old age." Boston Globe,
          January 25.
Coe, R.
  1980   "Professional perspectives on the aged." Pp. 472-481 in J.S.
          Quadagno (ed.), Aging, the Individual and Society. New
          York: St. Martin's Press.
Coffman, G.R.
  1934   "Old age from Horace to Chaucer: some literary affinities and
          adventures of an idea." Speculum 9:249-277.
Cohen, W.J.
  1957   Retirement Policies Under Social Security: A Legislative His-
          tory of Retirement Ages, the Retirement Test and Disability
          Benefits. Berkeley: University of California Press.
Cohodes, D.R.
  1982   "Where you stand depends on where you sit: musings on the
          regulation/ competition dialogue." Journal of Health Politics,
          Policy and Law 7:54-79.
Coll, B.D.
  1969   Perspectives in Public Welfare. Washington, D.C.: U.S. Gov-
          ernment Printing Office.
Coltin, W.
  1981   "Free care makes Barney Frank carefree." Boston Herald
          American, January 29.
Commission on Freedom of the Press
  1947   A Free and Responsible Press. Chicago: University of Chi-
          cago Press.

Comstock, G.S., N. Chaffee, N. McCombs, and D. Roberts
  1978   Television and Human Behavior, New York: Columbia University Press.
Comte, A.
  1896   The Positive Philosophy. Translated by H. Martineau. London: George Bell.
Congressional Budget Office
  1977a   Long-Term Care: Actuarial Cost Estimates. Washington, D.C.: U.S. Government Printing Office.
  1977b   Poverty Study of Families Under Alternative Definitions of Income. Washington, D.C.: U.S. Government Printing Office.
  1981   Paying for Social Security: Funding Options for the Near Term. Washington, D.C.: U.S. Government Printing Office.
Cooley, C.H.
  1902   Human Nature and the Social Order. New York: Charles Scribner's Sons.
Coriot, B.
  1980   "The restructuring of the assembly line: the new economy of time and control." Capital and Class 11(Summer):34-43.
Cottrel, F.
  1966   "Aging and the political system." Pp. 77-113 in J.C. McKinney and F.T. deVyver (eds.), Aging and Social Policy. New York: Appleton-Century-Crofts.
Coulton, G.G.
  1925   The Medieval Village. Cambridge, England: Cambridge University Press.
Crowley, M.
  1980   The View from 80. New York: Viking Press.
Cumming, E., and W. Henry
  1961   Growing Old: The Process of Disengagement. New York: Basic Books.
Currier, F.
  1975   "Aging and the media." Unpublished paper. Chicago: Center for Communication Analysis and Market Opinion Research.
Curtis, C.
  1983   "Machines vs. workers." New York Times, February 8.
Daly, C.
  1984   "Projects to test health plan for the elderly." Boston Globe, August 12.

Danowski, J.
  1975   "Information aging: implications for alternative futures of so-
          cietal information systems." Paper presented at the Annual
          Meeting of the International Communication Association,
          Chicago.
Darwin, C.
  1936   The Origin of the Species and the Descent of Man. New York:
          Modern Library.
Davidson, S.M.
  1980   The Cost of Living Longer. Lexington, Massachusetts: Lex-
          ington.
Davies, D.
  1975   The Centenarians of the Andes. New York: Anchor Double-
          day.
Davis, K.
  1938   "Mental hygiene and the class structure." Psychiatry 1:55-65.
Davis, K., and P. Van der Oever
  1981   "Age relations and public policy in advanced industrial so-
          cieties." Population and Development Review 7(1):1-18.
Davis, K., and C. Schoen
  1978   Health and the War on Poverty: A Ten-Year Appraisal.
          Washington, D. C.: The Brookings Institution.
Davis, M.
  1975   "The stopwatch and wooden shoe: scientific management and
          the IWW." Radical American 8(6):68-95.
Davis, N.J.
  1975   Sociological Constructions of Deviance. Dubuque, Iowa:
          W.C. Brown.
Davis, R.
  1971   "Television and the older adult." Journal of Broadcasting
          15:153-159.
  1975   "Television communication and the elderly." Pp. 315-335 in D.
          Woodruff and J. Birren (eds.), Aging: Scientific Perspectives
          and Social Issues. New York: Van Nostrand Reinhold.
Davis, R., A.E. Edwards, D.J. Bartel, and D. Martin
  1976   "Assessing television viewing behavior of older adults." Journal
          of Broadcasting 20:69-76.
Decker, D.L.
  1975   "Toward a critical perspective on aging." Paper presented at
          the Annual Meetings of the Gerontological Society, Louisville.

DeGrazia, S.
  1961   "The users of time," Pp. 113-154, R.W. Kleemeier (ed.), Aging and Leisure. New York: Oxford University Press.
Demkovich, L.E.
  1982   "Nobody's happy over administration's attempt to change nursing home rules." National Journal 11:508-510.
Dentzer, S., et al.
  1983   "The big business of medicine." Newsweek, October 31.
Derthick, M.
  1979   Policymaking for Social Security. Washington, D.C.: The Brookings Institution.
Devine, D.J.
  1972   The Political Culture of the United States: The Influence of Member Values on Regime Maintenance. Boston: Little, Brown and Company.
Dewey, J.
  1939   Freedom and Culture. New York: G.P. Putnam's Sons.
Dimmick, J.W., T.A. McCain, and W.T. Bolton
  1979   "Media use and the life span: notes on theory and method." American Behavioral Scientist 23:7-31.
Dobb, M.
  1963   Studies in the Development of Capitalism. Revised edition. New York: International Publishers.
Doolittle, J.
  1977   "Predictors of media use by older adults." Paper presented at the Annual Meeting of the Gerontological Society, San Francisco.
Doty, P., and E.W. Sullivan
  1983   "Community involvement in combating abuse, neglect and mistreatment in nursing homes." Milbank Memorial Fund Quarterly/Health and Society 61:222-251.
Dowd, J.J.
  1980   Stratification Among the Aged. Monterey, California: Brooks/ Cole.
DuBois, P.
  1980   The Hospice Way of Death. New York: Human Sciences Press.
Dubos, R.
  1959   Mirage of Health. New York: Harper and Row.
Duncan, D.
  1908   The Life and Letters of Herbert Spencer. New York: Appleton

and Company.

Dunlop, B.D.
1979   The Growth of Nursing Home Care. Lexington, Massachu-
        setts: Lexington.

Durkheim, E.
1938   The Rules of Sociological Method. Translated by S.A. Solo-
        vay and J.H. Mueller. Chicago: University of Chicago Press.
1951   Suicide. Translated by J.A. Spaulding and G. Simpson. Glen-
        coe, Illinois: Free Press.
1958   Professonal Ethics and Civil Morals. Translated by C. Brook-
        field. Glencoe, Illinois: Free Press.

Eastaugh, S.
1981   Medical Economics and Health Finance. Boston: Auburn
        House.

Edwards, R.
1978   "The social relations of production at the point of production."
        Union for Radical Political Economists 8(2-3):109-125.
1979   Contested Terrain: The Transformation of the Workplace in
        the Twentieth Century. New York: Basic Books.

Ehrenreich, B., and J. Ehrenreich
1971   The American Health Empire: Power, Profits and Politics.
        New York: Vintage.
1978   "Medicine and social control." Pp. 39-79 in J. Ehrenreich
        (ed.), The Cultural Crisis of Modern Medicine. New York:
        Monthly Review Press.

Engels, F.
1902   The Origins of the Family, Private Property, and the State.
        Chicago: Charles H. Kerr and Company.

England, P., A. Kuhn, and T. Gardner
1981   "The ages of men and women in magazine advertisements."
        Journalism Quarterly 58:468-471.

Enthoven, A.C.
1980   Health Plan: The Only Practical Solution to the Soaring Cost
        of Medical Care. Reading, Massachusetts: Addison-Wesley.

Estes, C.L.
1974   "Community planning for the elderly: a study of goal displace-
        ment." Journal of Gerontology 29:684-691.
1979   The Aging Enterprise: A Critical Examination of Social Poli-
        cies and Services for the Aged. San Francisco: Jossey-Bass.

Estes, C.L., and R.J. Newcomer
1983   "The future for aging and public policy." Pp. 249-270 in C.L.

Estes and R.J. Newcomer (eds.), Fiscal Austerity and Aging: Shifting Government Responsibility for the Elderly. Beverly Hills: Sage Publications.

Etzioni, A.
1976   "Old people and public policy." Social Policy 6:21-29.

Evans, L., and J.B. Williamson
1981   "Social security and social control." Generations 6:18-20.

Evans, R.
1974   "Supplier-induced demand: some empirical evidence and implications." Pp. 162-173 in M. Perlman (ed.), The Economics of Health and Medical Care. London: Macmillan.

Farrell, R.A., and V.L. Swigert
1982   Deviance and Social Control. Glenview, Illinois: Scott, Foresman and Company.

Feagin, J.R.
1975   Subordinating the Poor. Englewood Cliffs, New Jersey: Prentice-Hall.

Feagin, J.R., and C.B. Feagin
1978   Discrimination American Style. Englewood Cliffs, New Jersey: Prentice-Hall.

Feldstein, M.S.
1977   "Facing the crisis of social security." The Public Interest 47:88-100.

1981   Hospital Costs and Health Insurance. Cambridge, Massachusetts: Harvard University Press.

Feldstein, P.
1977   Health Associations and the Demand for Legislation. Cambridge, Massachusetts: Ballinger.

Felton, B.J., M. Moss, and R. Sepulveda
1978   "Two-way cable television programming for older people." Paper presented at the Annual Meeting of the Gerontological Society, Dallas, Texas.

Fine, S.
1956   Laissez-Faire and the General Welfare State: A Study of Conflict in American Thought, 1865-1901. Ann Arbor, Michigan: University of Michigan Press.

Fischer, D.H.
1978   Growing Old in America. Expanded edition. New York: Oxford University Press.

Fishel, L.
1967   "The problem of social control." Pp. 499-515 in M. Kranzberg

and C.W. Pursell (eds.), Technology in Western Civilization. New York: Oxford University Press.

Fisher, C.
1980   "Differences by age groups in health care spending." Health Care Financing Review 1(Spring):65-90.

Flaste, R.
1979   "Research begins to focus on suicide among the aged." New York Times, January 2.

Fontana, A.
1978   "Ripping off the elderly: inside the nursing home." Pp. 125-132 in J.M. Johnson and J.D. Douglas (eds.), Crime at the Top: Deviance in Business and the Professions. Philadelphia: J.B. Lippincott.

Foreman, J.
1980   "Dating after 55: it isn't easy." Boston Globe, February 3.

Fox, D.
1979   Economists and Health Care. New York: Prodist.

Fox, R.
1973   "A sociological perspective on organ transplantation and hemodialysis." Pp. 120-142 in R.W. Wertz (ed.), Readings on Ethical and Social Issues in Biomedicine. Englewood Cliffs, New Jersey: Prentice-Hall.

Fox, R., and J. Swazey
1974   The Courage to Fail: A Social View of Organ Transplants and Dialysis. Chicago: University of Chicago Press.

Francher, J.S.
1973   "'It's the Pepsi generation': accelerated aging and the television commercial." International Journal of Aging and Human Development 4:245-255.

Freeland, M.S., and C.E. Schendler
1983   "National health expenditure growth in the 1980s: an aging population, new technologies, and increased competition." Health Care Financing Review 4(March):1-58.

Friedman, B.
1976   "Mortality, disability and the normative economics of Medicare." Pp. 365-384 in R.N. Rosett (ed.), The Role of Health Insurance in the Health Services Sector. New York: Neale Watson.

Friedrich, C.J.
1963   Man and His Government. New York: McGraw-Hill.

Fuchs, N.E.
   1980   "What is CBA/CEA and why are they doing this to us?" New England Journal of Medicine 303:937-938.

Furniss, E.S.
   1965   The Position of the Laborer in a System of Nationalism. New York: Kelly.

Fusgen, I., and J. Summa
   1978   "How much sense is there to resuscitate an aged person." Gerontology 24:37-45.

Galbraith, J.K.
   1984   "The heartless society." New York Times Magazine, September 2.

Gamson, W., and K. Lasch
   1983   "The political culture of social welfare policy." Pp. 397-415 in S. Spiro and E. Yuchtman-Yaar (eds.), Evaluating the Welfare State. New York: Academic Press.

Gans, H.J.
   1981   "The uses of poverty: the poor pay all." Pp. 140-147 in J. B. Williamson, L. Evans, and A. Munley (eds.), Social Problems: The Contemporary Debates. Boston: Little, Brown and Company.

Garnham, N.
   1979   "Towards a political economy of mass communications." Media, Culture, and Society 2:123-146.

Gartman, D.
   1979   "Marx and the labor process." Insurgent Sociologist 8(2-3):97-108.

George, L.K.
   1980   Role Transition in Later Life. Monterey, California: Brooks/Cole.

Gerald, J.E.
   1963   The Social Responsibility of the Press. Minneapolis, Minnesota: University of Minnesota Press.

Gerbner, G.
   1961   "Press perspectives in world communication: a pilot study." Journalism Quarterly 38:312-322.

Gerbner, G., et al.
   1977   "TV violence profile no. 8: the highlights." Journal of Communication 27:171-180.

Gerbner, G., and L. Gross
   1976   "The scary world of TV's heavy viewer." Psychology Today

9(April):41-45, 89.

Gerbner, G., L. Gross, N. Signoriellie, and M. Morgan
1980   "Aging with television: images on television drama and conceptions of social reality." Journal of Communication 30:37-47.

Gerver, I.
1963   Lester Frank Ward, New York: Thomas Y. Crowell.

Gibson, R.M., D.R. Waldo, and K.R. Levit
1983   "National health expenditures, 1982." Health Care Financing Review 5(Fall):1-32.

Giddens, A.
1971   Capitalism and Modern Social Theory: Analysis of the Writings of Marx, Durkheim, and Max Weber. London: Cambridge University Press.

Gierke, O.
1927   Political Theories of the Middle Ages. Translated by F.W. Maitland. Cambridge, England: Cambridge University Press.

Gillespie, G.
1975   Public Access Cable Television in the United States and Canada. New York: Praeger.

Ginzberg, E.
1977   The Limits of Health Care Reform. New York: Basic Books.
1982   "Competition in health care: a second opinion." Hospitals 56(March 16):81-85.

Girshick, L.B.
1980   "The measurement of poverty: the case of the elderly." Paper presented at the Annual Meetings of the Society for the Study of Social Problems, New York.

Girshick, L.B., and J.B. Williamson
1982   "The politics of measuring poverty among the elderly." Policy Studies Journal 10:483-289.

Glasson, W.H.
1918   Federal Military Pensions in the United States. New York: Oxford University Press.

Glenn, N.
1978   "Age and attitudinal stability." Paper presented at the Annual Meetings of the American Sociological Association, San Francisco.

Glenn, N., and M. Grimes
1968   "Aging, voting, and political interest." American Sociological Review 33:563-575.

Goffman, E.
    1961   Asylums. Garden City, New York: Anchor/Doubleday.
    1963   Stigma: Notes on the Management of Spoiled Identity. Engle-
            wood Cliffs, New Jersey: Prentice-Hall.
Goldenberg, I.
    1978   Oppression and Social Intervention. Chicago: Nelson-Hall.
Gordon, A., A. Herman, and P. Schervish
    n.d.   Class and Class Struggle in the New Era of Capitalism: The
            Socialist Potential of New Work Arrangments, forthcoming.
Gordon, D.
    1976   "Capitalist efficiency and socialist efficiency." Pp. 19-39 in R.
            Baxandall et al. (eds.), Technology, Labor and the Working
            Class. New York: Monthly Review Press.
Gordon, D., R. Edwards, and M. Reich
    1982   Segmented Work, Divided Workers. New York: Cambridge
            University Press.
Gorz, A.
    1978   "The tyranny of the factory." Pp. 55-61 in A. Gorz (ed.), The
            Division of Labor. Sussex, England: Harvester Press.
Gough, I.
    ·1975   "State expenditure in advanced capitalism." New Left Review
            92:53-92.
    1979   The Political Economy of the Welfare State. London: Macmil-
            lan.
Goulder, A.W.
    1970   The Coming Crisis of Western Sociology. New York: Avon.
Graebner, W.
    1980   A History of Retirement. New Haven, Connecticut: Yale Uni-
            versity Press.
Graney, M.
    1974   "Media use as a substitute activity in old age." Journal of Ger-
            ontology 29:322-324.
Graney, M., and E. Graney
    1974   "Communications activity substitutions in aging." Journal of
            Communication 24:88-96.
Green, S.K.
    1981   "Attitudes and perceptions about the elderly: current and fu-
            ture perspectives." International Journal of Aging and Human
            Development 13:99-119.
Greenhouse, L.
    1980   "Congressional report predicts problems due to population

trends." New York Times, November 17.

Griffen, L.J., J.A. Devine, and M. Wallace
1981   "Accumulation, legitimation, and politics: the growth of welfare expenditures in the United States since the Second World War." Paper presented at the Annual Meetings of the American Sociological Association, Toronto.

Grimaldi, P.L.
1982   Medicaid Reimbursement of Nursing Home Care. Washington, D.C.: America Enterprise Institute for Public Policy Research.

Grinner, P.
1972   "Treatment of acute pulmonary edema: conventional or intensive care?" Annals of Internal Medicine 77:501-506.

Gubrium, J.
1975   Living and Dying at Murray Manor. New York: St. Martin's Press.

Gutman, H.G.
1976   Work, Culture and Society in Industrializing America. New York: Knopf.

Haber, W., and W. Cohen
1960   Social Security: Programs, Problems, and Policies. Homewood, Illinois: R.D. Irwin.

Hacker, H.M.
1975   "Women as a minority group." Pp. 505-520 in J. Freeman (ed.), Woman: A Feminist Perspective. Palo Alto, California: Mayfield.

Halamandaris, V.J.
1983   "Fraud and abuse in nursing homes." Pp. 104-114 in J. Kosberg (ed.), Abuse and Maltreatment of the Elderly, Boston: John Wright.

Hall, C.
1974   Medicaid Basic and Optimal Service: Impact on the Poor. Philadelphia, Pennsylvania: Temple University Press.

Hammond, J.L., and B. Hammond
1911   The Village Labourer. London: Longmans, Green.

Hamovitch, M., and J. Peterson
1969   "Housing needs and satisfaction of the elderly." Gerontologist 9:30-32.

Hampson, E.M.
1934   The Treatment of Poverty in Cambridgeshire 1597-1834. Cambridge, England: Cambridge University Press.

Handlin, O., and M.F. Handlin
 1969   Commonwealth. Cambridge, Massachusetts: Belknap Press.
Hapgood, D.
 1978   "The aging are doing better." Pp. 345-363 in R. Gross, B.
        Gross, and S. Seidman (eds.), The New Old: Struggling for
        Decent Aging. Garden City, New York: Anchor/Doubleday.
Haraszti, Z.
 1952   John Adams and the Prophets of Progress. Cambridge, Mas-
        sachusetts: Harvard University Press.
Harrington, M.
 1980   Decade of Decision: The Crisis of the American System. New
        York: Simon and Schuster.
Harris, A., and J. Feinberg
 1977   "Television and aging: is what you see what you get?" Geronto-
        logist 17:464-468.
Harris, L.
 1974   "A survey on aging: experiences of older Americans versus
        public expectations of old age." New York: Louis Harris and
        Associates.
Harris, L., and Associates
 1975   The Myth and Reality of Aging in America. New York: Na-
        tional Council on Aging.
Harris, R.
 1966   "Annals of legislation: Medicare." Part I. New Yorker, July 2.
Hartz, L.
 1955   The Liberal Tradition in America. New York: Harcourt,
        Brace.
Havighurst, C.C.
 1978   "The role of competition in cost containment." Pp. 285-323 in
        W. Greenberg (ed.), Competition in the Health Care Sector.
        Germantown, Maryland: Aspen.
Hayes, T.
 1980   "Panel suggests a retirement age of 68 for Social Security bene-
        fits." New York Times, November 19.
Health Insurance Association of America
 1982   Sourcebook   of   Health   Insurance   Data   1981-1982.
        Washington, D.C.: Health Insurance Association of America.
Hechter, M.
 1975   Internal Colonialism. Berkeley, California: University of Cali-
        fornia Press.

Hemming, S., and K. Ellis
  1976   "How fair is TV's image of older Americans?" Retirement Living 16(April):21-24.
Hendricks, J., and C. Hendricks
  1977   Aging in Mass Society: Myths and Realities. Cambridge, Massachusetts. Winthrop.
Henriques, U.R.Q.
  1979   Before the Welfare State: Social Administration in Early Industrial Britain. New York: Longmans, Green.
Herman, A.
  1982   "Conceptualizing control: domination and hegemony in the capitalist labor process." Insurgent Sociologist 11(Fall):7-22.
Hess, B.
  1974   "Stereotypes of the aged." Journal of Communication 24:76-85.
Hesse-Biber, S., and J.B. Williamson
  1984   "Resource theory and power in families: life cycle considerations." Family Process 23:261-278.
Hickey, T., and R.L. Douglass
  1981   "Neglect and abuse of older family members." Gerontologist 21:171-176.
Hirsch, B., H.A. Silverman and A. Dobson
  1982   Medicare Summary: Use and Reimbursement by Person 1976-1978. Baltimore, Maryland: Health Care Financing Administration.
Hobbes, T.
  1958   Leviathan. Indianapolis: Bobbs-Merrill.
Hobshawn, E.J.
  1959   Social Bandits and Primitive Rebels: Studies in Archaic Forms of Social Movement in the Nineteenth and Twentieth Centuries, Glencoe, Illinois: Free Press.
Hoffman, F.L.
  1906   "Physical and medical aspects of labor and industry." Annals of the American Academy of Political and Social Science 27:3-28.
Hofstadter, R.
  1944   Social Darwinism in American Thought 1860-1915. London: Oxford University Press.
Holtzman, J.M., and J.D. Beck
  1979   "Palmore's facts on aging quiz: a reappraisal." Gerontologist 19:116-120.

Homans, G.C.
    1961   Social Behavior: Its Elementary Forms. New York: Harcourt.
Hospitals
    1982   "Study describes state's long-term care as a 'bureaucratic nightmare." 56(May 1):50.
Huber, J., and W.H. Form
    1973   Income and Ideology. New York: Free Press.
Hudson, R.
    1981   "The graying of the federal budget and it's consequences for old-age policy." Pp. 261-281 in R. Hudson (ed.), The Aging in Politics: Process and Policy. Springfield, Illinois: Charles C. Thomas.
Hudson, R. (ed.)
    1981   The Aging in Politics: Process and Policy. Springfield, Illinois: Charles C. Thomas.
Hughes, E.C.
    1964   "Good people and dirty work." Pp. 23-36 in H. Becker (ed.), The Other Side. New York: Free Press.
Huntington, S.P.
    1968   Political Order in Changing Societies. New Haven, Connecticut: Yale University Press.
Hurst, J.W.
    1970   The Legitimacy of the Business Corporation in the Law of the United States, 1780-1970. Charlottesville, Virginia: University Press of Virginia.
Hwang, J.C.
    1974   "Aging and information." Communication 3:58-61.
Iglehart, J.K.
    1976   "Is it time for biomedical researchers to hunt for new fields?" National Journal 8:1217-1221.
    1981   "Drawing the lines for the debate on competition." New England Journal of Medicine 305:291-296.
    1982a   "Special report on Duke University Medical Center Private Sector Conference." New England Journal of Medicine 307:68-71.
    1982b   "Federal policies and the poor." New England Journal of Medicine 307:836-840.
    1982c   "Health policy report." New England Journal of Medicine 307:836-840.
    1983   "Another chance for technology assessment." New England Journal of Medicine 309:509-512.

Ikegami, N.
1982   "Institutionalized and non-institutionalized elderly." Social
        Science Medicine 16:2001-2008.
Illich, I.
1976   Medical Nemesis: The Expropriation of Health. New York:
        Pantheon.
Ingram, D.K., and J.R. Barry
1977   "National statistics on deaths in nursing homes." Gerontologist
        17:303-308.
Innis, H.
1951   The Bias of Communication. Toronto: Toronto University
        Press.
Institute of Medicine
1977   A Policy Statement: The Elderly and Functional Dependency.
        Washington, D.C.: National Academy of Sciences.
Israel, H., and J.P. Robinson
1972   "Demographic characteristics of viewers of television violence
        and news programs." Pp. 87-128 in E. Rubinstein, G. Com-
        stock, and J. Murray (eds.), Television and Social Behavior.
        Volume 4. Washington, D.C.: U.S. Government Printing Of-
        fice.
Jacobs, B.
1982   An Overview of the National Potential of Home Equity Con-
        version into Income for the Elderly. Madison, Wisconsin:
        Home Equity Conversion Project.
Jernegan, M.W.
1931   Laboring and Dependent Classes in Colonial America, 1607-
        1783. Chicago: University of Chicago Press.
Johnson, E.S. and J.B. Williamson
1980   Growing Old. New York: Holt, Rinehart and Winston.
Jones, J.M.
1972   Prejudice and Racism. Reading, Massachusetts: Addison-
        Wesley.
Jones, W., and W. Simpson
1966   NASA Contributions to: Cardiovascular Monitoring.
        Washington, D.C.: U.S. Government Printing Office.
Jordan, W.K.
1959   Philanthropy in England 1480-1660. London: Allen and Un-
        win.
1961   The Charities of Rural England 1480-1660. New York: Rus-
        sell Sage.

Judge, K.
    1982   "Federal expenditure for the elderly: a different interpretation
            of the past." Gerontologist 22:129-131.
Jules, H.
    1963   Culture Against Man. New York: Random House.
Kaercher, D.
    1984   "Amazing advances in medical technology." Better Homes and
            Gardens 62(January):15-21.
Kalish, R.A.
    1969   "The new ageism and the failure models: a polemic." Geronto-
            logist 19:398-402.
Kane, R., and R. Kane
    1982   Values and Long-Term Care. Lexington, Massachusetts: Lex-
            ington.
Kaplan, J.
    1982   "Three perspectives on the 1981 White House Conference on
            Aging." Gerontologist 22:125-128.
Katz, J., and A. Capron
    1975   Catastrophic Disease: Who decides What? A Psychosocial and
            Legal Analysis of the Problems Posed by Hemodialysis and
            Organ Transplantation. New York: Rusell Sage.
Kellner, D.
    1978   "Ideology, Marxism and advanced capitalism." Socialist Re-
            view 8:37-65.
Kelso, R.W.
    1922   The History of Public Poor Relief in Massachusetts, 1620-
            1920. Boston: Houghton Mifflin.
Kirchheimer, A.
    1981   "Abuse of the elderly: a growing social problem." Boston
            Globe, January 6.
Klapper, J.T.
    1960   The Effects of Mass Communication. New York: Free Press.
Klebaner, B.J.
    1952   "Public poor relief in America, 1790-1860." Unpublished doc-
            toral dissertation. New York: Columbia University.
Klemesrud, J.
    1980   "'If your face isn't young': women confront problems of aging."
            New York Times, October 10.
Knaus, W., et al.
    1981   "The range of intensive care services today." Journal of the
            American Medical Association 246:2711-2716.

Koch, L., and J. Koch
  1980   "Parent abuse — a new plague." Parade Magazine, January
          27.
Koetting, M.
  1980   Nursing Home Organization and Efficiency. Lexington, Mas-
          sachusetts: D.C. Heath.
Koff, T.
  1980   Hospice, A Caring Community. Cambridge, Massachusetts:
          Winthrop.
  1982   Long-Term Care. Boston: Little, Brown and Company.
Kogan, N.
  1961   "Attitudes toward old people." Journal of Abnormal and Social
          Psychology 62:44-54.
Kogan, N., and F.C. Shelton
  1962a   "Beliefs about 'old people': a comparative study of older and
          younger samples." Journal of Genetic Psychology 100:93-111.
  1962b   "Images of 'old people' and 'people in general' in an older sam-
          ple." Journal of Genetic Psychology 100:3-21.
Kolko, G.
  1971   "Conclusion: the last democracy." Pp. 141-150 in I. Unger
          (ed.), Beyond Liberalism: The New Left Views American
          History. Waltham, Massachusetts: Xerox College Publishing.
Korzenny, F., and K. Neuendorf
  1980   "Television viewing and self-concept of the elderly." Journal of
          Communication 30:71-80.
Kosberg, J.
  1973   "Differences in proprietary institutions caring for the affluent
          and nonaffluent elderly." Gerontologist 13:299-304.
Kosberg, J., and S. Tobin
  1972   "Variability among nursing homes." Gerontologist 12:214-219.
Kubey, R.W.
  1980   "Television and the aging: past, present, and future." Geronto-
          logist 20:16-35.
Lagerstrom, L.
  1976   Pension Systems in Sweden. Stockholm: Pension Guarantee
          Mutual Insurance Company.
Lalonde, M.
  1974   A New Perspective on the Health of Canadians. Ottawa: In-
          formation Canada.
Lamb, H., et al.
  1976   Community Survival for Long-Term Patients. San Francisco:

            Jossey-Bass.
Lasch, K.
    1984   "The political culture of medical technology assessment." Un-
           published doctoral dissertation. Ann Arbor, Michigan: Uni-
           versity of Michigan.
Laslett, P.
    1967   Locke's Two Treatises of Government: A Critical Edition with
           an Introduction and Apparatus Criticus. Cambridge,
           England: Cambridge University Press.
    1976   "Societal development and aging." Pp. 87-116 in R.H. Bin-
           stock and E. Shanas (eds.), Handbook of Aging and the Social
           Sciences. New York: Van Nostrand Reinhold.
Lave, J.R., and H.A. Silverman
    1984   "Financing the health care of the aged." Annals of the Ameri-
           can Academy of Political and Social Science 468:149-164.
Lazarsfeld, P.F., and R.K. Merton
    1971   "Mass communication, popular taste and organized social ac-
           tion." Pp. 554-578 in W. Schramm and D. Roberts (eds.), The
           Process and Effects of Mass Communication. Urbana: Uni-
           versity of Illinois Press.
Lefcourt, H.M.
    1976   Locus of Control: Current Trends in Theory and Research.
           Hillside, New Jersey: L. Erbaum Associates.
Leiby, J.
    1967   Charity and Corrections in New Jersey. New Brunswick, New
           Jersey: Rutgers University Press.
Leonard, E.M.
    1900   The Early History of English Poor Relief. Cambridge,
           England: Cambridge University Press.
Leonard, L.R.
    1982   "The lies that bind: life care contracts and nursing homes."
           American Journal of Law and Medicine 8:153-173.
Lerner, M.
    1963   "The triumph of laissez-faire." Pp. 146-166 in A.M. Schle-
           singer Jr. and M. White (eds.), Paths of American Thought.
           Boston: Houghton Mifflin.
Leutz, W.N.
    1978   "Work and aging: the relevance of Marxian labor process
           theory." Unpublished paper. Waltham, Massachusetts: Heller
           School, Brandeis University.

Levin, J., and W.C. Levin
  1977   "Perceived age and willingness to interact with an old person."
          Paper presented at the Eastern Sociological Society Meetings,
          New York.
  1980   Ageism: Prejudices and Discrimination Against the Elderly.
          Belmont, California: Wadsworth.
Liberkis, L.R.
  1981   "Factors predisposing to institutionalization." Acta Psychia-
          trica Scandinavica 63:357-366.
Lifton, R.
  1965   "Woman as knower: some psychohistorical perspectives." Pp.
          27-51 in R. Lifton (ed.), The Woman in America. Boston:
          Houghton Mifflin.
Linden, M.E.
  1956   "The relationship between social attitudes toward aging and
          the delinquencies of youth." Paper presented at the First Pan-
          American Congress of Gerontology, Mexico City.
Locke, J.
  1937   A Letter Concerning Toleration. Edited by C.L. Sherman.
          New York: Appleton-Century.
Lodge, G.C.
  1975   The New American Ideology. New York: Knopf.
Lombroso, C.
  1918   Crime: Its Causes and Remedies. Boston: Little, Brown and
          Company.
Lopata, H.Z.
  1974   "Living through widowhood." Psychology Today 7(July):86-
          92.
Lowell, J.S.
  1884   Public Relief and Private Charity. New York: G.P. Putnam's
          Sons.
Lowry, R.
  1982   "Doing good while doing well." The Social Report 3(June):2-
          3.
Lubove, R.
  1968   The Struggle for Social Security 1900-1935. Cambridge, Mas-
          sachusetts: Harvard University Press.
Luft, H.
  1982   "On the potential failure of good ideas." Journal of Health Poli-
          tics, Policy and Law 7:45-53.

MacPherson, C.B.
  1962   The Political Theory of Possessive Individualism: Hobbes to
         Locke. London: Oxford University Press.
Main, J.T.
  1965   The Social Structure of Revolutionary America. Princeton:
         Princeton University Press.
Marglin, S.
  1974   "What do bosses do: the origins and functions of capitalist hi-
         erarchy in production." Review of Radical Political Economics
         6(Summer):33-60.
Marmor, T.R.
  1981   "Enacting Medicare." Pp. 105-134 in R. Hudson (ed.), The
         Aging in Politics: Process and Policy. Springfield, Illinois:
         Charles C. Thomas.
Marshall, D.
  1926   The English Poor Law in the Eighteenth Century. London:
         Routledge, Kegan and Paul.
Marshall, V.W., and J.A. Tindale
  1978   "Notes for a radical gerontology." International Journal of Ag-
         ing and Human Development 9:163-175.
Martin, A.
  1977   "Sweden: industrial democracy and social democratic strat-
         egy." Pp. 49-96 in G.D. Garson (ed.), Worker's Self-
         Management in Industry: The West European Experience.
         New York: Praeger.
Martin, W.C., V.L. Bengtson, and A.C. Acock
  1974   "Aliention and age: a context specific approach." Social Forces
         53:266-274.
Marx, K.
  1906a Capital: A Critique of Political Economy. Volume I. Chicago:
         Charles H. Kerr and Company.
  1906b Capital: A Critique of Political Economy. Volume III. Chi-
         cago: Charles H. Kerr and Company.
  1961   Economic and Philosophic Manuscripts of 1844. Moscow:
         Foreign Language Publishing House.
  1968   Marxist Social Thought. Edited by R. Freedman. New York:
         Harcourt, Brace and World.
  1974   Capital. Volume I. London: Lawrence and Wishart.
McClure, W.
  1981   "Structure and incentive problems in economic regulation of
         medical care." Milbank Memorial Fund Quarterly/Health and

Society 59:107-144.

McCluskey, H.Y.
1978   "Designs for learning." pp. 169-184 in L.F. Jarvik (ed.), Aging into the twenty-first Century: Middle-Agers Today. New York: Gardner Press.

McCormick, T.R.
1976   "The medical nurse practitioner in the skilled care facility." Hospitals 50(October 1):176-180.

McGinley, L.
1984   "Study says his policy hurt poor." The Wall Street Journal, August 16.

McLuhan, M., and B. Nevitt
1973   "Technology and causality: the argument, causality in the electric world." Technology and Culture 14:1-18.

McTavish, D.G.
1971   "Perceptions of old people: a review of research, methodologies, and findings." Gerontologist 11:90-101.

Mead, G.H.
1918   "The psychology of punitive justice." American Journal of Sociology 23:577-602.
1934   Mind, Self, and Society. Chicago: University of Chicago Press.

Mechanic, D.
1974   Politics, Medicine, and Social Science. New York: Wiley.
1976   The Growth of Bureaucratic Medicine: An Inquiry into the Dynamics of Patient Behavior and the Organization of Medical Care. New York: Wiley.
1978   "Social justice." Pp. 253-273 in R.M. Battistella and T.G. Rundall (eds.), Health Care Policy in a Changing Environment. Berkeley, California: McCutchan.

Medicaid/Medicare Management Institute
1979   Data on the Medicaid Program: Eligibility, Services, Expenditures. Baltimore: U.S. Department of Health, Education and Welfare.

Meidner, R.
1981   "Collective asset formation through wage earner funds." International Labor Review 120(3):303-334.

Meltzer, H.
1962   "Age differences in status and happiness of workers." Geriatrics 17:831-837.

Mendelson, M.A.
  1974   Tender Loving Greed. New York: Knopf.
Merton, R.K.
  1970   "Discrimination and the American creed." Pp. 449-464 in P.I.
          Rose (ed.), The Study of Society. New York: Random House.
Message from the President of the United States
  1983   Health Incentives Reform Program. Washington, D.C.: U.S.
          Government Printing Office.
Meyersohn, R.
  1961   "A critical examination of commercial entertainment." Pp.
          243-272 in R.W. Kleemeier (ed.), Aging and Leisure. New
          York: Oxford University Press.
Miller, D.
  1980   "Swing beds can work — with good planning." Hospitals
          54(May 16):97-103.
Miller, L.
  1979   "Toward a classification of aging behaviors." Gerontologist
          19:283-289.
Mohl, R.A.
  1971   Poverty in New York: 1783-1825. New York: Oxford University Press.
  1973   "Three centuries of American public welfare: 1600-1932."
          Current History 65:6-10.
Montgomery, D.
  1980   Workers Control in America. Cambridge, England: Cambridge University Press.
Moos, F.
  1977   Too Old, Too Sick, Too Bad — Nursing Homes in America.
          Germantown, Maryland: Aspen.
Moreland Commission
  1976   Report of the New York State Moreland Commission on Nursing Homes and Residential Facilities. Albany.
Moss, M.
  1978   "Research on community uses." Journal of Communication
          28:160-167.
Munley, A.
  1983   The Hospice Alternative. New York: Basic Books.
Myles, J.F.
  1980   "Institutionalizing the elderly: a critical assessment of the sociology of total institutions." Pp. 257-268 in V. Marshall (ed.),
          Aging in Canada: Social Perspectives. Toronto: Fitzhenry and

Whiteside.

1981a "The aged and the welfare state: an essay in political demo-grapy." Paper presented at the Meeting of the International Sociological Association, Research Committee on Aging, Paris.

1981b "The trillion dollar misunderstanding." Working Papers 8:22-31.

1984 Old Age and the Welfare State. Boston: Little, Brown and Company.

Najam, L.M., and S. Levine
1981 "Evaluating the impact of medical care and technologies on the quality of life: a review and critique." Society, Science and Medicine 151:107-115.

National Center for Health Statistics
1977 Health, United States: 1976-1977. Washington, D.C.: U.S. Government Printing Office.

National Commission on the Cost of Medical Care 1976-1977
1978 Monroe, Wisconsin: American Medical Association.

National Research Council Committee on Technology and Health Care
1979 Medical Technology and the Health Care System: A Study of the Diffusion of Equipment-Embodied Technology. Washington, D.C.: National Academy of Science.

Navarro, V.
1976 Medicine Under Capitalism. New York: Prodist.

Nesselroade, J.R., K.W. Scaie, and P.B. Baltes
1972 "Ontogenic and generational components of structural and quantitive change in adult behavior." Journal of Gerontology 27:222-228.

Neugarten, B.L.
1982 "Policy for the 1980s: age or need entitlement." Pp. 19-32 in B.L. Neugarten (ed.), Age or Need?: Public Policies for Older People. Beverly Hills: Sage Publications.

Neuwirth, G.
1969 "A Weberian outline of a theory of community: its application to the 'dark ghetto.'" British Journal of Sociology 20:148-163.

Newcomer, R.J., C. Harrington, C.L. Estes, and P.R. Lee
1982 "State adjustments in Medicaid program policies and expenditures: implications for health and human services for the elderly." Working Paper No. 20. San Francisco: Aging Health Policy Center, University of California.

Newhouse, J.P., W.G. Manning, and G.N. Morris
1981 "Some interim results from a controlled trial of cost sharing in

health insurance." New England Journal of Medicine 305:1501-1507.

Newhouse, J.P., and C. Phelps
  1976   "New estimates of price and income elasticities of medical services." Pp. 261-313 in R.N. Rosett (ed.), The Role of Health Insurance in the Health Services Sector. New York: Neale Watson.

New York Times/CBS Poll
  1982   "Party choices of voters 1982 vs. 1978." New York Times, November 8.

Nicholls, Sir G.
  1898   A History of the English Poor Laws. New edition. Volume I. A.D. 924 to 1714. London: P.S. King.

Nielsen, A.C.
  1974   Nielsen Estimates National Audience Demographic Report. Chicago: A.C. Nielsen Company.
  1976   Nielsen Estimates National Audience Demographic Report. Chicago: A.C. Nielsen Company.

Northcott, H.C.
  1975   "Too young, too old — age in the world of televisoin." Gerontologist 15:184-186.

Northrop, F.S.C.
  1946   The Meetings of East and West. New York: Macmillan.

Oberleder, M.
  1969   "Emotional breakdown in elderly people." Hospital and Community Psychiatry 20:191-196.

O'Connor, J.
  1973   The Fiscal Crisis of the State. New York: St. Martin's Press.
  1981   "The fiscal crisis of the state revisited: a look at economic crisis and Reagan's budget policy." Kapitalistate 9:41-61.

Offe, C.
  1975   "The theory of the capitalist state and the problem of policy formation." Pp. 125-144 in L. Lindberg et al. (eds.), Stress and Contradition in Modern Capitalism. Lexington, Massachusetts: Lexington.

Oliphant, T.
  1983   "Federal spending by function." Boston Globe, February 1.

Olson, L.K.
  1982   The Political Economy of Aging: The State, Private Power and Social Welfare. New York: Columbia University Press.

O'Neill, K.E.
  1984   Family and Farm in Pre-Famine Cavan: The Parish of Kil-
          lashandra. Madison: University of Wisconsin Press.
Opinion Research Corporation
  1957   The Public Appraises Movies: A Survey for the Motion Pic-
          ture Association of America. Princeton. New Jersey: Opinion
          Research Corporation.
Ossowski, S.
  1963   Class Structure in the Social Consciousness. London:
          Routledge, Kegan and Paul.
Ovenstone, I.M., and P.T. Bean
  1981   "A medical, social assessment of admission to old people's
          homes in Nottingham." British Journal of Psychiatry 139:226-
          229.
Owen, D.
  1965   English Philanthropy, 1660-1690. Cambridge, Massachusetts:
          Harvard University Press.
Oxley, G.W.
  1974   Poor Relief in England and Wales 1601-1834. London: David
          and Charles.
Palliox, C.
  1976   "The labor process: from Fordism to Neo-Fordism." Pp. 46-67
          in The Labor Process and Class Strategies. London: Con-
          ference of Socialist Economists.
Palmer, B.
  1975   "Class, conception and conflict: the thrust for efficiency mana-
          gerial views of labor and the working class rebellion 1903-
          1922." Union for Radical Political Economists
          7(Summer):31-49.
Palmore, E.
  1971   "Attitudes towards aging as shown by humor." Gerontologist
          11:181-186.
Palmore, E., and K. Manton
  1973   "Ageism compared to racism and sexism." Journal of Gerontol-
          ogy 28:363-369.
  1974   "Modernization and the status of the aged: international corre-
          lations." Journal of Gerontology 29:205-210.
Panati, C.
  1980   Breakthroughs. New York: Berkley Books.
Parkhurst, E.
  1937   "Poor relief in a Massachusetts village in the eighteenth cen-

tury." Social Service Review 11:446-464.

Parsons, T.
  1949   The Structure of Social Action: A Study in Social Theory with
          Special Reference to a Group of Recent European Writers.
          Glencoe, Illinois: Free Press.
  1951   The Social System. Glencoe, Illinois: Free Press.
  1953   "Illness and the role of physicians: a sociological perspective."
          Pp. 609-617 in C. Kluckholn and H.A. Murray (eds.), Per-
          sonality in Nature, Society, and Culture. New York: Knopf.

Pauly, M.V.
  1978   "Is medical care different?" Pp. 11-35 in W. Greenberg (ed.),
          Competition in the Health Care Sector. Germantown, Mary-
          land: Aspen.

Pearlin, L.I.
  1959   "Social and personal stress and escape television." Public Opin-
          ion Quarterly 23:255-259.

Pechman, J., and B.A. Okner
  1974   Who Bears the Tax Burden? Washington, D.C.: The Brook-
          ings Institution.

Pegals, C.C.
  1980a   Health Care and the Elderly. Rockville, Maryland: Aspen.
  1980b   "Institutional vs. noninstitutional care for the elderly." Journal
          of Health Politics, Policy and Law 5:205-212.

Perry, S., and J. Kalberer
  1980   "The NIH Consensus Development Program and the assess-
          ment of health care technologies: the first two years." New
          England Journal of Medicine 303:169-172.

Petersen, M.
  1973   "The visibility and image of old people on television." Journal-
          ism Quarterly 50:569-573.

Peterson, I.
  1982   "More of the aged seek work for extra money." New York
          Times, November 1.

Piro, P., and T. Lutens
  1973   "Utilization and reimbusement under Medicare for persons
          who died in 1967 and 1968." Health Insurance Statistics, U.S.
          Department of Health, Education and Welfare, Social Secu-
          rity Administration. Washington, D.C.: U.S. Government
          Printing Office.

Piven, F.F., and R.A. Cloward
  1971   Regulating the Poor: The Functions of Public Welfare. New

York: Random House.
1977   Poor People's Movements, Why They Succeed, How They Fail. New York: Pantheon.

Plato
1930   The Republic I. Translated by P. Shorey. Cambridge, Massachusetts: Harvard University Press.
1935   The Republic II. Translated by P. Shorey. Cambridge, Massachusetts: Harvard University Press.

Polanyi, K.
1944   The Great Transformation. New York: Rinehart.

Pollack, W.
1977   "Long-term care facility reimbursement." Pp. 103-142 in J.F. Holahan et al. (eds.), Altering Medicaid Provider Reimbursement Methods. Washington, D.C.: Urban Institute.

Poulantzas, N.
1973   Political Power and Social Classes. London: New Left Books.

Powell, L.A., and J.B. Williamson
n.d.   "The mass media as legitimizers of control: implications for the aged." Social Policy, in press.

Pratt, H.J.
1976   The Gray Lobby. Chicago: University of Chicago Press.
1981   "The politics of Social Security." Pp. 135-150 in R. Hudson (ed.), The Aging in Politics: Process and Policy. Springfield, Illinois: Charles C. Thomas.

President's Commission
1983   President's Commission for the Study of Ethical Problems in Medicine and Biomedical and Behavioral Research: Decision to Forego Life-Sustaining Treatment. Washington, D.C.: U.S. Government Printing Office.

President's Commission on Pension Policy
1980   Towards a National Retirement Income Policy. Washington, D.C.: U.S. Government Printing Office.

Press, A., J. Huck, and P. Clausen
1981   "The Betamax imbroglio." Newsweek, November 2.

Pryga, E., and H. Bachofer
1983   Hospice Care Under Medicare. Office of Public Policy Analysis, Working Paper. Chicago: American Hospital Association.

Public Law 93-406
1974   "Employment Retirement Income Security Act of 1974." Pp. 829-1035 in 93d Congress, 2d session, United States Statutes At Large. Volume 88. Part I. Washington, D.C.: U.S. Gov-

ernment Printing Office.

Public Law 95-623
  1978   "Health Services Research, Health Statistics and Health Care
          Technology Act of 1978." Pp. 3443-3458 in 95th Congress, 2d
          session, United States Statutes At Large. Volume 92. Part 3.
          Washington, D.C.: U.S. Government Printing Office.

Pumphrey, R.E., and M.W. Pumphrey
  1961   The Heritage of American Social Work. New York: Columbia
          University Press.

Randall, J.H., Jr.
  1970   The Career of Philosophy. Volume I. New York: Columbia
          University Press.

Real, M., H. Anderson, and M. Harrington
  1980   "Television access for older adults." Journal of Communication
          30:80-88.

Redish, M.
  1978   "Physician involvement in hospital decision making." Pp. 217-
          243 in M. Zubkoff, I.E. Raskin, and R.S. Hanft (eds.), Hos-
          pital Cost Containment. New York: Milbank Memorial Fund.

Reid, A.
  1977   "New telecommunications services and their social implica-
          tions." Paper presented at the Royal Society Symposium on
          Telecommunications in the 1980s and After, London.

Reif, L., and C.L. Estes
  1982   "Long-term care: new opportunities for professional nursing."
          Pp. 147-181 in L.H. Aiken (ed.), Nursing in the 1980s:
          Crises, Opportunities, Challenges. Philadelphia: J.B. Lippin-
          cott.

Reinhard, H.
  1970   "The administrative aspects of organ transplantation." Paper
          presented at the First International Symposium on Organ
          Transplantation in Human Beings, Dallas, Texas.

Relman, A.S.
  1980   "The new medical-industrial complex." New England Journal
          of Medicine 303: 963-970.

Renshon, S.
  1974   Psychological Needs and Political Behavior: A Theory of Per-
          sonality and Political Efficacy. New York: Free Press.

Report of the Joint AMA/ANA Task Force
  1983   "Improvement of health care of the aged chronically ill." Paper
          presented at the Annual Meeting of the American Nurses As-

sociation, Kansas City, Missouri.

Rettig, R.
1979   "End-stage renal disease and the 'cost' of medical technology."
        Pp. 88-115 in S.H. Altman and R. Blendon (eds.), Medical
        Technology: The Culprit Behind Health Care Costs?
        Washington, D.C.: U.S. Government Printing Office.

Ricardo, D.
1951   The Works and Correspondence of David Ricardo. Edited by
        P. Sraffa. New York: Cambridge University Press.

Rice, D., and J. Feldman
1983   "Living longer in the United States: demographic changes and
        health needs of the elderly." Milbank Memorial Fund
        Quarterly/Health and Society 1:362-390.

Richard, E.C., and L. Miedema
1977   "The nurse practitioner in the nursing home." Journal of Nurs-
        ing Administration 7:11-13.

Riesenfeld, S.
1955   "The formative era of American assistance law." California
        Law Review 43:175-223.

Riley, M.W., and A. Foner
1968   Aging and Society. Volume I. New York: Russell Sage.

Rivers, W.L., and W. Schramm
1969   Responsibility in Mass Communication. New York: Harper
        and Row.

Rivkin, J., and R. Barber
1978   The North Will Rise Again: Pensions, Politics and Power in
        the 1980s. Boston: Beacon Press.

Roberts, A.H., and M. Rokeach
1956   "Anomie, authoritarianism, and prejudice: a replication."
        American Journal of Sociology 61:355-358.

Rose, M.E.
1966   "The allowance system under the new poor law." Economic
        History Review 19:607-620.
1971   The English Poor Law, 1780-1930. New York: Barnes and No-
        bel.

Rosen, B., and T.H. Jerdee
1976   "The influence of age stereotypes on managerial decisions."
        Journal of Applied Psychology 61:428-432.

Rosenblum, R.
1983   "Out-of-pocket health expenses and the elderly." Health Care
        Management Review 8:77-87.

Rosenstock-Hussey, E.
    1949   The Driving Power of Western Civilization: The Christian Revolution of the Middle Ages. Boston: Beacon Press.
Ross, E.A.
    1928   Social Control: A Survey of the Foundation of Order. New York: Macmillan.
Rossiter, C.
    1953   Seedtime of the Republic. New York: Harcourt, Brace and World.
Rossman, I., and I. Burnside
    1975   "The United States of America." Pp. 85-111 in J.C. Brockle-hurst (ed.), Geriatric Care in Advanced Societies. Lancaster, England: Blackburn Times Press.
Rothman, D.J.
    1971   The Discovery of the Asylum. Boston: Little, Brown and Company.
Rothschild, E.
    1981   "Reagan and the real economy." New York Review of Books 28:12-18.
Rotter, J.B.
    1966   "Generalized expectancies for internal versus external control of reinforcement." Psychological Monographs 80:1-28.
Roucek, J.S.
    1956   Social Control. New York: D. Van Nostrand.
Rubin, J.H.
    1984   "Home TV taping legal — high court: sale of VCRs doesn't violate copyright law." Boston Globe, January 17.
Russell, L.
    1979   Technology in Hospitals: Medical Advances and Their Diffusion. Washington, D.C.: The Brookings Institution.
Sacks, K.
    1974   "Engels revisited: women, the organization of production, and private property." Pp. 207-222 in M.A. Rosaldo and L. Lamphere (eds.), Women, Culture, and Society. Stanford, California: Stanford University Press.
Samuelson, R.J.
    1978   "The withering freedom to govern." Washington Post, March 5.
Schalinske, T.
    1968   "The role of television in the life of the aged person." Unpublished doctoral dissertation. Columbus, Ohio: Ohio State

University.

Schieber, S., and P. George
1981   Retirement Opportunities in an Aging America: Coverage
        and Benefit Entitlement. Washington, D.C.: Employment
        Benefit Research Institute.

Schlender, R., P. Schaughnessy, and I. Yslas
1983   "The effect of case mix and quality on cost differences between
        hospital-based and freestanding nursing homes." Inquiry
        20(Winter):361-368.

Schmitt, R.
1979   Private Pension Plan Reform: A Summary of ERISA.
        Washington, D.C.: Congressional Research Service.

Schneider, D.M.
1938   The History of Public Welfare in New York State 1609-1866.
        Chicago: University of Chicago Press.

Schrag, P.
1978   Mind Control, New York: Pantheon.

Schram, S.
1981   "Title XX implementation and the aging." Pp. 220-235 in R.
        Hudson (ed.), The Aging in Politics: Process and Policy.
        Springfield, Illinois: Charles C Thomas.

Schramm, W.
1969   "Aging and mass communication." Pp. 353-375 in M.W. Ri-
        ley, J.W. Riley Jr., and M.E. Johnson (eds.), Aging and So-
        ciety. Volume 2: Aging and Professions. New York: Russell
        Sage.

Schulz, J.
1974   Providing Adequate Retirement Income. New Hampshire:
        University Press of New England.

Schulz, J.H.
1985   The Economics of Aging. Second edition. Belmont, Califor-
        nia: Wadsworth.

Schwartz, R.
1982   "The blue diamond coal case." The Social Report 3(June):5-6.

de Schweinitz, K.
1943   England's Road to Social Security. Philadelphia: University of
        Pennsylvania Press.

Sclar, E.
1980   "Aging and economic development." Pp. 29-38 in E. Markson
        and G. Batra (eds.), Public Policy for an Aging Population.
        Lexington, Massachusetts: Lexington.

Scoy-Mosher, M.
    1982   "An oncologist's case for no-code orders." Pp. 14-18 in A.E. Doudera and J.D. Peters (eds.), Legal and Ethical Aspects of Treating Critically and Terminally Ill Patients. Ann Arbor, Michigan: Aupha Press.

Scull, A.T.
    1977   Decarceration: Community Treatment and the Deviant — A Radical View. Englewood Cliffs, New Jersey: Prentice-Hall.

Seeger, R.
    1983   "Technology assessment: a look at initiatives." American College of Surgeons Bulletin 68(11):16-17.

Seligman, M.E.P.
    1975   Helplessness: On Depression, Development, and Death. New York: W.H. Freeman and Company.

Shannon, W.V.
    1982   "Forget the scaremongers — the Social Security outlook is not all bleak." Boston Globe, November 3.

Sheehan, T.
    1976   "Senior esteem as a factor of socioeconomic complexity." Gerontologist 16:433-440.

Siebert, F.S., T. Peterson, W. Schramm
    1956   Four Theories of the Press. Urbana: University of Illinois Press.

Signorielli, N., and G. Gerbner
    1977   "The image of the elderly in prime-time network television drama Report No. 12." Philadelphia: University of Pennsylvania, Institute for Applied Communication Studies, Annenberg School of Communications.

Silfren, N.P.
    1980   "Legislative comment: nursing home patients' rights in Massachusetts — current protection and recommendation for improvement." American Journal of Law and Medicine 6:315-333.

Silverman, M., and J.C. Townsend
    1977   "Effects of implied attitude similarity on stereotype of aging: a pilot study." Perceptual and Motor Skills 45:894.

Simmons, J.L.
    1965   "Public stereotypes of deviants." Social Problems 13:223-232.
    1969   Deviants. San Francisco: Boyd and Fraser.

Simmons, L.
    1945   The Role of the Aged in Primitive Society. New Haven, Con-

necticut: Yale University Press.

Simmons, R., S.D. Klein, and R. Simmons
   1977   The Social Impact of Transplantation. New York: Wiley.

Skillman, J. (ed.)
   1975   Intensive Care. Boston: Little, Brown and Company.

Sloan, F.A., and R. Feldman
   1978   "Competition among physicians." Pp. 45-102 in W. Greenberg
          (ed.), Competition in the Health Care Sector. Germantown,
          Maryland: Aspen.

Smith, A.
   1937   The Wealth of Nations. New York: Random House.

Smith, M.D.
   1979   "The portrayal of elders in magazine cartoons." Gerontologist
          19:408-412.

de Sola Pool, I.
   1968   "The communication revolution: social trends." Science and
          Technology 76:87-97.
   1976   The Social Impact of the Telephone. Cambridge, Massachu-
          setts: Massachusetts Institute of Technology Press.

Somers, A.
   1980   "Rethinking health policy for the elderly: a six point program."
          Inquiry 17(Spring):3-17.
   1982   "Long-term care for the elderly and disabled." New England
          Journal of Medicine 307:221-226.

Sontag, S.
   1972   "The double standard of aging." Saturday Review 55(Septem-
          ber 23):29-38.

Sorenson, T.
   1965   Kennedy, New York: Harper and Row.

Soroka, M., and R. Newcomb
   1981   "Vision care for the nation's elderly: a plea for policy direc-
          tion." Journal of Health Politics, Policy and Law 6:73-86.

Spasoff, R.R., et al.
   1978   "A longitudinal study of elderly residents of long-stay institu-
          tions." Gerontologist 18:281-292.

Spencer, H.
   1868   Social Statics. London: Williams and Norgate.
   1961   "The nature of society." Pp. 139-143 in T. Parsons et al. (eds.),
          Theories of Society. Volume I. New York: Free Press.

Spitzer, S.
   1975   "Toward a Marxian theory of deviance." Social Problems

22:638-651.

Srole, L.
  1956   "Social integration and certain corollaries: an exploratory
          study." American Sociological Review 21:709-716.
Stannard, C.I.
  1980   "Old folks and dirty work: the social conditions for patient
          abuse in a nursing home." Pp. 500-515 in J.S. Quandagno
          (ed.), Aging: The Individual and Society. New York: St. Mar-
          tin's Press.
Stark, D.
  1980   "Class struggle and the transformation of the labor process."
          Theory and Society 9:89-132.
Starr, P.
  1982   The Social Transformation of American Medicine. New York:
          Basic Books.
Steiner, G.Y.
  1971   The State of Welfare. Washington, D.C.: The Brookings Insti-
          tution.
Steiner, R.L.
  1972   Visions of Cablevision: The Prospects for Cable Television in
          the Greater Cincinnati Area. Cincinnati, Ohio: Stephen H.
          Wilder Foundation.
Stephens, J.D.
  1979   The Transition from Capitalism to Socialism. New York: Mac-
          millan.
Stevens, R., and R. Stevens
  1974   Welfare Medicine in America: A Case Study of Medicaid.
          New York: Free Press.
Stone, K.
  1975   "The origins of job structures in the steel industry." Pp. 27-84
          in D. Gordan, R. Edwards, and M. Reich (eds.), Labor
          Market Segmentation. Boston: D.C. Heath.
Stults, B.
  1982   "Digoxin use in the elderly." Journal of the American Geriatric
          Society 30:158-164.
Sudnow, D.
  1967   Passing On: The Social Organization of Dying. Englewood
          Cliffs, New Jersey: Prentice-Hall.
Sundquist, J.L.
  1968   Politics and Policy: The Eisenhower, Kennedy and Johnson
          Years. Washington, D.C.: The Brookings Institution.

Swank, C.
    1979   "Media uses and gratifications: need salience and source dependence in a sample of the elderly." American Behavioral Scientist 23:95-117.

Sweezy, P.
    1976   "A Critique." Pp. 33-56 in R. Hilton (ed.), The Transition from Feudalism to Capitalism. London: Verso.

Szasz, T.S.
    1963   Law, Liberty, and Psychiatry. New York: Macmillan.
    1970   Ideology and Insantiy. Garden City, New York: Anchor/Doubleday.

Tawney, R.H.
    1954   Religion and the Rise of Capitalism. New York: Mentor Books.

Thibault, A., et al.
    1980   "Medical intensive care: indications, interventions, and outcomes." New England Journal of Medicine 302:938-942.

Thompson, E.P.
    1967   "Time, work-discipline and industrial capitalism." Past and Present 38:56-97.

Thurow, L.C.
    1980   The Zero-Sum Society: Distribution and the Possibilities for Economic Change. New York: Penguin.

Tierney, B.
    1959   Medieval Poor Law. Berkeley: University of California Press.

Tishler, H.S.
    1971   Self-Reliance and Social Security, 1870-1917. Port Washington, New York: Kennikat Press.

Tomayko, J.
    1978   "The role of labor in containing health costs." Pp. 85-88 in Proceedings of a Conference Sponsored by Blue Cross and Blue Shield Associations, Health Care in the American Economy: Issues and Forecasts, 1978. Chicago: Health Services Foundation.

Townsend, C.
    1971   Old Age: The Last Segregation. New York: Crossman.

Trattner, W.I.
    1974   From Poor Law to Welfare State. New York: Free Press.

Trausch, S.
    1981   "Retired but still working." Boston Globe, November 3.

Treas, J.
  1979   "Socialist organization and economic development in China: latent consequences for the aged." Gerontologist 19:34-43.
Trichard, L., A. Zabow, and L.S. Gillis
  1982   "Elderly persons in old age homes: a medical, psychiatric and social investigation." South African Journal of Medicine 61:624-627.
Tuckman, J., and I. Lorge
  1953   "Attitudes toward old people." Journal of Social Psychology 37:249-260.
U.S. Bureau of the Census
  1977   "Characteristics of the population below the poverty level." Current Population Reports, Series P-60. Washington, D.C.: U.S. Government Printing Office.
  1979   "Money income and poverty status of families and persons in the United States: 1978." Current Population Reports, Series P-60, No. 120. Washington, D.C.: U.S. Government Printing Office.
U.S. Department of Health and Human Services
  1981   "Usual sources of medical care and their characteristics." National Health and Expenditures Study. Hyattsville, Maryland: National Center for Health Services Research.
U.S. Department of Health, Education and Welfare
  1969   Task Force of Prescription Drugs Final Report. Washington, D.C.: U.S. Government Printing Office.
  1973   Totally Implantable Artificial Heart: Economic, Ethical, Legal, Medical, Psychiatric, Social Implications. Washington, D.C.: Heart Assessment Panel.
  1975   Selected operating and financial characteristics of nursing homes in the United States: 1973-1974. Rockville, Maryland: National Center for Health Statistics.
  1978a Facts About Older Americans. Washington, D.C.: U.S. Government Printing Office.
  1978b Major Initiative: Long-Term Care/Community Services." Memorandum of July 14, 1978 from the Office of the Secretary. Washington, D.C.: U.S. Government Printing Office.
  1981   Social Security Area Population Projections: 1981. Office of the Actuary. Washington, D.C.: U.S. Government Printing Office.
U.S. Department of Labor
  1980   Employment and Earnings. March.

U.S. House of Representatives

1978a   "Health services research statistics and technology." Congressional Record, September 25, H10585-10597.

1978b   Statement by Julius Richmond, before the Subcommittee on Domestic and International Scientific, Planning, Analysis, and Cooperation of the Committee on Science and Technology, October 6. Washington, D.C.: U.S. Government Printing Office.

1983a   Proceedings of the Conference on the Future of Medicare, before the Committee on Ways and Means, November 29. Washington, D.C.: U.S. Government Printing Office.

1983b   Hearing on Pension Legislation, before the Subcommittee on Labor-Management Relations of the Committee on Education and Labor, December 13, 1982. Washington, D.C.: U.S. Government Printing Office.

1984   Proceedings of the Conference on the Future of Medicare, before the Subcommittee on Health of the Committee on Ways and Means, February 1. Washington, D.C.: U.S. Government Printing Office.

U.S. House of Representatives Select Committee on Aging

1977   Age Stereotyping and Television. Washington, D.C.: U.S. Government Printing Office.

1978a   Economic Plight of the Elderly. Washington, D.C.: U.S. Government Printing Office.

1978b   Televised Advertising and the Elderly. Washington, D.C.: U.S. Government Printing Office.

1980   Retirement: The Broken Promise. Washington, D.C.: U.S. Government Printing Office.

1982a   Every Ninth American. Washington, D.C.: U.S. Government Printing Office.

1982b   Cost of Living Adjustments Under the Old Age Survivors and Disability Insurance (Social Security) Program. A Report by the Chairman, April 23. Washington, D.C.: U.S. Government Printing Office.

1983   Proposals to Address the Financing Problem of Social Security: Memphis, Tennesee. Washington, D.C.: U.S. Government Printing Office.

1984   Pension Asset Raids. Washington, D.C.: U.S. Government Printing Office.

U.S. National Center for Health Statistics

1973   Current Estimates from the Health Interview Survey: 1971.

Rockville, Maryland: U.S. National Center for Health Statistics.

U.S. News and World Report
1980   "Life begins at 55." September 1.

U.S. Senate
1978   "National Institutes of Health Care Research Act of 1978." Congressional Record, August 9, S12934.

1983a   Health Benefits: Loss due to Unemployment. Staff Report to the Committee on Finance, April. Washington, D.C.: U.S. Government Printing Office.

1983b   Hearing on Retirement Equity Act of 1983, before the Subcommittee on Labor of the Committee on Labor and Human Resources, October 4, Washington, D.C.: U.S. Government Printing Office.

1984a   "Medicare solvency and Health Care Financing Reform Act of 1984." Congressional Record, March 13, S. 2424.

1984b   Hearings on Social Security Disability Program Reform, before the Committee on the Budget, March 16. Washington, D.C.: U.S. Government Printing Office.

U.S. Senate Special Committee on Aging
1974   Nursing Home Care in the United States: Failure in Public Policy. Washington, D.C.: U.S. Government Printing Office.

1975   "Doctors in nursing homes: shunned responsibility." Pp. 319-354 in Nursing Home Care in the United States: Failure in Public Policy. Washington, D.C.: U.S. Government Printing Office.

1979   The Proposed Fiscal 1980 Budget: What It Means for Older Americans. Washington, D.C.: U.S. Government Printing Office.

1980   Development in Aging: 1979. Part I. Washington, D.C.: U.S. Government Printing Office.

1981   Social Security in Europe: The Impact on an Aging Population. Washington, D.C.: U.S. Government Printing Office.

1982   Congressional Action on the Fiscal Year 1983 Budget: What It Means to Older Americans. Washington, D.C.: U.S. Government Printing Office.

Vladeck, B.C.
1980   Unloving Care: The Nursing Home Tragedy. New York: Basic Books.

Vladeck, B.C., and L.P. Firman
1983   "The aging of the population and health services." Annals of

the American Academy of Political and Social Science
468:132-148.

Vogel, M.
    1980   The Invention of the Modern Hospital. Chicago: University
        of Chicago Press.

Wald, M.L.
    1980   "When abuse adds to woes of the old." New York Times,
        August 24.

Ward, R.B.
    1977   "The impact of subjective age and stigma on older persons."
        Journal of Gerontology 32:227-232.

Waters, H.F., G. Hackett, E. Gelman, J. Huck, and L. Howard
    1981   "Cable TV: coming of age." Newsweek, August 24.

Weaver, J.L.
    1981   "Issue salience." Pp. 30-46 in R. Hudson (ed.), The Aging in
        Politics: Process and Policy. Springfield, Illinois: Charles C
        Thomas.

Weaver, W.
    1982   "Age discrimination charges found in sharp rise in U.S." New
        York Times, February 22.

Webb, S., and B. Webb
    1910   English Poor Law Policy. New York: Longmans, Green.
    1927   English Poor Law History: Part I. The Old Poor Law. New
        York: Longmans, Green.
    1929   English Poor Law History: Part II. The Last Hundred Years.
        Volume I. New York: Longmans, Green.

Weber, M.
    1947   The Theory of Social and Economic Organization. Translated
        by A.M. Henderson and T. Parsons. New York: Oxford Uni-
        versity Press.
    1958   The Protestant Ethic and the Spirit of Capitalism. Translated
        by T. Parsons. New York: Charles Scribner's Sons.

Weinberger, L.E., and J. Millham
    1975   "A multi-dimensional, multiple method analysis of attitudes
        toward the elderly." Journal of Gerontology 30:343-348.

Weissert, W.G., T.T.H. Wan, and B.B. Livieratos
    1980   "Effects and costs of day care and homemaker services for the
        chronically ill: a randomized experiment." Hyattsville, Mary-
        land: Department of Health, Education, and Welfare.

Wellman, D.M.
    1977   Portraits of White Racism. Cambridge, England: Cambridge

          University Press.

Wells, R.V.
    1975   The Population of the British Colonies in North America Be-
              fore 1776. Princeton, New Jersey: Princeton University Press.

Wenner, L.
    1976   "Funcational analysis of TV viewing for older adults." Journal
              of Broadcasting 20:77-78.

White House Conference on Aging
    1981   "Toward a national policy on aging." Final Report.
              Washington, D.C.: White House Conference on Aging.

Wilder, C.S.
    1971   Chronic Conditions and Limitations of Activity and Mobility:
              United States, July 1965-June 1967. Rockville, Maryland:
              U.S. National Center for Health Statistics.

Williams, J.
    1982   "Why are blacks less suicide prone that whites?" New York
              Times, February 9.

Williams, W.A.
    1966   The contours of American History. Chicago: Quadrangle.

Williamson, J.B.
    1984   "Old age relief policy prior to 1900: the trend toward restric-
              tiveness." American Journal of Economics and Sociology
              43:369-384.

    n.d.   "Old age relief policies in the New Land." In B.B. Hess and
              E.W. Markson (eds.), Growing Old in America. Third Edi-
              tion. New Brunswick, New Jersey: Transaction Books, in
              press.

Williamson, J.B., and K.J. Branco
    n.d.   "The origins of English aging policy: a re-examination of the
              cyclical theory of social relief." Journal of Sociology and Social
              Welfare, in press.

Williamson, J.B., L. Evans, and A. Munley
    1980   Aging and Society. New York: Holt, Rinehart and Winston.

Williamson, J.B., L. Evans, and L.A. Powell
    1982   The Politics of Aging: Power and Policy. Springfield, Illinois:
              Charles C Thomas.

Wolf, S., and B. Berle (eds.)
    1981   The Technological Imperative in Medicine. New York:
              Plenum Press.

Wolfe, A.
    1974   "New directions in the Marxist theory of politics." Politics and

Society 4:131-160.

1977   Limits of Legitimacy: Political Contradictions of Modern Capitalism. New York: Free Press.

Wood, V.

1971   "Age-appropriate behavior for older people." Gerontologist 11:74-78.

Woodworth, W.

1981   "Forms of employee ownership and worker control." Sociology of Work Occupations 3(2):195-200.

Wortman, P., A. Vinokur, and L. Seechrest

1982   "Evaluation of NIH consensus development process: final report." Ann Arbor, Michigan: Center for Research on Utilization of Scientific Knowledge.

Wright, E.O.

1979a   Class Structure and Income Determination. New York: Academic Press.

1979b   Class, Crisis and the State. London: Verso.

Wrong, D.H.

1979   Power: Its Forms, Bases, and Uses. New York: Colophon.

Young, P.

1981   "New scanner boon to body research." Portland Oregonian, July 12.

Young, T.

1979   "Use of the media by older adults." American Behavioral Scientist 234:119-136.

Zimbalist, A. (ed.)

1979   Case Studies on the Labor Process. New York: Monthly Review Press.

NAME INDEX

SUBJECT INDEX

A

Administration on Aging (ACA), 133, 147
Advertising, 106, 113, 176, 181-183, 185, 189, 200-201, 201n, 203n, 224-225
Age consciousness, 8
Ageism, 6, 180-181, 191, 200-201, 206-244, 236
  definition, 206, 218
Aging vote, 2547-248
AFL-CIO, 90
America-Colonial Relief Policy, 56-67, 183
  comparison with England, 57-58, 62-63, 96
  County Poorhouse Act, 61
  definition of poor, 59
  influence of the Church, 57, 62-63, 66n-67n, 96, 122, 212-213, 216, 237n-238n
  institutionalization, 59-62, 65, 66n, 96-97
  laissez-faire liberalism, 66-67n, 121, 207-208, 212-218, 228-229, 237n-238n, 255, 258
  scientific charity movement, 63-64, 67n
  Yates Report (1824), 60
American Association of Retired Persons (AARP), 247, 255-256
American College of Cardiology, 159
American College of Physicians, 171
American Dental Association (ADA), 129
American Express Company, 73
American Geriatric Society, 126
American Hospital Association (AHA), 129, 141n, 158, 164, 171, 249, 256, 259

American Medical Association (AMA), 23, 127-132, 141n-142n, 157-158, 171, 249, 256, 259
American Nurses Association (ANA), 129, 141n, 157
American Nursing Home Association (ANHA), 129
Amalgamated Clothing Workers, 82
Attitudes about the aged, 29, 33-34, 66n, 106-107, 111, 121, 206, 217-226, 229-230, 232, 235, 238n-241n, 245
  mass media, 182, 188, 193-194, 198 (*see also* Stereotyping; Ageism)
Attitudes of the aged, 8, 30
  political, 194-195
  self-concept, 182, 189, 191-192, 200, 228, 240n
Autonomy, 5, 8, 13, 32, 45, 89, 121, 160, 165, 178-179, 215, 218, 230
Authority, 3, 4, 8, 10, 25, 176, 181
  and ageism, 207, 217, 227-228

B

Blue Cross and Blue Shield Association, 171, 249-250, 256

C

Capitalism, 14-23, 36n, 51, 55n, 62, 65, 98, 237n, 258
  and ageism, 5, 9, 85, 112, 207-209, 219-221, 228-229, 231, 235-236, 238n
  control of the labor process, 10, 19-21, 46, 68-72, 74-75, 92n, 97-98, 100, 103, 215, 255
  health care, 23-24, 121-122, 125-126,

325